MOST DOPE

MOST DOPE
THE EXTRAORDINARY
LIFE OF MAC MILLER

PAUL CANTOR

Abrams Press, New York

ABRAMS The Art of Books
195 Broadway, New York, NY 10007
abramsbooks.com

For my wife and daughter, my extended family, and most importantly, you.

AUTHOR'S NOTE

In 2009, long before anyone really knew who Mac Miller was, I received a message from a gentleman named Arthur Pitt, who was working as a publicist for an up-and-coming independent record label out of Pittsburgh called Rostrum Records.

The label was the brainchild of Benjy Grinberg, a former assistant to legendary record exec L.A. Reid, and had endured some early struggles with an artist they were trying to break—his name was Wiz Khalifa.

Very early in Wiz's career—August of 2006—I interviewed the baby-faced rapper for a short profile that was to run in a forthcoming issue of *XXL* magazine, at the time hip-hop's most important publication. Capable of minting stars overnight, *XXL* was initially enthusiastic about Wiz, but after my article was written, they changed their mind and declined to publish. He just wasn't popular enough yet.

But there I was that day some years later, sitting alone in my Staten Island apartment, when my AOL Instant Messenger alerted me to a new message from Arthur, whom most everyone colloquially referred to as Artie. Rostrum had gone to the mat with Wiz, and after numerous independent releases and a botched deal for him with Warner Bros. Records, Wiz was beginning to experience real success.

Artie wanted me to check out a new artist he was working with. He sent me a YouTube clip; in it, a young rapper—a white kid, no less—sat with the camera close to his face, freestyling aggressively in a pained effort to impress anyone who might be watching.

"I'm thinking of working with this kid," Artie said. "Tell me what you think."

Back then, I was already half a decade into writing about rap music; with a popular blog that I penned on *XXL*'s website, and freelance work for outlets like *Vibe*, *Complex*, and MTV—to say nothing of my work as an aspiring record producer—music industry people were always asking me to check something or someone out.

A tough critic who had been a hip-hop obsessive since the early nineties, I was often let down by what I heard or saw, and I expected very little from what Artie had sent me. I considered Artie a friend, and I liked Wiz Khalifa, but wasn't terribly impressed with some of the newer artists Artie was working with.

That day, though, when I pressed play, I immediately thought the rapper before me—Mac Miller—had "bars," that at a time when being super-lyrical was not trendy, he was clearly an above-average lyricist using the most time-honored tool of the hip-hop trade, the "freestyle," to make his name known. Moreover, there was a kernel of something there. He was young, still in high school, but you could see a spark, the undeniable and indefinable "it" factor that the music industry is built on. I told Artie he should work with him, and while I'm certain I wasn't the only person he consulted for advice, he wisely decided to do so.

Unlike Wiz, Mac took off quickly. It seemed that as soon as Rostrum began working with him, he was everywhere. I couldn't help but feel that so much of the work the label had done with Wiz had helped Mac out—in the end, though, a label was only as good as the artists on its roster. And Mac was an unbelievable talent. He could write, produce, perform, and so much more. But even that is often not enough to turn someone into a star, let alone a legend.

What set Mac apart, I think, is that he was genuinely interested and enthusiastic, perhaps to an unhealthy degree, about what he did. He seemed to be unflinchingly nice and charismatic, a genuine human who endeared himself to everyone he met. But the thing that made him truly great, the thing that allows his name to echo from this generation to the next and beyond, is that he just wanted it more.

He wasn't afraid or embarrassed or too cool to say he wanted to be great. And he didn't just want to be great for himself, he wanted to be great for you, for me, and for everyone else. He also saw greatness in other people, wanted it just as badly for them, even when they did not want it bad enough themselves. Life, to him, was something you had to live to its fullest potential.

I met Mac a few times. We didn't have a close relationship, though I have no doubt that between our mutual friends and my profile as a writer, he was aware of me in some regard. He was complimentary when I reviewed his second album for *VIBE*, which I appreciated (especially because it wasn't the most flattering review). And since he seemed to have a long career ahead of him, I always assumed I would one day write something substantial about him. I certainly didn't know it would be this.

Working on this book was an unbelievable challenge. Mac was an endlessly fascinating character, someone whose perspective on life interested me as much as his art. He seemed to have grown up in public, and was open about many of his struggles. But when he died on September 7, 2018, I—like many others—felt it was a terrible tragedy. He had just released the best album of his career, *Swimming*, and there were still so many questions unanswered.

Still, while I thought I was familiar with his story, it wasn't until I began traveling back and forth to Pittsburgh, spending time walking the very same streets he grew up on, and talking to his close friends, that so much of this book started to come together. Even then, though, it was difficult; the pain of having lost him was still so raw for many, and the challenge of asking people questions was something that I, for one of the first times in my life, had moral concerns about. *Too soon*, I seemed to keep telling myself, *it's too soon*.

But then I noticed something. Despite what my inner voice was telling me, the people I had reached out to for interviews kept wanting to talk. The pain of losing their friend, Mac Miller, was still fresh. But they wanted to share. They had all these memories, all these experiences, all this life that they had lived with him. Not all of it was good, some of it was bad, and, of course, some of it existed in that vast space in between.

However, the thing that really drove home how important this book was to write, how essential this was book was to write, came on the one-year anniversary of Malcolm's passing. That night, there was a party held in his honor; it was in Pittsburgh, and his longtime DJ, Clockwork, was manning the decks. All proceeds were being donated to the Mac Miller Fund, a charity that "supports programming, resources and opportunities to youth from underserved communities, helping them recognize their full potential through exploration in the arts and community building."

After spending the duration of the party inside the venue, enjoying the music, as one is wont to do, I ventured outside, and began interviewing many of Mac's fans. These were Mac Heads—as they are colloquially known—some new, some old, but all of them sharing between them an undying passion for Mac Miller and his art. Perhaps because of the date, it being the anniversary of his death, emotions were running high, and the stories being shared moved me to such a degree that, till this day, still reverberate.

These were stories about how Mac's music had saved their lives, how at their lowest moments, when they felt that they were at the end of their rope, they heard his voice, something he said, something he, too, seemed to be going through—and felt a sudden urge to keep on living. I, too, knew what those moments felt like, and I, too, knew what it felt like to receive a sign.

I made the decision that night that I would continue working on this book, writing this book, finishing this book, and ultimately publishing this book, because I knew what stories and biographies did for me once, how—even in the moments when they became uncomfortable—they provided a third dimension of understanding about the lives and times of whomever, in that moment, I was reading about. That understanding brought so much to my life, and helped me in times of need just as, I know, Mac Miller's music had done for other people.

A quick note: Before you move on to the story itself, let it also be known that this book was written without the participation of Mac Miller's family and estate. With respect to their grieving process, they were approached very early on, with the hope that—at least on my behalf—they would ultimately contribute. They opted not to, and I respected that. Nevertheless, many people close to Mac chose to participate. And I appreciate them for it.

So, although as the author my name is on the cover, this book is not for me—this book is for you. You are a Mac Miller fan, or you are a music fan, or maybe you are simply an inquisitive person who wants to read more about a dynamic individual. Know this: Mac Miller was a complex guy, a rapper who spent his life using his art to explore the space between his own madness and genius; all the while, he battled untamable forces inside him that were beyond his control. Now, we may not all be mad geniuses, but on that last note, I'm certain many can relate.

—Paul Cantor, 3:14 A.M., August 10, 2021

PROLOGUE

On May 17, 2018, Mac Miller was at a bar. He was out with friends, knocking back a few drinks.

To him, it may have seemed like just another day. But to the public, Mac at a bar was odd. A year earlier, he would not have been there. A year earlier, things were different.

Back then, he was in a good place. He was dating one of the most famous singers in the world, Ariana Grande, and he was happy. *The Divine Feminine*, his fourth album (released in the fall of 2016), had been well received, and he had just performed at Coachella, a career highlight.

Most importantly, though, after years of substance abuse, that part of his life was behind him.

"It's amazing," he said. "I am actually completely sober for the first time."[1]

This was a revelation. For much of his career, it seemed, he had been under the influence of one substance or another. But he always appeared to have things under control.

"He did drugs," a longtime fan who got to know him socially told me. "But it wasn't an addiction, it was a lifestyle."[2]

The lifestyle had brought him tremendous success. At the time, he had released four studio albums, numerous mixtapes, and countless collaborations, earning him worldwide fame, millions of dollars, and a legion of die-hard fans.

He had started independently, with Rostrum Records, then moved to a major label, Warner Bros., inking a ten-million-dollar deal. But success hadn't come easy. Hailing from Pittsburgh, Pennsylvania, he was a white rapper in a traditionally Black musical genre; respect wasn't given, it had to be earned, and it took work—years of pounding the pavement, years of nonstop touring, and years of releasing music, all in a quest to be taken seriously.

When he finally achieved a modicum of respectability—arguably around 2013, after the release of his second album—he struggled to adapt. "Being famous used to just defeat me," he said. "I wouldn't leave my house because I was worried about someone being like, 'Oh, are you Mac Miller?' and then the rest of the night I couldn't be myself."[3]

If he was uncomfortable with fame, dating Ariana, a paparazzi magnet, was unlikely to have helped. A former Nickelodeon star, she'd parlayed her TV fame into a pop music career, notching multiple hits along the way. Like Mac, she had a passionate fan base who obsessed over her every move.

Their fans seemed generally supportive of their relationship, though, and the pair kept up appearances. They performed at each other's shows, were spotted on each other's social media accounts, and showed up at events. For a year and a half, things seemed to be good; until, well, they weren't.

On May 9, 2018, the celebrity industrial complex was shaken up when Ariana announced, via Instagram story, that she and Mac had broken up. For his part, Mac remained mum, offering no public comments. But within days, Ariana was rumored to have moved on, dating *SNL* comedian Pete Davidson.

By the time the seventeenth had rolled around—the day Mac sat at that bar—a week had gone by, a week in which gossip columns went crazy speculating about Ariana and Pete's new relationship, with the budding couple doing little to dispel the rumors. Instead, they simply stirred the pot, flirting the way their generation did best: by liking each other's old photos on Instagram, and posting pics of their matching tattoos.

Had Mac seen this? It was difficult to tell, though he was an extremely online person, active on Twitter, Instagram, Facebook—even Vine, when it was popping. He was also prone to reading negative comments about himself online, which affected him deeply. Then again, it was also possible he hadn't seen it at all.

Regardless, Mac was at the bar, downing drinks. It is not clear what he drank—maybe Knob Creek, Jameson, Rémy Martin, or Hennessy, all brands he was fond of. It is possible, based on information revealed later, that he had more in his system than alcohol. But as the night grew darker and the spring cold came in, as it does in LA, where the wind bites at the skin when it rolls off the Pacific, it was time to roll.

The bar was not far from his house. He would later tell his longtime DJ, Clockwork, that it was "mad close"; so close, in fact, that he saw no problem with leaving that bar with his car keys in hand, and putting those keys into the ignition of his white 2014 Mercedes G63 AMG—the "G-Wagon," as it is colloquially known—and doing something they tell you not to do when you've been drinking, let alone drinking the way Mac was known to drink.

He got into the car with two passengers and tried to drive his drunk ass home.

Around one A.M., as he got closer to his house, he rounded a bend. He had come around this bend countless times before, but this time, things were different.

"Something just told me to floor it," he told Clockwork.[4]

He pressed his foot down on the gas, all eight cylinders fired, five hundred forty-four horsepower of German steel booming around the corner, zero to sixty in five seconds, four seconds, three seconds, two seconds . . . boom, into the curb Mac crashed, the car spinning back onto the other side of the road, up over the opposite curb, right into a telephone pole. The telephone pole then cracked, collapsing in a heap against some trees.

Mac Miller opened the driver's side door of the G-Wagon, and out into the darkness he went. Through a fence he dashed, escaping, only to be arrested at his house hours later, charged with driving under the influence and a hit-and-run. After posting fifteen thousand dollars' bail, he was released the next day.

The rapper Bun B, a friend and mentor, called him after the accident became headline news.[5]

"I'm all right, Unc," Mac said. "It was just a rough day."

"If you need to talk to somebody about what's going on . . ." Bun said.

"Nah, OG—I promise I'm good," Mac said.

Bun took him at his word. So did other people who spoke to him then.

"At that point, there's really not much more that you can do," Bun said. "I know that there was this concerted effort to help him fight his demons, trying to help him deal with what he was dealing with. And when people are fighting addiction, it's always easy to put on the public face like, 'Nah, man, I'm good. I'm working on it, I'm addressing it.' You can say everything that you want people to hear you say. You think it will stop them from asking you about it. And then go right back to whatever it is that you told them that you weren't doing."

The crash seemed out of character, though. Perhaps it was a sign.

Just over a week after the crash, while still at work on the album that would become *Swimming*, he would sit in the backyard of his house in Brentwood, staring out at the mountains, the great big sky above, and the row of houses built below. On most mornings, the scene brought him great tranquility.

"Bro, what happened?" Clockwork asked him. "What happened with the accident?"

Mac sucked on a cigarette. He looked away, failing to make eye contact.

"I don't know why I did it," he said. "I don't know what the fuck I was thinking."

He took another drag.

"Luckily, we hit that tree. And the tree stopped us from going down the hill."

He bounced his knee against his hand. He seemed nervous now, hitting the cigarette harder and faster.

"I don't know, man."

Then there was a pause, something said without saying it. Mac looked out further, searching.

"You ever feel invincible?" he said.

More silence.

"I just felt invincible."

ONE

In Point Breeze, Pittsburgh, the leafy streets are clean, the air quiet and peaceful. Stately homes dot neat, well-manicured blocks. The most visible hardship here, you'd think, is the never-ending saga of maintaining one's lawn.

"This neighborhood is filled with children and dogs," one resident told me. "Everyone wants to live in Point Breeze."

"Some of the wealthiest people in the history of the United States lived there," said Arthur Pitt, a Point Breeze native who, depending on whom you're talking to, can lay claim to having been the one to *discover* Mac Miller. "It fluctuates. From the wealthier side, if you cross the main avenue, it's not as wealthy. It's a mix. Point Breeze is an interesting place."

Indeed, it is. Long before Pulitzer Prize–winning writer Annie Dillard's memoir about Point Breeze—*An American Childhood*, published in 1987, detailing her coming-of-age in the Pittsburgh suburb in the 1950s and wrestling with the neighborhood's complicated legacy—and long before doctors, lawyers, and politicians—today's upper middle class—called it home, Point Breeze was just a bunch of trees in the midst of a great, unsettled wilderness.

Historians trace its post–Native American history to 1758, when it was settled by Europeans. Back then, the neighborhood was neither breezy nor pointy. But there was a hotel—the Point Breeze Hotel—that stood at the center of present-day Fifth and Penn Avenues. Some two hundred years ago, a traveler from a distant land, perhaps New York or Philadelphia, might have been riding along in their pimped-out stagecoach. They'd be tired; a trip west could take, literally, months, and so they'd stop, have a hearty meal, catch some z's, then wake to the sound of birdsong in the morning before continuing on their journey.

In those days, the only way through Point Breeze was the Greensburg Pike, a Native American trail paved in the early nineteenth century. At once rustic and remote, it wasn't long after it got paved that the Pittsburgh gentry discovered the area; they saw it as a refuge from the hustle and bustle of the city rapidly growing around it.

Among the esteemed folks who landed in Point Breeze was Judge William Wilkins. The son of a captain in the American Revolution, Wilkins held many positions of high social importance. He was president of the Bank of Pittsburgh, a member of the House of Representatives, a senator, congressman, secretary of war, even the US minister to Russia; in his day, he was kind of a big deal.

Wilkins liked Point Breeze. And in 1835, he built himself a grand, *MTV Cribs*-style house there. This would be a mansion—a big, sprawling thing, fashioned in the Greek Revival style, with four Georgian columns fronting a stately entrance. Surrounded by 650 acres of open land, a house such as this would not do with just an address. It needed to be more than that, for it *was* more than that. It was a big home surrounded by woods—Wilkins dubbed it "Homewood."

At Homewood, Wilkins hosted important people. Daniel Webster, Henry Clay, even the seventh vice president of the United States, John Calhoun, all came by the mansion to eat and chitchat—politics as usual. All the while, the world outside Homewood, outside of Point Breeze, was rapidly changing. America was a young country, and Pittsburgh was a young city. But it was already proving to be one of the most important locations in the Union.

Pittsburgh sat at the confluence of the Allegheny and Monongahela Rivers, which met and became the Ohio River, then flowed 981 miles southwest to Cairo, Illinois, where it connected with the Mississippi. In the early 1800s, the big business in Pittsburgh was boats, because railroads were still in their infancy, and traveling on the rivers was how people got around.

To wit, it was from Pittsburgh, not St. Louis, as it's commonly thought, that Lewis and Clark departed on their landmark eight-thousand-mile expedition exploring the territories obtained by the United States from France in the Louisiana Purchase. The legendary explorers floated down the Ohio River to Missouri, and from there they went on to discover the rest of the country.

Because of this, Pittsburgh, in the 1800s, was known as the "Gateway to the West." All of America was to soon head in that direction; through Pittsburgh is how they would get there.

But Pittsburgh also had other things working in its favor, like a wealth of natural resources. In the late 1700s, for example, large coal deposits were discovered a few miles west of Point Breeze, across the Ohio River, in a neighborhood largely settled by German immigrants called Mount Washington. Coal had many uses and led to the development of a variety of industries. It could be used for fuel, and with fuel there was a world of opportunity. All around the city, factories and foundries were being built. Iron, brass, tin, glass, textiles, furniture, booze, even oil refining—if it could be made, Pittsburgh would make it.

Along with the boom in industry came a boom in population; immigrants arrived—Welsh, Scottish, German, Irish, and others. Many of them would work in the factories, while the veterans of the Revolutionary War were literally handed plots of land. As for Black people, the year 1780 saw enslavement abolished in Pennsylvania, though it remained in another form, indentured servitude, which held back former enslaved people and the children of enslaved people from taking part in the great Pittsburgh land grab.

Perhaps the most famous of the Pittsburgh strivers was Andrew Carnegie. Carnegie was born in Scotland, but early in his life, after his parents had fallen on hard times, they borrowed money and in 1848 moved with Andrew to Pennsylvania. They took up residence in "slab town," a noisy, overcrowded immigrant community that came with only the finest accoutrements—no natural gas, no water, streets that remained cloaked in darkness at night, and where, at all times of day, one would encounter wild hogs and dogs roaming free.

There was also little concern for the conditions the factories created. "The smoke permeated and penetrated everything," Carnegie wrote. "If you washed your face and hands they were as dirty as ever in an hour. The soot gathered in the hair and irritated the skin, and for a time . . . life was more or less miserable."[1]

Carnegie was not overly educated, having ended his studies around the time he immigrated, but was industrious and hardworking. As a youth, he worked in a cotton factory, then got a job as a messenger. It was through this job that he met Thomas A. Scott, president of Pennsylvania Railroad, who took him on as his secretary, paying him thirty-five dollars a month. It was at this job, now with more money, that he began investing, taking up interests in coal, iron, and oil.

When the Civil War broke out, demand increased for iron, helping Carnegie turn a profit; when the war finally ended, he turned his interests to iron almost exclusively, resigning from the Pennsylvania Railroad to start the Keystone Bridge Company in 1865, making a small fortune in contracts to build iron bridges in place of the more common wooden ones. But by then, Carnegie had already moved up in the world, living with his family far from the grime and pollution that hung like a thick cloud over the city, in a house on Homewood Street, just a stone's throw from Judge William Wilkins, which he'd purchased in 1862.

In his early thirties, having made enough money to no longer be poor but still lacking in some sense the luxuries that wealth could afford, Carnegie wrote himself a memo. During his lifetime it was never shared, and it was only after his death, when his wife donated it to the New York Public Library, that it became public. The memo detailed Carnegie's plans to retire at age thirty-five; at that point he would aim to become a learned, sophisticated man, and by forty, his mind flush with all the literary knowledge he'd since then consumed, he'd move, in his newly cosmopolitan life, to London, he thought, and devote himself to more serious matters—maybe he'd run a newspaper, all the while putting his money to good use, helping those who were less fortunate.

"To continue much longer overwhelmed by business cares and with most of my thoughts wholly upon the way to make more money in the shortest time, must degrade me beyond hope of permanent recovery," he wrote. The pursuit of money, it seemed, wasn't all it was cracked up to be.[2]

But early retirement never came. A few years later, Carnegie began turning iron into steel, which in turn led him to buy up steel mills. In the late 1800s, he formed Carnegie Steel Company, and in 1901 sold it, at the behest of J. P. Morgan, to U.S. Steel, netting him 226 million dollars—an amount worth more than 7 billion dollars today.

Among Carnegie's partners in the steel business was Henry Clay Frick, whose acquaintance he made while Frick was honeymooning with his wife in New York. Despite a twenty-five-year difference in age, the two became fast friends. Frick, too, was an industrialist, but his main trade was coke—not the white stuff, but what became of baking coal in a brick beehive oven, and which was a key component in the manufacture of steel.

According to R. Jay Gangewere, the editor at *Carnegie* magazine: "Frick adroitly took control of the coal fields of Connellsville in the 1870s and expanded his control of mining and coking operations until he became a millionaire by the age of 30. The finest metallurgical coke in the world was his to sell, and he sold it to Carnegie Steel, eventually becoming a partner in that firm as well as remaining the King of Coke."[3]

At Carnegie Steel, Frick rose to become chief executive, all the while serving in a kind of Tom Hagen role to Don Andrew. But over time, after fortunes were made many times over, the two had a falling-out. Carnegie tried forcing Frick from the company, so Frick raised the price of his coke. Carnegie balked and fired him. In turn, Frick tried kicking Carnegie's ass; instead, he had to settle for a good old-fashioned lawsuit, said to be—at that time, at least—the largest in American history. Frick won the lawsuit and pocketed thirty-one million dollars.

The two men would remain bitter enemies for the rest of their lives, though they continued to be neighbors, as Frick, too, called Point Breeze his home. From 1882 to 1905, he lived along with his family in a twenty-two-room mansion called the Clayton, which he purchased for twenty-five thousand dollars, and where he received visitors, among them titans of industry, politicians, and other members of the upper crust.

In fact, in 1902, as part of an executive committee looking to bring the president to Pittsburgh, Henry Clay Frick sent an invite to Theodore Roosevelt.

Roosevelt accepted and soon traveled to the city, where he gave a speech at Schenley Park to a crowd of more than 750,000 people. Afterward, in lieu of returning to Washington, he departed for the Clayton, where he dined with the Fricks. Such was the appeal of the Fricks' home, and such was the allure of Point Breeze. Presidents walked its streets.

When Frick died, nearly twenty years later, he left much of his wealth to be used for the public good—including the home, and the land that would become Frick Park, the largest municipal park in all of Pittsburgh. As the twentieth century progressed, the robber barons who made their mark in Pittsburgh would leave for elsewhere, like New York City, and before long the era of great wealth they'd brought to American life would decline. The mansions that for a hundred years once stood in Point Breeze would be, in many instances, demolished. The streets would be built up and expanded as the neighborhoods around it, like East Liberty, Squirrel Hill, and Shadyside grew.

But the legacy of achievement would forever remain in Point Breeze. In the decades after Frick and Carnegie were long gone, in the years when Judge William Wilkins's last name would be known only to historians, the people in Point Breeze would, unknowingly, walk in their image. In a city where the cost of living was, compared with the rest of the United States, relatively low, the neighborhood would remain, unlike much of Pittsburgh proper, affluent and aspirational.

In Point Breeze, politicians, artists, educators, scientists, doctors, and lawyers—the best and the brightest—came to live. The Steel City could boom and bust, as it so famously did throughout the second half of the 1900s, but in Point Breeze, a dependable, upper-middle-class life known as the American Dream was attainable. And that was the world into which, decades later, one young boy was born.

TWO

Malcolm McCormick was born at 8:46 A.M. on January 19, 1992. He was exactly eight pounds. And from that day on, it seemed he was destined to become the center of attention.[1]

His mother, Karen, was a photographer by trade. One of her clients was University of Pittsburgh Medical Center, and when the hospital needed a face for one of its billboards—*We need a cute kid*, they said—Malcolm said his mother thought: *Well, I've got one right here.*[2]

And that's how, at the age of five, not yet even able to tie his own shoes, Malcolm McCormick's cherubic face ended up on a billboard.

"He had a thermometer in his mouth," Karen said in interview with *Complex*. "All his friends that were in preschool would see it, 'cause it was on the highway coming back from the airport. They'd say, "Is Malcolm sick?"[3]

The house he grew up in, in Point Breeze, was full of art and music. Karen's photography work kept her busy, and his dad, Mark, was an architect. He served on the city's Art Commission and ran his own firm, which was prominent in the redevelopment of many landmarks in and around Pittsburgh.

But Mark was not a Pittsburgh native; in fact, he had grown up in Silver Lake, Ohio, an affluent suburb of Akron. In the early seventies, he graduated from Miami University of Ohio with a dual degree in psychology and philosophy. After some years working as a carpenter in Denver, Colorado, he found his way back to school and graduated with a master's degree in architecture in 1979.

In Denver, Mark quickly found employment with the firm Barker Rinker Seacat & Partners; in 1984, he became a partner, but it wasn't long before he was on the move again, this time to Pennsylvania. By then, he had met Karen, who had grown up in Pittsburgh, and in 1986 they were married.[4] Karen's father was an engineer, her mother a homemaker, and she went to school in Massachusetts—Boston University and Emerson College, specifically—where she studied English and art history.

Public records reveal that two years after getting married, with Mark working as the city architect of Pittsburgh, they bought a house in Point Breeze on Rosemary Road. Built in 1855, the four-bedroom house was a shade under 2,500 square feet—not overly large, but perhaps just the right size, because not long afterward, in 1988, Karen gave birth.

The family's first son was named Miller, perhaps for his maternal grandmother, Marcia, who was born Marcia Miller before changing her last name to that of her first husband, William "Ted" Meyers (the last name Karen appears to have taken and kept upon marrying Mark), and later Weiss (for her second husband, Mickey Weiss).

In the early nineties, the McCormicks were a prosperous bunch. Mark had, by then, left his city job and gone back into the private sector, buying out his previous employer, Oliver Design Group. When Malcolm arrived in 1992, one of Mark's big projects was redesigning the Heinz 57 Center, an historic building formerly housing Gimbels' flagship department store, rechristened under the corporate banner of German ketchup entrepreneur and onetime Point Breeze resident, Henry J. Heinz.

For the most part, Malcolm's childhood was idyllic. In 1998, the family moved a few blocks to a new house, which was larger—five bedrooms. Things were going well. A few years earlier, Mark had completed a big project, the redevelopment of the public library in Mount Lebanon, a Pittsburgh suburb.

The work was significant. It involved stripping the library's original structure, built in 1965, to its bones, then building it back up again, making it bigger—more than doubling it from 13,000 square feet to 26,500—and filling it with natural light. Ample space was dedicated for reading and individual study.

"We love the light," Cynthia Richey, the library's director, said at the time. "The building is spacious but there are nooks for reading. I also like the pitched and beamed roof. This is nirvana for us!"[5]

Another big design plus was room for computers—sixty-two of them—without sacrificing space for books and library stacks. In fact, now there was even more room for books.

"We still have books," Richey said. "Libraries call them the cockroaches of civilization: You can't get rid of them. I don't think they will ever disappear."

Upon its completion, the former commissioner of Mount Lebanon, Barbara Logan, said of Mark's firm: "You have won much-deserved recognition, and a standard of quality has been established for the community."

The project netted Mark a Design Excellence award from the Pittsburgh chapter of the American Institute of Architects.

• • •

Mark and Karen didn't necessarily push their children to be creative, but it wasn't a stretch that they would be.

"I'm a photographer and my husband's an architect," Karen told *Complex*. "There's a lot of genetic disposition towards creativity."[6]

Karen and Mark were baby boomers, part of the post-hippie generation that defined so much of American life in the second half of the twentieth century. Music, art, and culture—they were into it all. When the kids were young, they took them to jazz concerts in the park; at home, they hipped the boys to the music of their youth and anything else that caught their ears.

"My dad plays guitar," Malcolm said. "And my mom always had music blasting in the house. All kinds of music, everything from the Talking Heads to Lauryn Hill to Aretha Franklin. Crazy stuff. So, I was like—instantly into music."[7]

Malcolm was particularly keen on the Beatles, whose album *Sgt. Pepper's Lonely Hearts Club Band* would, over time, become one of his favorites. Malcolm loved the band so much that he got two Beatles tattoos—John Lennon on his right forearm, and the word "Imagine" on his right inner bicep.

"I love what [the Beatles] represent," Malcolm would say many years after the band's music had been seared into his memory. "I love all the shit when they started getting really weird. I kind of identify with them, not in massiveness, but in their journey."[8]

As for Lennon—and that tattoo—he flat-out believed the man from Liverpool was the second coming of the messiah.

"He's Jesus," he said. "John Lennon is my favorite."[9]

Then there was Dylan. His dad loved Bob Dylan so much that he brought the boys to see Dylan on his Never Ending Tour when Malcolm was still a child. The family's tickets were general admission, but Malcolm was so entranced by the performance that he snuck down to the front row,[10] where he could take it all in.[11]

And back at the house, it wasn't uncommon to find Mark hanging out with the kids, guitar on his hip, singing and strumming one of Dylan's tunes. "It all helped me see that you didn't need a whole lot of things to make an impact," Malcolm said. "Sometimes, you just need a guy and a guitar speaking his own truths."[12]

But it was more than Dylan and his truth that affected Malcolm. It was Dylan's voice, that nasal, midrange drone. Whether he was belting out his material or singing low and controlled, if Dylan's music was playing, you could tell it was him. Dylan's voice was as much a part of his act as the guitar or harmonica.

"Bob Dylan is someone who had a voice that was unlike anyone [else's]," Malcolm said. "He wasn't hitting the wildest falsetto runs. . . . He just put his soul in it."[13]

Years later, Malcolm would seek to emulate this. "When I sing, it's a very vulnerable state," he said. "Very raw. It's me not worrying about where I fall on the spectrum of good singing, and more like how my voice is my instrument."[14]

But that was yet to come. Still a kid, Malcolm exuded a natural charisma. In home videos and photos, friends aren't just embraced; they're hugged as if life depends on it. Many people who knew Malcolm as a child say that he radiated happiness.

Take one particular video, where he raps the lyrics to the Sugar Hill Gang's "Rapper's Delight." He delivers the lyrics with a wry smile, his eyes wide and teeth big, hair falling just above his ears.

In her interview with *Complex*, Karen recalled that Malcolm had always been magnetic, relishing any opportunity to put on a show.[15]

Dylan Reynolds met Malcolm when he was five, at a Little League game. Malcolm's face was painted like Spider-Man, and he was surrounded by other kids; even then, he was the center of attention.

The pair became fast friends and were soon sleeping over at each other's houses regularly. In an article for NextPittsburgh.com,[16] Reynolds remembered a particular moment, back when they played youth football together.

"Our coach told us that on defense we should all try to touch the ball carrier. This was supposed to teach us how to be involved in a play and follow through until the play was over. Malcolm, who was the littlest guy on the field, took this literally and would often be the last one to jump on the dog pile . . . to which the announcer would say 'Mac Attack!' He always wanted to be involved in the action. He hated to be left out."

Other friends who played youth sports remembered him spending more time messing around than actually playing the game. For Malcolm, the real action wasn't on the field; it was off of it.

"You have those guys in the dugout that are making everyone laugh and are always grabbing people's attention, probably taking people's attention away from the game," said Ben Cohen, who played with Malcolm in a baseball league in nearby Squirrel Hill (the neighborhood famous for being the home of Mr. Rogers). "He was a good athlete but a better entertainer."[17]

Malcolm was interested in music as soon as he was old enough to recognize it. He was always dancing around the house; if it had a beat, he'd move to it. Then, around the age of five or six years old, things got turned up a notch. It was the holiday season, and he wasn't really looking forward to another pair of socks.

He told his parents that he wanted to make music; like, for real.

So that year, on one of Hanukkah's eight nights, he unwrapped a gift and found something life-altering staring back at him—a brand-new keyboard. "I hooked that thing up and never stopped playing it,"[18] he said.

Next came piano lessons. Malcolm took to it; still, he had to add his own twist.

"At piano recitals, I would never play Beethoven or Mozart—I would play my own shit," he said. "Which wasn't as good as Beethoven or Mozart, but you had to respect the effort."[19]

Then there was that bellwether of every child's upbringing—religion. Mom was Jewish, and Dad was Catholic. For Malcolm, like many kids of interfaith marriages, this complicated things. His sense of identity was in flux and was shaped by the world around him.

Early on, he attended Catholic schools. First, it was elementary at St. Peter & Paul. After that, middle school at St. Bede, where the philosophy espoused is "that each child is a unique human being endowed by God with special gifts," and where learnings are peppered with Roman Catholic influences with a focus on "Faith, Family, Community, Love and Service."

The goal, in the end, was to model "Christ-like behaviors through actions and words."[20] But Malcolm also went to Hebrew school. At thirteen, he had his bar mitzvah at Rodef Shalom,[21] an historic synagogue with the distinguished privilege of being the oldest Jewish congregation in western Pennsylvania.

And he spent many summers at the Emma Kaufmann Camp, a Jewish sleepaway camp near Morgantown, West Virginia, where at night he slept in a dorm and during the day he engaged in summery activities—barn fires and sing-alongs, swimming, waterskiing, canoeing, horseback riding, and arts and crafts. It was your typical summer jam.

Malcolm made many close friends at the camp and was influenced by its outings, daily trips where the kids boarded a yellow school bus, then traveled to places like Cincinnati and Washington, DC.

It was a way to break up the monotony of the days spent in the great outdoors, but it also provided an opportunity for Malcolm to entertain his pals; like in a video taken when Malcom was a teenager, where he sits on the bus with his friends. Dressed in togas, their fitted caps twisted backward, the scene has all the gravitas of a frat house.

"The Togas—Quad 5, homie," Malcolm shouts. And the kids start shouting back—"Toga! Toga! Toga!" Then he quiets them down. "Do the beat." Sitting across from Malcolm, a kid begins beatboxing. Like a comic version of *8 Mile*, Malcolm smiles, his braces tight against his big white teeth. He pushes his medium-length hair back, fixes the blue toga resting against his white tank top. His eyes wide, he jumps in: "On the bus sitting here in a toga. . . ."[22]

The rhyme is otherwise inoffensive—just a kid saying things to impress his friends on a hot summer day. It is hardly the stuff from which deep meaning could be extracted, though the lyric "I spit a few lines and they act like it's a crime" suggests something unspoken at play.

Malcolm attended the Emma Kaufmann Camp until he was fifteen; on weekends, he'd perform at the camp's Shabbat talent shows.

"People say he got his start at Shabbat Concert," Sam Bloom, a former camp director, told the *Jewish Chronicle*. "If it wasn't, it was darn close to where it began."

He did more than rap at these concerts.

Jeremy Goldman, another former camp director, told the *Chronicle* that he remembered telling Malcolm his favorite song was "Send Me on My Way" by Rusted Root. And when Saturday night came, sure enough, there was Malcolm with the guitar, belting out the song. "At 13 years old, he was cooler than anyone I had ever met—and I was 31 at the time," Goldman said. "Whenever it was his turn to do his act, he brought the house down."[23]

But Malcolm never made much of a *real* fuss about Judaism or Christianity. On a song titled "S.D.S.," released in 2013, he rapped that he was a "Jewish Buddhist tryna consume the views of Christianity." More than just a clever boast, it seemed to be a summary of his spiritual life; Judaism—which he would later mine for both comedic and creative effect—was just another footnote in the countless things that made him who he was.

Fans seized on his Judaism though. In an early interview, when told people were calling him the "greatest Jewish rapper of all time," he chuckled.

"I'm Jewish . . . that's how I was raised; I had a bar mitzvah," he said. "[But] I'm not a very religious person. So it's humorous to me when people do this big Jewish rapper thing. This is a world filled with so much variety of cultures. Every time something different is out, it's good. Because then it's just like, oh, a Jewish rapper! I didn't think there could be a Jewish rapper. But there could be any kind of rapper. Religion has nothing to do with that."[24]

You see, people were billing him as a "Jewish" rapper when he was just a rapper who happened to be Jewish. Were they confused? Perhaps. But then, Malcolm wore Judaism—literally—on his sleeve.

On his upper left arm, he had a tattoo, the Jewish symbol of a Chai. In Judaism, the Chai is made up of two letters, Chet and Yod; together, they are said to mean "alive" or "living." The Chai commemorates life.

He got the tattoo for two reasons. He wanted it to remind him who he was[25]—a Jew. But also to remember one crucial thing: that in life, no moment was greater than any other; to be alive, breathing, that was a beautiful thing.

Life was something he hoped to never take for granted.

THREE

Life in Point Breeze was peachy. It was a "front porch" community, where neighbors kept tabs on other people's kids, and where, when an adult suspected someone from the "other side"—like, say, neighboring Homewood, just across Penn Avenue—of casing the place, they walked right over and let them know they were being watched, then walked them out of the neighborhood, assuming they hadn't already taken the hint.

Arguably the most liberal part of town, its houses were filled with academics and artists, and its relative safety and progressive politics came with its own set of problems; namely, the long leash some parents gave their kids. In the neighborhood, Malcolm was one of many kids who stayed out of trouble but tested the limits.

Will Kalson lived not far from Malcolm, in nearby Squirrel Hill.

"I would be in Point Breeze all the time, playing basketball, playing football," Kalson said. "Malcolm would always be around. He was just this little kid that ran around the neighborhood. He said things that he shouldn't have been saying at his age, and you, like, remembered him."[1]

They first met on the basketball court at Sterrett middle school, down the street from Malcolm's home, right across from Frick Park.

"He came down on the court and was trying to play with us. He must've been eleven years old. And so he came over. And he was, like, way smaller. I mean, we were in middle school and he was in elementary school."

After Malcolm hooped for a little bit, the game came to its end. The boys meandered around the court. That was when Malcolm cut in.

"What you doing tonight?"

The boys looked at one another, confused. What could this little kid care about what they were up to?

"I dunno," Kalson said. "What are *you* doing tonight?"

Malcom didn't miss a beat.

"I'm gonna go smoke some blunts," he said. "Yeah, that's right—I'm gonna go smoke some blunts with these bitches."

In the neighborhood, it wasn't uncommon for kids to begin smoking weed by thirteen or fourteen years of age. Malcom began even earlier. He started with cigarettes in the third grade; then, two years later, when he was ten, came weed.[2]

Now, if Malcolm seemed a bit bold—well, he was a colorful kid, and was already knee-deep into hip-hop, rife with its adult themes. The first rap album he ever listened to was Outkast's *Aquemini*, which he had picked up rifling through his brother's CD collection. To him, the album served as a kind of North Star.

"That's the bar for me, it's my guiding light," he said. "I heard it when I was super young. . . . My brother had it and the cover was just so unbelievable that I grabbed it. I remember locking myself in my grandma's guest room and listening to it on repeat all day. Being that young, and having an idea of what I thought music should be, then hearing *Aquemini* completely shifted things."[3]

The thing that he loved about *Aquemini* was that it had a central theme. The subject matter itself was wide-ranging, but it had a specific tone, a real *sound*; its tracks brim with live instrumentation and an experimental, trippy vibe. Southern rap was still in its infancy, and the album, released in 1998, cut against the grain. It wasn't Wu-Tang, Bad Boy, Ruff Ryderz, or Roc-A-Fella. It was Outkast. And it was art.

"It's a whole, complete album, not just a collection of songs," he said. One track he loved was "Hold On, Be Strong," the album's intro. On it, singer Tony

Hightower gently repeats the lyrics—"Hold on, be strong"—over an ethereal guitar lick and plaintive kalimba, played by group member André 3000 himself. "It makes me feel like I'm in water," Malcolm said, "which is my favorite feeling."[4]

When he wasn't spacing out to Outkast, he was jamming to indie rock, stuff like Jack Johnson, Bright Eyes, and Dave Matthews, among other eclectic interests.

"One of my last middle school memories is of him with long, curly hair with a guitar under his arm while singing some Dave Matthews song to a girl at our school," James Rudolph, a fellow student at St. Bede, recalled. Around his neck was not a diamond-encrusted pendant, no hip-hop bling. "I even think he was wearing a puka-shell necklace, those bead necklaces that were a hallmark of the early 2000s, while doing it."[5]

The look fit with his MO. His original goal, in fact, was to be more of a singer-songwriter. "When he was going through puberty, he was going really hard on the guitar," Jimmy Murton, one of his closest friends, told *Complex*. "He wanted to be a singer-songwriter."[6]

He played in bands, even competed in some local competitions. At one battle of the bands in 2004, at the Jewish Community Center, he played the acoustic guitar and sang—people who were there remember it being an impressive little performance. Maybe there was a future in this. He could grow up and have a rock career; he'd play guitar in a jam band, tour college campuses, and make a killing.

"I thought I was gonna be like a G-Love type of person," he would later say. "That's what I thought I was gonna do."[7]

But the band dream got put on hold. People weren't enthused about his voice, an acquired taste, and before long he was finding other ways to express himself.

FOUR

Growing up, Malcolm had a diverse group of friends. On the one hand, the nice Jewish boys he went to camp with in West Virginia; on the other, his pals from Point Breeze and its surrounding neighborhoods.

One of his best friends was Derek Green. Derek's mom, Marina, grew up in Pittsburgh. Her dad—Derek's grandfather—was Wesley Posvar, a decorated air force veteran and later the chancellor of the University of Pittsburgh; his grandmother was Mildred Miller, a mezzo-soprano with the Metropolitan Opera who later founded the Opera Theater of Pittsburgh.

Derek's mom went to middle school with Malcolm's mom, Karen. When she got married, the family began moving around a lot. His dad was a sports television producer, and every few years his job found him uprooting the whole family to wherever the work went. One year it was New York, the next Maryland, after that Oklahoma, and finally, after many years, the parents got divorced. Which is when they moved back to Pittsburgh.

"It was like, 'Oh, I'm gonna reconnect with my old crew—you got kids, I'm gonna bring my kids around your kids,'" said Derek's older brother, Brian. "Malcolm's a year younger than my brother, Derek. So they became super, super close. And he was at our house every weekend, sleeping over, or vice versa."[1]

Even back then, there was something about Malcolm that made him seem special. "He was very much an old soul," Brian said. "As a kid—despite his amount of years on Earth—he felt more in touch with the base elements of human contact and emotion. He could relate to people who were way older than him. When I was in high school—ninth grade, tenth grade—he would be cool with seniors in high school, dappin' 'em up and cuttin' up with them. He exceeded beyond his years."

Plus, he was entertaining. "He was very charismatic and funny," Brian said. "He was ten and I was fourteen, whatever the age difference was, but I still found him hilarious to talk to. He always had a smile on his face. He was almost always laughing. He could brighten up everybody's smile in a room, no matter how old you were. You either were gonna laugh at him or laugh with him."

Bill Niels was another friend. He went to school with Malcolm's brother, Miller—they were in the same grade—and he, too, would sleep over at Malcolm's house. "My first memory of Mac, he was about ten or eleven," Bill said. "And we were all laughing in his parents' kitchen. I had just spilled milk out of my nose."[2]

The next time their paths crossed, things were a little more tense. It was a weekend and they were out at the country home of Brian's grandparents, in Ligonier, PA, about an hour southeast of Pittsburgh. It's Brian and Bill, a bunch of their high school friends, and Malcolm and Derek, and a bunch of their middle school friends. Bill, for whatever reason, decided to take acid. "And we were just fuckin' trippin' our balls out," Bill said. Malcolm and his friends were off in a separate corner of the house—not high on acid, but certainly up to their own unique brand of mischief.

"We were all leaving the next morning," Bill said, "and I was like, broke." But Bill had a BB gun on him. And Malcolm just happened to cross his line of sight. "So I go up. I put the gun to Mac's head. 'Give me your money.'"

Malcolm was scared shitless!

"I wasn't actually going to hurt him," Bill said. "But then he gave it to me. Twenty dollars or something. And I was like, all right, cool—and I just left."

Malcolm never harbored any ill feelings. That wasn't his style. He was too easygoing and carefree, saw too much of the good in people. He could never hold a grudge.

"Years later, he showed up at my mom's apartment. He bought some shirt off me for twenty dollars. But he never paid me. And he was like, that's for that."

Then there was TreeJ. TreeJ grew up in Pittsburgh's Hill District, just a fifteen-minute drive from Malcolm's house, but in many ways a world away. "Up there, they sell dope their whole lives, go to jail," said TreeJ. "That's all anyone does in the Hill District. I got lucky making it out."[3]

It was a mixture of good and bad fortune that led TreeJ to that outcome.

"There was a school across the street from my mom's house, and I got kicked out of that. I was so young, it had to have been something stupid. So, my mom sent me to another school. And I got kicked out of there. I was fuckin' around with the principal's daughter. Not in a sexual way or anything. I was in like third grade; I just liked picking on her, I guess. Anyway, the principal gave me the boot."

After that, TreeJ's mom told him she would be sending him to a much nicer school. He would have to take a bus there—but maybe it'd put him in the right kind of learning environment, around the right kind of people to set him on a better path. "You fuck up again," she told him, "I'm just gonna whoop your ass."

So TreeJ went to St. Bede, one of a handful of Black students at a mostly white school. "That's the first time I was really around white people," he said. And it was at St. Bede, with its focus on small classes—just thirty-two students per grade level—where he became close with a pair of white kids. Their names: Jimmy Murton and Derek Green.

Like Derek, Jimmy had known Malcolm since he was a child. He had met him at a friend's house around the time he was eight, and they would often play together in the neighborhood. As TreeJ began traveling from the Hill District to hang with Derek and Jimmy, he inevitably fell in with the little kid who was always around them.

"Malcolm would be there," TreeJ said. "So, we became this little group. Me, Jimmy, Derek, and Malcolm."

"I was like the connecting friend," Malcolm said.[4]

The friends spent a lot of time at Derek's house. The house was a relatively carefree kind of place, with little parental supervision. There, they would smoke weed, listen to music—Lil Wayne and Dipset got a lot of play—and generally run amok.

"Brian's mom's house was basically like, you could do whatever you wanted there," said Will Kalson, who would frequent the spot when he came home from college. But the freedom had its drawbacks. Malcolm and Derek, who were still relatively young, could keep their shit under control; Derek's older brother, Brian, however, was another story.

"I was selling drugs on a very small level," Brian said. "Just weed, and maybe something randomly, like mushrooms. I wasn't trapping on the block or nothing like that."

School wasn't of much interest to him, so he dropped out. "It wasn't like, 'Oh, I'm rich, I don't need to do this' or anything like that," he said. "I was just doing that and was like, 'eh, fuck school.' I wasn't looking out for my future at that point, I was just making reckless decisions."

Before long, Brian's mother's boyfriend had had enough. "You gotta stop sleeping all day," he told Brian.

"People would be in and out of the house partying, drinking late, doing stupid shit," Brian said. "So, he was just like, 'You gotta get the fuck out of here.'"

And so Brian moved out and went to stay at Bill's, where he shacked up for a few months. He got a job washing dishes for eight dollars an hour at a restaurant called Point Brugge, saving money for an apartment. But privately, he was plotting the start of a rap career: He'd pen lyrics in the morning before work and at night when he came home.

Meanwhile, with Brian out of the house, there was a vacancy at Derek and Brian's mother's. His former room was a full apartment up in the attic, where he had run of the place. Malcolm, Derek, Jimmy, TreeJ—the whole gang couldn't wait to take it over.

"There was a living room," Malcolm said in an interview for MTV's *When I Was 17*. "[Then] there was this room called the shroom room, with like a little mushroom with chairs around it, where usually we would go to test out some of the chemicals that we were working on. We had the storage room. It was basically a room with a couch and a TV and if you were tripping out real hard you would just go in that room."[5]

But the most important room was a simple space with two spare beds next to each other and stars on the ceiling. The stars glowed in the dark when the lights were turned off, and the boys would sit there gazing up at them, high on weed, mushrooms, acid—whatever they could get their hands on that day.

They called it the "Star Room."

Like the keyboard he got as a child, the Star Room would change Malcolm's life. Up there in the attic, away from home, school, parents, and teachers, away from the "real world" and all the high school talk of where you'd go to college and what you—a teenager with nothing figured out yet—were going to do with your life, the space functioned as a sanctuary.

In the Star Room, Malcolm could do many of the things kids do when nobody is watching.

"I became a man in the attic," he said.[6]

He played video games and watched movies like *How High*, the stoner comedy starring Redman and Method Man. He watched the movie so many times that he learned every word to it. He drank forty-ounce beers and messed around with local girls. He got his first blow job in the Star Room. And after losing his virginity while watching *Nacho Libre* at age fourteen to a girl who his older brother, Miller, as well as a few of his friends, had previously had sex with, in the basement of her parents' house,[7] it was inside the Star Room that he had sex for the second time.

It was easy to see why this place was a teenage dream. Malcolm remembered a typical night in the attic going as follows: The boys would be sitting around. They were young and broke. But they'd want to get high. Girls in the neighborhood knew about the Star Room. And they'd call the house.

"What are you doing?" they'd ask.

"Hanging out," Malcolm would reply. "Do you have sixty dollars?"

"We only have forty," they'd say.

No dice.

"Call us back when you have sixty."

And before long, they'd call back. "We've got the sixty dollars."

"OK, you can come over." And then they'd come, pay for the drugs, and make a night of it.[8]

One time, a girl came over. She was high on acid, so high that she began taking off all her clothes. When she was done, she sat there, naked on the couch. There were twenty guys in the room, and, according to Malcolm, she was down for whatever.

Then Derek's mom barged into the room, so they shoved the girl in a closet. *Nothing improper happening here, no ma'am.* When Derek's mom exited, they busted out laughing. They needed to get her out of there. So out of the house she went, into a car, to be dropped off at a friend's house. Crisis averted.

"She was our homie," Malcolm said. "We wanted to make sure she was straight."[9]

In his interview on MTV's *When I Was 17*, he told two versions of the same story—a clean version and a dirty version, with the dirty one unpublishable by modern standards; however, he implored the interviewer to use the dirty version. It was clear, from this early interview, that he was already aware there could be two versions of the same story and that, when given the choice, most people would choose the one with less edge.

He gave that interview in 2012; however, by then he appeared to have matured, admitting that in hindsight, "We did a lot of scumbaggy things. . . . My friends and I were not— are not—proud of the things that went on."[10]

But mostly, the Star Room was best known for one thing. It was where Malcolm McCormick really became a rapper.

He spit his first-ever freestyle there, rapping over Dr. Dre's "Xxplosive," and when he finished, it was like something for him and his friends had changed. They stared at one another, amazed.

"It was one of those moments. I rapped and we were like—all right, this is real." And from then on, he could be found up in the attic.

"I would rap as entertainment," he said. "Because really that's all we had to do. We would just throw on instrumentals and I used to freestyle. One time, I freestyled for two hours straight."

It didn't matter how long it was. Malcolm loved it.

"Beat after beat after beat after beat."[11]

He couldn't stop.

FIVE

One day, when he was fourteen years old, Malcolm was at Derek Green's house, freestyling in the attic, as he was known to do in his free time. Malcolm was just messing around, but on this day, Derek pulled out a Canon PowerShot camera and pressed record. When he was done, Derek emailed the video to Brian.

"They knew I was into rap and they just thought—Hey, it'd be cool to show him this," Brian said. "It was cheesy, but dope. Malcolm had braces, he was wearing a fake BAPE hoodie. It was goofy, but it was so him. It was authentic to who he was. Which was just this goofy ball of energy. I thought it was awesome. Because if you knew him as a kid, you would just think, this kid's a star."[1]

Brian was impressed by Malcolm's rapping abilities. On a technical level, they weren't brilliant. Just a lyrical workout of sorts, rhyming words that went together, as rappers do. The thing that sold Brian was how fast Malcolm thought of things to rap about. Freestyling—that is, true freestyling, where a rapper improvises lyrics on the spot—is something of a lost art, having fallen out of favor sometime around the mid-nineties. But there Malcolm was, dropping bars off the top of his head.

"He's got a big smile on his face. And he was pretty skillful at how he could quickly come up with the words. I was impressed. I thought—OK, you can actually kinda freestyle; this is pretty good."

At the time, Brian had a friend named Nils. Nils was absolutely horrible at rapping but was one of those kids who, if you were to hang around with him long enough, would eventually want to get a cypher going. "We gotta get him over and freestyle," Nils said. So they invited Malcolm over to Brian's apartment, across the street from the Star Room.

"That was literally how it started," Brian said. "The three of us just kicking it, rapping. We were like—'this is fun!' Then, one time me and Malcolm decided we were gonna make a song. Then we did a couple more."

They cut the tracks on Brian's old G4 computer, recording into GarageBand through a cheap microphone he had purchased for a hundred dollars. They didn't know what the hell they were doing; they were simply figuring it out as they went along.

"There was no YouTube to go check out a tutorial at the time," Brian said. "People now, they can just do whatever. I see people get started and already have a SoundCloud hit and they just learned how to record themselves that day."

All the songs were more or less "freestyles" in the modern sense of the word—tracks with written verses then layered over instrumentals to songs that had already been released. You strung enough of these freestyles together, you had a mixtape. Sometimes a mixtape would have original songs on it and have the feel of a complete vision, like an album. Sometimes it was a mix of freestyles and original music. In the end, there was no formula for a mixtape; they could be sold, but they could also be distributed for free as promotional items. For a young artist just starting out, they were like demo tapes for the public, a business card announcing to whomever came in possession of one: *Hey, I'm a rapper, check me out!*

The mixtape format had existed for years, first on actual tapes, then on CDs. They were a boon to many hip-hop artists and DJs, including 50 Cent, Young Jeezy, The Diplomats, Lil Wayne, and countless others. So Malcolm, rapping under the name Easy Mac (sometimes stylized as EZ Mac), decided he would take the tracks he made with Brian, plus some songs he'd recorded solo, and drop a mixtape of his own.

For the cover, he draped himself in an oversize blue-and-gold Pittsburgh Panthers basketball jersey. On his head he wore a blue fitted cap, twisted to the back. He walked up to the Star Room and sat on the bed. It was littered with papers and spindles of CD-Rs, but Malcolm didn't care. He threw both hands up and sucked in his bottom lip, pretending to be a tough guy. Then he told Brian to take a picture.

"He pressed up copies," Will Kalson said, estimating that there are about fifty of them in existence. "He was burning 'em one by one," Brian told me. "You know, you'd buy like a twenty-pack of CD-Rs."

Kalson said that though the mixtape is rare, those who heard it were put onto Mac's talent right away. "It was an amateur mixtape. But anyone who heard it was like, he's funny, he's charismatic, he's really good for how young is. He was like fourteen when he made that."

Original copies of the mixtape are scarce. A nine-track version exists online—you can hear it on YouTube, or the website DatPiff—but that's not the actual mixtape. Rather, it's just a collection of songs that Malcolm uploaded to DatPiff because he thought the original version was so bad.[2] "[The actual mixtape is] way worse than the version that's online," said Brian.

And yet, listening to it now, *But My Mackin' Ain't Easy* shows signs of early promise and unlocks clues to the teenage feelings Malcolm was experiencing. To be sure, his flow lacks polish, his breathing is occasionally labored; at times, he seems to be freestyling, literally, off the top of his head (which is impressive in a live setting but often less interesting once committed to tape). Still, these early recordings have an elusive, charming quality.

Over Jay-Z's "Dead Presidents" instrumental, he raps about disappointing his parents, apologizing to his dad for not bringing home "medallions" like other kids. He says his mother doesn't understand him—"She got me trapped like a cell," he raps. He cites their disapproval of his lifestyle, how they hate his fitted caps (Dad called him "The Mad Hatter"), and the way his pants hang off his ass ("thought I act Black 'cause I'm sagging jeans"). He's upset, a teenager venting.

Elsewhere, rapping over Yung Joc's "Coffee Shop," he acknowledges his limitations: "Chill, I will improve, drugs, I will abuse . . . too high, I can touch the sky, my mom knows I rap, but she still wonder why." And on "Good Days Are Gone," over a soulful Nicolay beat, he says that music is his outlet for voicing that which cannot be said in real life. "Thanks for Coming Out," a freestyle over the Roots' jazzy instrumental of "What They Do," closes the mixtape, the mix so amateur that at times you can hear where different parts of the beat have been spliced together; however, the point is made: "Shit's for Pittsburgh, that 412," he says. He sends shots to his haters, says his life was altered after hearing Nas's debut album *Illmatic*, and hints that his inner demons escape through writing.

•••

If Malcolm believed *But My Mackin' Ain't Easy* would change his life, he was sorely disappointed. It got him some attention at Winchester Thurston, the prep school he was now attending. But that was about it.

The former owners of the Frick Park Market, a small bodega-style store located a block and a half away from Malcolm's home, remember him bringing the mixtapes around, trying to peddle them outside to local kids after school.

The owners—a husband and wife—were supportive, even if they weren't exactly fans. The husband thought Malcolm's early music was crap; he'd joke with him about it, telling him he had to do better.[3]

Malcolm would later name a song on his debut album after the market (and shoot its accompanying music video inside the store), but at the time he seemed to take the criticism to heart. "I guess I gotta work harder," he said. Look, if you get better, then you can charge six bucks instead of three, the owner told him. Malcolm got a chuckle out of that; that's what the owners recalled, how he laughed and kept a positive attitude no matter what they said.[4]

But becoming a successful rapper was no laughing matter. If Malcolm was going to make his mark, he'd have to work much harder at getting better. Technology had made it so that anyone with a computer could produce a mixtape in their bedroom. And in the future, that bedroom-style aesthetic would come to define so much of the music that would become popular.

He could string words together, sure, but anyone could do that. "Rapping is easy," Bun B said. "Writing words that rhyme, saying them in music, that's fairly easy—you can teach that. Like playing football, I can teach you the rules of football, I can throw you a football and you'll probably catch it. But to be considered one of the greatest football players of all time, you have to go above and beyond. You have to practice at it and work at it more than other people do. It's not a casual effort; it's a very concerted effort, and there's a lot of hours, and a lot of time, and a lot of thought put into the process."

Brian and Malcolm had a good working chemistry. When recording, they'd often trade lyrics back and forth. Malcolm would rhyme a few lines, then Brian would rhyme a few, and they'd continue like this, their two distinct voices serving one sound. Old-school hip-hop groups like EPMD, A Tribe Called Quest, and Kid 'n Play had done this frequently.

"It felt like a lost art in a way," Brian said. "We were listening to [EPMD], Souls of Mischief, a bunch of nineties shit, all the Duck Down [Records] stuff."

Soon, the idea to become a group began to crystallize. "We were just like—'Yo, we should just fuckin' start a group,'" Brian said. "I drove my car out to meet him at his mom's house one day, like, late night. We were gonna go over some shit and he said something about 'the Ill Spoken.' I said, 'That shit is like a group name. It's some backpacker-sounding shit, "the Ill Spoken."'" And that was that.

As the Ill Spoken, they decided they would make a mixtape. Then Will Kalson got wind of what they were up to.

"I was going to Indiana University in Bloomington, Indiana," Kalson recalled. "I wasn't going there for anything specific; I just wanted to go and party, basically. So I was at IU. And Brian had started rapping. And he was sending me his music. At the same time, he was also sending me Malcolm's music."

When Kalson heard Malcolm's music, he really liked it. Kalson was a serious hip-hop head. He had an almost encyclopedic knowledge of different rap scenes in different cities. He kept up with new producers, new artists; whatever was happening in hip-hop, in "the culture," he was aware of it.

He liked what he heard from Malcolm, and told Brian, who shared that information with his young padawan. In late 2007, Kalson came home from college for the winter break. He was visiting Brian when Malcolm walked in.

"I heard you fuck with my music," Malcolm said.

"'Yeah, I fuck with your music, it's dope,'" Kalson remembered telling him. "I could see potential in him. And he knew how much I knew about hip-hop, how much I loved hip-hop. The fact that I liked his music was, I think, a big deal to him. He was fifteen years old and he looked up to me and Brian. From there, it was like we never stopped talking."

Shortly afterward, Kalson came on as a kind of de facto manager of the Ill Spoken. He felt the group had what it took to become something.

"We were like, yeah, we're gonna do this Ill Spoken project, it's going to be crazy," he said. "It's going to be Malcolm and Brian and it's going to be nuts."

On paper, Kalson did not exactly have what it took to be a manager. At least not in the traditional sense. He had never worked at a record label, nor did he have much in the way of industry connections. But he was hungry, and digitally savvy. He was particularly attuned to what was happening on the forums at RapMullet.com; in those years, the mid-aughts, many popular mixtape DJs would browse the forums, searching for new music.

"Kay Slay had an account, DJ Enuff, all the big New York DJs had accounts on there and they would like, talk shit on each other in the forums," Kalson recalled. "And this was the early stages, even before social media. Before blogs."

Kalson had an idea. If he could get the Ill Spoken's music on the forums, maybe the group would make some noise. So he, Brian, and a high school friend named Zachary Lipshitz (who put up roughly five thousand dollars as an initial investment) started a company. They called it East End Empire.

"Zach was living in Ohio or something at that time," Kalson said. "We drove halfway and met him on the highway at a truck stop. We sat in the truck stop and talked about what we were gonna do. He agreed to fund the Ill Spoken mixtape, pay for the logo, shit like that."

When it came to the business, Malcolm didn't want to be too involved, opting instead to focus solely on the art. He had a mixtape to make and the funding to record it. It was time for the Ill Spoken to hit the studio.

The spot where they recorded was called Tuff Sound. It was owned by an engineer named Soy Sos, and run out of his house on Trenton Avenue, just outside of Pittsburgh, in nearby Wilkinsburg. Technically still in the Pittsburgh metro area, it was only a stone's throw from Point Breeze, but in a town with a median household income of 26,621 dollars, it felt like it was a world away from the streets Malcolm grew up on.

Soy was skeptical. Born and raised in Pittsburgh, he not only knew the city but had worked with many of the area's hip-hop artists. Most (but certainly not all) hailed from neighborhoods like Braddock, Garfield, Homewood, and the Hill District. These were Black communities where the pipe dream of rap stardom held strong, for along with professional sports, it could potentially provide a way out of the hood.

Among these groups there were Pimp Player Union, who Soy described as "some pretty badass guys," the D-Boys, whose subject matter was "mostly drug selling and gun shit," and F-Block, who became Traptastic, then Trap Illustrated. These groups weren't very organized, but were determined.

"A lot of those projects were crews of six, eight, ten guys—with various spin-offs and combinations," Soy said. "I worked with everybody and I was just considered, like, a white guy that 'got it.' I was cool, reliable, and would do right by your project."[5]

Now there was the Ill Spoken, Easy Mac and B-Dub (later Beedie), the name Brian had chosen for himself, who hailed from the mean streets of Point Breeze, and who also happened to be white.

"I was definitely suspect of white rappers," Soy said. "The white kids I almost was not rooting for as hard because I'm just like, 'we have all the advantages,' I just wanted these other Black kids I was working with to get a break. I'd worked with other white rappers and I'd [always] be like—this kid's fucking trash."

If it wasn't their lack of talent that bothered him, it was something else that white rappers would do. Like one group from Braddock, whose members were Black but had a lone white member. "His name was Tony, but they called him White Tone, and they authorized him to use the N-word," said Soy. He recorded the music, but thinking back on it makes him cringe. Another time he had to listen to a white rapper from a well-to-do neighborhood spitting lyrics about how hard it was "out here on these streets."

In his estimation, when it came to white rappers, there was Eminem and . . . well, that was it.

"To me, Eminem was the moment," he said. "My clients were sitting around going—Oh, you hear about this guy, man? The thing that sold Eminem, from what I saw, was that he was considered working-class. He worked off of that image of 'I'm from Detroit and I'm poor and I'm white trash. I'm crazy.' And he's good; he was really good. Black kids respected Eminem in a way that I hadn't seen before. All those other rappers were kind of a joke. 3rd Bass was good, but they weren't great. Obviously, everybody hates Vanilla Ice."

But it didn't take long for Soy's skepticism to recede. The Ill Spoken worked diligently. Song after song, it seemed they kept improving.

"These guys started coming more steadily, then they were building up a catalog of stuff, and I was like, 'oh, this is good,'" he said.

Soy liked that they were kids—Brian was nineteen and Malcolm just fifteen—and they were hungry. That they were getting better with each recording session only sweetened the deal. They were clients, after all, and he was running a business, but he was also a fan. He remembered Malcolm, especially, being very inquisitive. He wanted to know what each thing in the studio did.

"He wasn't one of those kids that was disinterested," said Soy. "Some people just come and they're like, 'I just need to lay my fucking voice down.' But he was interested in the process. He was patient. He wanted to get it right. He would do multiple takes to make sure it wasn't just a throwaway verse. Everything that he was doing was very purposeful, very much intentional. He was a student of the craft."

The sessions with Brian and Malcolm were fun. Time was money, and they learned that quickly in the studio, so they would write the songs together before they got there, then lay them down rather expediently. Because the sessions moved fast, they got a lot of work done. "He was a natural," Brian said. "He didn't really need to do a lot of shit over. He would maybe redo it a couple times—like, 'oh, let me do another take'—but would rarely revise the whole thing. He was just on to the next."

Beginning in October of 2007, they spent nine months in the studio. The first song they recorded was called "Come Around." The producer was named Anwar; he was from Sweden and Brian met him on Myspace. "He didn't believe in Mac," Brian said. "I went to war with people all the time. People would be like, 'Yeah, I mean, you're dope, but what's up this young dude?' I'd be like, 'No, this kid's dope, trust me.'"

Often, Brian and Malcolm would work on music late at night, after Malcolm was supposed to be in bed. Brian would take his mother's car and drive to Malcolm's house, at which point Malcolm would sneak out. The car parked, they'd sit inside and work on songs together.

One night, Malcolm decided he'd do the driving.

"I can actually grab my mom's car and I'll come meet you," he said. He didn't even have a driver's permit, but he took the car anyway, making a dangerous left turn onto a main road, into oncoming traffic, almost wrecking the car—and himself—in the process.

But he escaped unharmed, and when he pulled up to Brian's house, he said—"Dude, I almost just got into a car wreck. I almost just died."

He was smiling.

"All this would have been over," he said.

"What do you mean?" Brian asked.

"The journey," Malcolm said. "The music!"

Brian sat there quietly.

"He believed that he was gonna be a huge artist," Brian said. "In that moment, you could see it in him."

SIX

It was the early 2000s, and Benjy Grinberg was graduating from the University of Pennsylvania. A local Pittsburgh kid, Benjy grew up not far from Malcolm's family, in nearby Squirrel Hill.

Some fifteen years earlier, Benjy had been on a trip to Israel. A bunch of families from Pittsburgh had gone together, and he was all of seven years old—it was 1985—when one of the kids on the trip handed Benjy a pair of headphones and said: "Check this out." A Run-DMC song was playing.

"That was the beginning of my love affair with hip-hop," Benjy told *Tablet* magazine."[1]

Over time, Benjy's passion intensified.

"He was really into music—he was like a music junkie," said Arthur Pitt, who met Benjy as a teenager, and played with him on the basketball team at the local Jewish Community Center. "He'd drive me home from practice sometimes, and we became friendly."[2]

Benjy drove a Dodge Caravan then, a car littered with cassettes and CDs. To Artie, the overwhelming selection of music was something to marvel at. "It was unbelievable," Artie said.

On those drives back from practice, Artie would sit in the passenger side of the Caravan, their heads bobbing in unison as Benjy pumped up the volume on the latest hip-hop albums; staring out the window as the streets of the Steel City zipped by, Artie's mind would drift.

"I was always trying to figure out why there was no one from Pittsburgh that was dope," Artie said. "It wasn't like New York. Like, we had nothing here. It always frustrated me. I was like—damn, why aren't there any serious rappers from Pittsburgh?"

There had been some. In 1991, Tuffy Tuf had a minor hit with a track called "Ghetto Soundchek," and the rapper Sam Sneed signed to Death Row Records in 1994, releasing the Dr. Dre–assisted "U Better Recognize." Producer/ rapper Mel-Man also fell in with Dr. Dre, rapping on *Dr. Dre Presents . . . The Aftermath* in 1996 before becoming an in-house producer at the Doc's label.

But by and large, unlike previous generations, the Pittsburgh rap scene hadn't produced many musical icons. It was a break from tradition, for the city had a rich musical history. In the 1800s, Lawrenceville native Stephen Foster, the songwriter behind "Oh! Susanna," "Old Folks at Home," "Nelly Bly," and dozens of other tunes now deem racist by many, was largely considered the "father of American music."[3] In 1916, from his garage in Wilkinsburg, Dr. Frank Conrad conducted one of the very first broadcasts of music over the radio; then, in 1920, Pittsburgh became home to one of the first commercial radio stations in the entire world, KDKA.[4] From the early 1920s until 1960s, the Hill District was a locus for Black music and art; nightclubs and ballrooms produced jazz greats like Errol Garner, Mary Lou Williams, Art Blakey, and Earl Hines, among others.[5] Later, Pittsburgh became a doo-wop stronghold; classics of the genre, like the Skyliners' "Since I Don't Have You," the Del-Vikings' "Come Go With Me," and perhaps most famously, the Marcels' "Blue Moon," all came out of Pittsburgh.[6]

When it came to rap, though, there was an underground scene, but it hadn't amounted to much. That was the thought Artie had that day in the car. Little did he know that his compadre in the seat next to him, Benjy, seemed to be having the exact same thought. But what could do they about it? They were just kids.

That is, until Benjy got out of college and headed to New York, where much of the music industry was still headquartered, and where, in the early 2000s, you could turn on HOT 97 or Power 105 FM and hear Jay-Z, DMX,

Nas, Cam'ron, and just about anyone who was anyone in the world of hip-hop, playing all day long. The Internet was ascendant, but record stores were still in abundance, and what you didn't buy at a traditional music store you got from a mixtape, purchased from a mixtape stand, found on many Manhattan street corners—be it downtown on Canal Street or uptown on 125th Street—or from a bootlegger, who walked around soliciting, "Mixtape . . . DVD . . . mixtape . . . DVD."

In New York, Benjy lived with his brother, sleeping on his couch. He got a job working in artist relations for a company called Digital Club Network; launched in 1998, its primary focus was webcasting concerts from venues around the country—places like CBGB and Tramps in New York; the 9:30 Club in Washington, DC; and the Great American Music Hall in San Francisco, among other locations.[7]

One of Digital Club Network's founders, Andrew Rasiej, got the idea while working at New York's Irving Plaza. Year after year there, night after night, he'd watch artists perform—Hootie & the Blowfish, the Dave Matthews Band, and many others who would go on to be big. The concerts were legendary, but they were fleeting; without recording them, would anyone know they actually happened? Rasiej told the *New York Times* in 2001 that the lightbulb went off when he realized, "Every one of these concerts is going to be lost forever."[8]

In the early years, Digital Club Network built a sizable catalog of live performances, and they were webcast, in a pre-YouTube world, through America Online. Benjy's primary task was getting artists to sign the contracts that would allow Digital Club Network to webcast their shows. The job wasn't glamorous. Webcasting technology was crude, connecting to the Internet still largely took place via dial-up modem, and with slow connection speeds, quality was poor. These were not yet the days of artists logging on to Instagram during the COVID-19 pandemic and performing their entire catalog from their patio.

For Benjy, the job was a grind, and though he wasn't opposed to getting his hands dirty, it didn't seem as if he particularly liked it.

One night, Benjy was walking downtown in New York City when he bumped into an old friend. They began talking about what they were both up to. Benjy said he was working at the Digital Club Network; what he really wanted, however, was to work at a record label, because that was where the action was, and that was where he wanted to be. Coincidentally, his friend was with a pal who had a temp job at Arista Records.

Arista Records was an exciting place to be at the time. In 2000, the company had come under new leadership, with Antonio "L.A." Reid taking over for Clive Davis as president and CEO. Reid was a unicorn. He was a songwriter and producer with a remarkable ear for talent. He could also operate in the c-suite. In the nineties, his label, LaFace Records, had turned Usher, Outkast, TLC, and many others into stars. At Arista, Avril Lavigne and Pink, two of his first signings, had both achieved multiplatinum success. He was one of the hottest executives in the business.[9]

After Benjy's friend hooked him up with Arista, he was put through a series of interviews. On his fifth interview, he was referred to Reid. Benjy was thrilled, but Reid wasn't, and he didn't give the young man much time to make his case. "We'll let you know," Reid said, dismissively. It is likely Benjy knew that if he walked out of Reid's office that day, he might have never walked back in. So he decided, in that moment, that he had to shoot his shot.

"I'm here right now," he said. "Is there anything I can do for you while I'm here?'"

Reid asked Benjy to compose a letter to another record executive. When it was done, Reid looked it over. He must have been pleased, because he wound up using it.

The experience landed Benjy a job as L.A. Reid's executive assistant. Working for one of the most powerful executives in music was a transformative experience. It not only connected Benjy with anyone who was anyone in the industry, but, more importantly, it gave him an opportunity to learn from Reid himself.

"... I was basically the gatekeeper," Benjy said. "All music kind of went through me to him, and I got more confident in myself and my ear, so to speak."[10]

For three years, Benjy was L.A. Reid's right-hand man. He was thrown in with the sharks and found a way to swim. But entrepreneurship and the music business go hand-in-hand, it's an industry built on hustle, so to truly advance, Benjy seemed to believe that he would have to venture out on his own. With that in mind, he decided he'd form his own label. He'd call it Rostrum

Records. A rostrum is a raised platform—a podium, so to speak—where someone stands and gives a speech, delivering a message. It was an apt name for a record company.

Though his company was technically started elsewhere, Benjy's heart and soul remained in Pittsburgh. "When I started Rostrum, even though I was living in New York, it was like my dream was to find an artist from Pittsburgh, to develop an artist from Pittsburgh, to represent Pittsburgh," he said.[11]

So, in 2004, he signed a rapper named Nitty, who was—well, not from Pittsburgh. In fact, he hailed from the Fort Apache section of the Bronx and trafficked in a brand of rap descended from the likes of Will Smith, Tone Loc, and even MC Hammer. Which didn't stop him from landing a minor hit that year with a song called "Nasty Girl," built around a sample of "Sugar, Sugar," the bubblegum pop song ostensibly credited to the fictional rock group the Archies—as in the *Archie* comic books—released way back in 1969, when it was a certified smash, rising to the top position on the *Billboard* Hot 100.

Considering that the Archies, technically, did not exist, "Sugar, Sugar" becoming such a big hit was a surprise. "The year of Woodstock, the year that we landed on the moon, the year everyone was talking about Charles Manson and the Beatles were breaking up and they had that concert on the roof—there was this song that just showed up," Andy Kim, one of the song's cowriters, told NPR.[12] Even when the record was made, nobody thought much of it. "I had no idea what was going on except a lot of people were putting the song and the record down, as if it was fluff," he said. "As if it didn't mean anything, there was no value to it."

Ironically, the original tune would go on to become a rock classic, a bellwether of the era when 45 singles reigned supreme; meanwhile, Nitty's "Nasty Girl" arrived thirty-five years later, cribbing the melody and all, for a frivolous pop rap song that went: "Hey girl, I like your flavor, wish I could be your neighbor . . ."

It was hardly the stuff from which rap legends were made. But then, that never seemed to be Nitty's goal. According to an interview he did with a music television show in Australia—where "Nasty Girl" had been warmly embraced—Nitty's intent was simply to make hip-hop fun again. He wanted to be a "nice guy rapper, with lighthearted songs and videos."[13] This was music that was meant to go down easy—and hopefully move some units.

Which "Nasty Girl" did. The song reached platinum status in Australia, with more than seventy thousand copies sold, was featured on a handful of Hollywood soundtracks (*Domino* and *Tammy*), and could even be heard kicking off the second season of the popular HBO series *Entourage*. It was enough momentum to have Universal Music Group sign on to distribute Nitty's first album, *Player's Paradise*, making it Rostrum Records' first official release.

Back home, the news was met with applause. "In Pittsburgh that was a big deal," said Artie. "That a guy from Pittsburgh could manage a platinum artist. What Benjy was doing with Nitty, I just thought that was so cool."

But Benjy still wanted to find some homegrown talent. Nobody from Pittsburgh had really made it big yet, and he figured he was as plugged-in as anyone—why shouldn't Rostrum be the label to make it happen? One day in late 2004, Benjy was listening to a mixtape put out by ID Labs, a small studio back in Pittsburgh, run out of a storefront, that periodically released mixtapes featuring songs by the artists who recorded there.

One song on the mixtape caught Benjy's discerning ear. It was by a rapper he had never heard before. His real name was Cameron Jibril Thomaz, but when he rapped he shortened a nickname his uncle had given him—Wisdom—and added the Arabic word for "leader." Thus, he became Wiz Khalifa.[14]

Wiz had sauntered into ID Labs rather inauspiciously two years earlier. At the time, he was fifteen years old. His parents, who were in the military, divorced when he was just a baby, then moved around a lot when he was growing up. He was born in North Dakota, spent time in places like Georgia, South Carolina, England, and Germany, but it was while staying with his dad in Oklahoma that he learned to record and make beats on studio equipment his pops had purchased.

Back in Pittsburgh, living with his mom in Hazelwood, Wiz was looking for a place to record, somewhere that could help take his work to the next level. He settled on ID Labs, and began frequenting it with his friends. All his friends rapped, but to ID Labs owner Eric "E.Dan," Dan, Wiz stood out the most.

"Yo, there's this kid who comes to ID Labs studio after school with a group of kids," he told his friend DJ Bonics.[15] "He's pretty tight. His name is Cam. The other guys stink, but he's real good."

At first, Wiz was just a paying customer, another client. But increasingly, E. Dan and another producer, Chad Glick, felt he possessed real star qualities and wanted to nurture them. So they offered him a job answering phones and sweeping floors in exchange for free studio time.[16]

Wiz took them up on their offer. Which made sense because the pair held some sway in the nascent Pittsburgh hip-hop scene. In the late nineties, along with rappers Masai Turner and MC Sied (who would later rechristen himself Pittsburgh Slim and notch a solo hit in 2007 with "Girls Kiss Girls"), they had been part of a group called Strict Flow, which met with local success, selling cassettes for five dollars apiece before, in 1999, dropping a twelve-inch single ("People on Lock") through New York–based indie label Raw Shack Productions. The single didn't make them stars but the group toured regionally, and became a popular opening act when artists like Nelly, Nas, Usher, The Roots, Jurassic 5 and Ja Rule came through the area. Their debut album, *Without Further Ado*, was released independently in 2003.

Veterans of a sort, they spied opportunity in Wiz, whose talent impressed them nearly as much as how mature he seemed to be. "He has an old soul," Glick said.[17] They likened Wiz to rapper Nas, who at age seventeen had appeared on the Main Source song "Live at the Barbecue," and made a name for himself rapping lines like: "When I was twelve, I went to hell for snuffin' Jesus."

The Nas comparisons may have been unfounded, as any similarities between the two artists' styles were difficult to identify; however, wanting to work with Wiz in earnest took a leap of faith.

"We don't . . . nurture every artist who comes in the door," E. Dan told the *Pittsburgh City Paper* in 2005.[18] "Wiz was the one guy we felt like was the most talented, and also the easiest to work with as a person. There are a lot of people that I would say are talented, but I wouldn't necessarily want to hole up in a room and make a record with them."

Glick came on as Wiz's first manager. Wiz was in the studio every day, and with a slew of songs banked for a future mixtape, ID Labs began thinking about next steps.

"The trouble with Pittsburgh is there's nobody to get your music out there," Glick said. "I don't think there was anyone in a position like Benjy before."[19]

So Glick hipped him to Benjy. And when the pair finally connected in person, sparks flew.

"When I met him I immediately knew I needed to work with him," Benjy said. "He was sixteen, an amazing lyricist, and even though he wasn't all the way developed you could just tell that he was a diamond in the rough, and that with some polishing, guidance, and backing he could become something special."[20]

In early 2005, Benjy signed Wiz Khalifa to Rostrum Records. Wiz was a hometown kid, had gone to Taylor Allderdice High School. The flagship artist of Rostrum: That's who Wiz Khalifa was slated to be. And Wiz was primed for it.

"I definitely want to be one of the big icons of music and hope to start a movement that will be well-respected from Pittsburgh," Wiz told reporter Ed Masley at the *Pittsburgh Post-Gazette*. "I'm super confident that we can make happen what needs to happen. We've got a football team. But we really don't have too many musicians, especially in hip-hop, where you can say 'That dude's from Pittsburgh. That's Pittsburgh right there.' There's nobody out there like that. And I hope to be one of the first to step out and put us on the radio."[21]

With Benjy committed to turning Wiz into a star, it was the label, Rostrum, that needed its roster filled. The company was little more than Benjy himself. If Wiz was ever going to be anything, he'd need help, someone who could push his work to the hip-hop audience, which was thus far unfamiliar with anything coming out of Pittsburgh.

That's where Benjy's old basketball buddy, Arthur Pitt, came in. Artie was born in New Haven, Connecticut, and moved to Pittsburgh when he was eight. He grew up in Point Breeze—his dad was a professor of pharmacology and his mother did social work—and after high school he went to Allegheny College, ninety miles north, intent on becoming a lawyer. But once there, he wound up studying history and creative writing—and also got in a shit-ton of trouble.

"The town the school was in—it's called Meadeville. It was pretty rough. Very rural. A lot of farmland around it. Meadville's known for being home of the zipper. There was a zipper factory there in the eighties and I think when the zipper factory fell apart, the economy and the town collapsed. It was a big deal to go to Perkins for dinner and Perkins is like, a diner. I studied and I went to school, but I partied a lot. I got into fights. My freshman year my parents gave me this crappy old Volvo that was breaking down and I was able to come back to Pittsburgh and see my boys when I wanted to. I felt really stuck up there. I was doing too much drinking. I was just bored as hell in a small town. So, I got arrested. And ended up doing hundreds of hours of community service, and I got put on probation with the college."[22]

Artie ended up graduating, though, with honors. And after college he returned to Pittsburgh, where he landed a job at a law firm. It was a low-maintenance gig, a clerk job, but it gave him time to prepare for the LSAT. Maybe he'd go to law school after all. But he scored poorly on the test and the job turned out to be a dead end.

"Honestly, I was kind of lost," he said. "I was bored. I wasn't making any money. But I always liked strip clubs. A friend of mine owned a company—rest in peace, he was actually murdered a couple of years ago—called Extreme Entertainment. And I started doing security, driving the strippers he represented and managed. I was doing that at night, four nights a week, maybe. We had about thirty girls. I'd work the door and there was a whole routine. A lot of the girls that work in the clubs are miserable and mistreated; so, we'd go to these strip clubs and recruit the girls out of there—which was actually kind of dangerous, we had some problems with that. But we'd get the girls and they'd either come in pairs or there'd be two of them, then three of them, then four of them, and I'd get them to parties. But these weren't bullshit parties—they were private parties. They were high-end, wealthy people, professional athletes. And I'd run the parties. I'd collect the money. I'd count the money. I was responsible for keeping the girls safe, driving them to and from home."

Artie did this for a couple of years while juggling random jobs and working toward a master's degree in creative writing. Once a year or so, he'd run into Benjy at a bar, while he was back from New York visiting family and friends. They'd say hello and remained cordial. Then one day Artie ran into another old friend, Chad Glick. Glick said he was managing Wiz and invited Artie to meet him at the studio. "Benjy Grinberg's thinking about signing him," Glick said.

Artie knew Benjy had some success working with Nitty; he also knew that he, himself, was very confused about the direction his life was heading.

But then he went to the ID Labs studio one day in June of 2005, and everything changed.

"I met Wiz and I was blown away. I was just like—holy fuck, this guy is dope. And I thought: I gotta figure out how to do something with these guys. The energy was really cool. It felt special to me right when I walked in. It's strange. I could tell looking at Wiz that he was really special: confident, tall, and a ton of swagger."

Artie asked Benjy and Glick if he could write Wiz's bio, a biographical sketch used by record labels to help market their artists to radio programmers, journalists, and other music industry tastemakers. They said he could, and afterward Artie kept brainstorming.

"I said to myself, 'I need to think of more ideas so I can keep staying around these guys. I knew a lot of people involved in nightlife around Pittsburgh and I was pretty well connected. I thought I could get his music playing in clubs and I could get him press. So, I started hitting up newspapers and I started going to the radio stations, getting his music to all the DJs and just being really active."

What Artie remembers fondly from this period is how local journalists would visit ID Labs and find themselves bowled over with excitement about Wiz and Rostrum. When it came to music, there hadn't been anyone from Pittsburgh to be excited about in years; now, a bunch of hometown kids were on the cusp of something.

"Wiz had a five-song demo that we were going to take to the majors," Artie recalls. "And these local writers would be like, 'Oh shit, this is the best shit I ever heard from a local rapper.' They'd be like, 'Damn! He's got mad charisma, he looks like a star'; Benjy's very intelligent, he's got some success under his belt with [Nitty]; E. Dan, and Chad, people know them. So around here, we were kind of like a little all-star team. Maybe not in the music industry overall—but in Pittsburgh we were."

In July of 2005, Artie landed Wiz on the front page of the *Pittsburgh Post-Gazette*. Benjy told the paper that he saw Wiz having a long career; he wouldn't just have a hit single and disappear. "It's the kind of thing where people are gonna love *him*, not just his music, and want to keep hearing what he has to say, much like a Jay-Z or a Nas, who can be, like, 10 albums in, and everyone still wants to hear what they have to say," he said.[23]

Afterward, Artie put the word in to Benjy. "Make the company bigger," he said. "We're ready to go, dude. We're huge. Wiz is on the front of the *Post-Gazette*." In reality, it wasn't much to be excited about. Just local press in a local paper in a city that not many people were paying attention to. But after Wiz dropped a mixtape (*Prince of the City: Welcome to Pistolvania*) then followed with a full-length album (*Show and Prove*), his buzz grew bigger. Still, his music was a hard sell.

"There had never been a famous rapper out of Pittsburgh or even a rapper that was really known," Artie said. "A lot of people just laughed at his name. I'll give you an example. He did a show at SOBs for AllHipHop.com Week. It was 2007. Not only did Noreaga, who was hosting, butcher his name, but he ended up being the last performer of the night; there was nobody there except for me, Benjy, and a few of our friends. But I believed in him. I had blind faith in Wiz. I thought he was so fucking dope and I just committed to keep pushing him. Then my friend Katy Longmire took a liking to him. She worked at Warner Bros."

By then, Artie had moved to New York. He was living in Sunnyside, Queens, and Katy was dating his roommate. She worked in branding and marketing at Warner Bros., and passed Wiz's music around the office. The label was vaguely familiar with him; if they had heard about him at all, it was from the press coverage Artie got him. In particular, the websites of magazines like *Rolling Stone* and *XXL* had shown Wiz a lot of love.

"I met Brendan Frederick on Myspace," Artie said. "It was the spring of 2006. He was working for *XXL* mag at the time. And he asked me if *XXL* could premiere a Wiz Khalifa song. The song was called 'Damn Thing.' And that's the first song Wiz got on the radio in Pittsburgh. The radio stations around here didn't support anybody. We really broke down some doors with that. He was on high rotation."

So, Warner Bros. was interested. And when, in March of 2007, Wiz was opening a show for Nas at Fitzgerald Field House in Pittsburgh, the label sent an A&R scout, Kenny "Tick" Salcido, to scope it out. That night, draped in a black hoodie and baggy jeans, Pirates cap atop his head, Wiz stalked the stage like a young veteran, his lean frame belying his thick drawl, belting out lines like: "A dude grind, in due time, he's gonna blow / To make paper it takes patience, so walk it slow . . ."

Tick seemed to be floored by the performance, and the Rostrum gang, having watched their young leader tear the place down, was excited. After the show, they went to a local club to celebrate. They bought a couple of bottles and huddled in the VIP, away from the college kids and weekend warriors sipping their watered-down rum and Cokes. There, they toasted to success, finally within their grasp.

"It felt like we were on *Entourage* or something," Artie said. "It was just those early days of good feelings and dopamine rushes. All I kept thinking was—we're gonna get a million dollars!"

SEVEN

While Rostrum Records was hustling hard to turn Wiz into a star, the Ill Spoken were hustling too. They were camped out in the studio—150 recording sessions down, and 48 songs complete.

Their manager, Will Kalson, began circulating their material on RapMullet.com's forums, and the group started performing. The first show was in 2007, at Moondog's, a blues bar across the Allegheny River in Blawnox, Pennsylvania. It was not exactly ground zero for hip-hop, but they did the show anyway, performing with other local artists.

For these early performances, the goal was simple: Try things out, see what works and what doesn't.

For Malcolm, performing came naturally. From his time with his earlier bands, he had experience onstage, and he seemed to intuitively grasp basic concepts.

"He knew how to face the crowd and communicate," said Brian. "He was confident. He had already performed a lot. He had done a bunch of shows. He had a musical background. I knew more [of] the technical side of things—we learned from each other."

Which isn't to say the shows were packed. Sometimes they'd perform to crowds that could barely qualify as crowds at all. "There would be people," said TreeJ. "But they'd be at the fucking bar, more concerned about getting a drink. And like, two other stragglers."

Malcolm remembered these performances fondly. He was so unknown then that he had to pay just to get onstage.

"I used to pay fifty dollars to perform at super-hood clubs in Pittsburgh for two people that had their back to me. Or like perform for ten people that were just the rapper's friends that were on the stage," he said. "That is the hardest performance you'll ever do. It's not fun. It's awkward."[1]

When not performing to empty bars, the Ill Spoken were briefly embroiled in that most time-honored hip-hop tradition—beef. It was a minor beef, but a beef nonetheless, one of Malcolm's first real challenges as he embarked on his journey.

As it turned out, there was a rapper who lived up in Alberta, Canada, lobbing disses at Malcolm on the Internet. He also went by the name Eazy Mac, and felt the moniker belonged to him.

Malcolm hadn't gone looking for a fight. Who was this kid? He had no clue. But one day Malcolm had gone to get some footage from a camcorder digitized. When he got home, he dumped the footage onto his computer. The footage was to be used for a promotional video, the kind of clip that finds its way onto the Internet every five seconds.

"Yo, I'm Easy Mac," he said, puffing on a cigarette in the bathroom at Brian's house while music played in the background.

It was a simple clip, nothing fancy, and he thought it looked cool. So he put it on YouTube.

"But this dude found it—the Canada guy," Brian said. "And started dissing him in the comments."

The aggression caught Malcolm by surprise. All this over a name?

"I mean, 'Easy Mac' is not the best fuckin' name, let's be real," said Brian. "You're going to fight it out over 'Easy Mac?'"

But it was a challenge, and beef was central to hip-hop culture, dating back to the original dance battles between B-boys at park jams and in neighborhood rec rooms, graffiti crews who competed to see who could bomb the most trains, neighborhood DJs trying to outdo one another with the loudest sound systems, and MCs who spit bars about one another at parties for neighborhood props.

Battling, beef, competition—it was all part of the hip-hop game. And whether it was Roxanne Shanté dissing UTFO to declare herself "The Real Roxanne," KRS-One dissing MC Shan on "The Bridge Is Over," or even more contemporary battles, like Jay-Z vs. Nas and 50 Cent vs. Ja Rule, the unwritten rule of rap was that when someone called you out, you couldn't back down.

Malcolm followed suit. "At the time, I was super real about it," Malcolm said. "I set up the camera at the crib, put on 'Ten Crack Commandments' or something, and I was like . . . Look, son, you fucked up."[2]

"So we made a diss video, then a second diss video, and we were roasting him," Brian said. "We rallied all our homies up to roast [him] in the comments like, '[You're] wack.' 'You're so weak, bro,' shit like that."

Then the Canadian Eazy Mac, who had a small following in Calgary, posted an antagonistic video on YouTube: "I'm calling out this other rapper named Easy Mac, who is kinda fronting, and he's really kinda pissing me off," he said. He continued, "The border is closed, bro."[3]

The Ill Spoken responded one more time, then the flames that had been fanned just sort of died out. "It wasn't beef," said Brian. "Let's get it straight: It was a joke. The icing on the cake was on Malcolm's first Canadian tour, he did a show in Calgary, and who is opening up? Eazy Mac! He texts me like, 'I'm in Canada, Eazy Mac is sucking my dick right now, trying to get backstage. We kicked him out.'"

Their spat with Eazy Mac behind them, the Ill Spoken still had a mixtape they were trying to release. Inspired by Redman and Method Man's 2001 stoner comedy, which they'd watched in the Star Room until their eyes bled, they dubbed it *How High*—a clever nod to their actual lifestyle.

"*How High* shaped so much of my childhood," Malcolm said. "Being a young stoner."[4]

While working on *How High*, the Ill Spoken began rounding out their unofficial crew, the East End Empire. It was made up of local rappers, one of whom called himself Franchise, and in the mid-aughts had been an up-and-coming artist in the then-nascent Pittsburgh scene. He was from Braddock, a suburb only fifteen minutes south of tony Point Breeze, but in some senses a world away.[5]

"Braddock is rather poverty-stricken," Franchise said. "It's very similar to somewhere like Detroit. Detroit had the motor industry, which failed. In the early 1980s, the same thing happened in Braddock. Braddock had the steel mills, and the steel mills failed. A lot of people were left without jobs. Now, they call it one of the ghost towns of the rust belt. There isn't much opportunity there. Not many people make it out. People sell drugs, play football, or do some type of entertainment. Growing up, it was pretty rough."[6]

Franchise wasn't all that different from anyone else in Braddock. Hip-hop, he figured, could be his ticket to a better life. He had begun making music in the early 2000s with friends Vinny Radio, Palermo Stone, and others. Around the same time that Wiz Khalifa became a regular at ID Labs, Franchise became a client at the studio as well. "That was the thing that made me wanna go to ID Labs, to keep it real," he said. "At that time, Wiz and another group called the Govament was bubbling. I'm hearing how good they shit sound. I don't wanna rap like them or sound like them, but I want my shit to sound as good as theirs."

Often, Franchise would look at the credits on mixtapes. A couple names kept popping up—E. Dan at ID Labs, and a producer, Johnny Juliano, who lived in the studio's basement. He purchased some beats from Juliano, and soon began recording at ID. Juliano was so impressed with what Franchise was doing on his beats, he began forking them over, sometimes for free, or, at the very least, a reduced rate.

"You're next, bro," Juliano told him.

One night, Franchise traveled to a club on the outskirts of the city, a large skating rink refashioned into a concert venue. "For like two months or so, every Saturday, Wiz was headlining—they would have S Money and Chevy Woods open up. This one time, after the club let out, I was outside. I was sitting on the hood of my girl's car, passing out CDs of my mixtape, *Perfect Storm*. This small, short, white kid comes up. *Franchise, right? I'm Easy Mac, bro. I've been hearing your shit, bro. I fuck with your shit.* I said I had been hearing about him, I just never put a face to the name."

They parted ways but within days reconnected on Myspace, a popular social networking platform at the time. The Ill Spoken had an open space on a song called "What It Is," which was to appear on *How High*. They sent Franchise the track, with plans to meet up at Sos's Tuff Sound studio. That they were a pair of white boys didn't matter to Franchise, he only cared that they were dope.

"I guess you could look at them like, *these dudes are just tryna be [Black], they're tryna fuck with our culture*, but they ain't even like that. I never heard none of them dudes say 'ni**er,' nothing," Franchise said. "I don't really see color, especially when you're giving it up in the right way. I thought they were genuinely good. It was authentic. I chopped it up with them, we recorded, smoked bud, listened to jams; I really seen it was genuine what they was doing, and that's what made me fuck with them."

Franchise figured that if they liked him, they'd also like his boy Vinny Radio, and his inkling was right.

"I came back to the hood," Franchise recalls. "I say to Vinny—get down with these boys, they're nice and they're on the same type of time we are. They want it and they're dedicated. A week later, Vinny came through and did the same thing; recorded a verse, which they loved. Again, we smoked some weed. And from that point on, we were glued to each other."

The next addition to their crew was Palermo Stone (rapping under the name Tip Tha-Ill Spit), who palled around with Vinny and Franchise.

"There wasn't too many white rappers in Pittsburgh at this time," Stone recalled. "But Franchise was always telling me—yo, there's this little white kid, man, you'd wanna fuck with him, he's actually really dope. One night, I got a show at this spot called the Shadow Lounge. I'm walking out of the show, and there's a cypher going on. There's a big crowd. Someone is in the middle of this cypher going off. This dude is killing it. But I couldn't see who it was. Afterward, the crowd split up. I look and it's this little short-ass white dude. I asked him his name—'Easy Mac,' he says."[7]

Like Franchise and Vinny, Stone fell in quickly with Malcolm and Brian. He thought they were cool kids, but, more importantly, he liked their music. "It was super unique—it was so New York," Stone said. "Everything was really authentic to hip-hop. They actually had a *sound*."

How High was released online in October of 2008. "We put it on iTunes and we're seeing people buy it in China and shit like that and we're like, 'What the fuck?'" Brian recalled. "I think that was when we first started taking it seriously. I mean, we were taking it seriously in our heads before that, but now people were playing it across the world."

The Internet allowed for such things—people from parts unknown could tap into music being made by relatively undiscovered kids in Pittsburgh—but that didn't mean much. The Ill Spoken were still on their grind. But it was a start. And if you looked closely enough, there was something there.

Soy Sos was a fan of both rappers. Recording them at Tuff Sound, he saw them up close. Brian, he felt, had a stronger command of technique. "I thought Beedie was the more serious rapper; he had a more grown-up voice," he said. "Malcolm was goofy . . . I liked both of them, but I never really understood Malcolm until I saw him live. They did a show at the Shadow Lounge and I was like—this kid's got mad charisma. His onstage banter was really good and comfortable and people were having a good time. He was likable."

Some of the differences between the two rappers can be heard on *How High*. Brian's flow is sharp and polished, his vocals smacking crisp against the beats. Malcolm, too, exudes confidence. He has a deft ability for delivering clever punchlines, an all-important component in any rapper's tool kit. But his voice, while clear and present, is notably adolescent, full of air and the addled breath control of someone guilty of sucking on far too many cigarettes.

Most glaring at the time was Malcolm's sense of mimicry: flows and patterns of rappers who had come before him, the way a young basketball player learns by copying the moves of their favorite ballers.

He could have copied anyone, though. In 2008, the sounds of Kanye West, 50 Cent, and Lil Wayne dominated the airwaves. But his inspiration was an unlikely source. "My biggest influence was Big L," Malcolm said. "When I first started rapping on a serious tip that's all I was listening to."[8]

Big L died tragically in 1999, shot nine times on a street corner in Harlem. In his short life he left a rather large imprint on hip-hop culture, and while it may seem odd for Malcolm to have been inspired by him, of all rappers, he couldn't have picked anyone better, because Big L certainly had his moments.

Like in late February 1995, when he traveled not far from his Harlem home to Manhattan's West Side for a late-night freestyle session on the *Stretch Armstrong and Bobbito Show*. The show aired on Columbia University's radio station WKCR, and he was joined in the studio by another MC, a guy from Brooklyn who, when he got on the microphone, said he had just left a club downtown that had been raided by shotgun-toting members of the NYPD.

He, too, was an underground phenom, with just a few records under his belt. He called himself Jay-Z.

That night, the two rappers freestyled for ten minutes, each one spitting two verses a piece. L, it seemed, shined brightest. He was polished and precise, and jaws dropped when he made his clever boasts.

"Big L is the ni**a you expect, to catch wreck on any cassette deck / I'm so ahead of my time, my parents haven't met yet," he rapped. It was enough to make you pause and ask, *Did he really say that?*

The following month, Big L dropped his debut album, *Lifestylez ov da Poor & Dangerous*. Powered by the singles "Put It On" and "M.V.P.," the project earned him a reputation as a fierce lyricist, among the best in the game. The industry was on notice. Nas was on the heels of having released his landmark debut, *Illmatic*, but after hearing Big L, he claimed he was "scared to death." "There's no way I can compete," Nas remembered thinking. "If this is what I gotta compete with—there's no way."[9]

When it came to rapping, L had the special sauce.

"His wit and his imagination in putting rhymes together—he'd take a punchline and go left field with it; you wouldn't even see it coming," said Lord Finesse, who worked closely with L as a producer and in the rap collective D.I.T.C. (Diggin' In The Crates). "From a lyrical standpoint, those are the most incredible punchlines. The key is to make you rewind. Big L's rewind factor made you go, 'Goddamn, wait up, he said what?' And you have to go back. You have to. He took the time to make it rhyme flawlessly and it's just so masterfully put together."[10]

The most influential tastemakers in hip-hop couldn't deny that, back when being a lyricist meant something, Big L had the game in a chokehold. The ferocity with which he rapped, the way his lines made you double back. Every verse was a tour de force. He was simply on another level.

"Big L was the best lyricist at the time," said DJ Funkmaster Flex. "He was a better lyricist than Biggie and Jay-Z."[11]

The problem was, for all the respect Big L commanded, props only went so far. His debut album peaked at number twenty-two on *Billboard*'s hip-hop charts, and ultimately failed to sell; before long, L was dropped from his label, Columbia Records. If L was going to succeed, he would have to make hits—and his label, assuming he signed another contract, would have to give him a push.

He wasn't waiting around though.

Guys he had come up with—Cam'ron and Mase, with whom he was in a childhood rap group, Children of the Corn (which also included rappers Herb McGruff and Bloodshed) were blowing up—so in 1998 he launched his own label, Flamboyant Entertainment, and dropped a single, "Ebonics." The song broke street lingo down to its simplest terms, a kind of proto–Urban Dictionary.

"Ebonics" wasn't a hit single, but the creativity of it, the concept, garnered him attention. A few years before, L was ice-cold; now, executives were calling, wanting to do a deal. One was a guy he knew from Harlem, Damon Dash, who had gone on to help turn Jay-Z into a formidable artist. They had their own label together, Roc-A-Fella Records.

"We were about to sign him right before he passed away," Jay-Z said. "We were about to sign him to Roc-A-Fella. It was a done deal . . . he was a very talented writer. [And] once you have that, as you grow as a writer, depends on whether you're gonna be a star and keep going, or just write in your own box. I think he had the ability to write big records."[12]

But then Big L was killed. And that was that. "We were all just numb," said the producer Showbiz, who had worked closely with L. "The world didn't even get to see his full talent on display. L was in a class by himself. It was just crazy."

Almost a decade later, there Malcolm was, starting the very first Big L fan page on Facebook, trying to emulate his style.

"He really inspired me to be clever and witty," said Malcolm, who was only six years old when L died. "My early stages of rapping, I was basically trying to be like Big L—trying to be a super-raw MC. That's what he really inspired in me: to always keep that MC factor about myself and about my music."[13]

To be an MC meant more than merely rapping over beats. A real MC saw the craft of rapping as an art form unto itself. MCs approached rapping almost as sport, practicing it and perfecting it with a studied seriousness. In the end, the difference between a rapper and an MC was not unlike the difference between a cook and a Michelin-starred chef; one simply served the people, while the other used their talents to become best in class.

Malcolm wanted to be not only an MC, but one of the very best MCs. At times, he was so focused on it, he seemed possessed. On school nights, after the skies of western Pennsylvania had darkened, after his parents had retired to bed and the house had turned quiet, Malcolm sat alone in his bedroom, scribbling into a notebook, the crisp pages filling with rhyme after rhyme.[14] The kid would barely sleep. He hoped, one day, his hard work would pay off.

•••

Offstage, just as the Ill Spoken were building steam, the relationship between Malcolm and Brian was breaking down. In the long run, perhaps it was inevitable. Their commitment to the group was nominal. They were a group, yes, but also solo artists. They'd make music as a group, as well as apart. And their careers were still in the vast space between nowhere and somewhere; really, they were throwing a bunch of shit at the wall, hoping something would stick.

"We would talk about how we'd be like how Mos Def and Talib Kweli were Black Star, but we would do more than one project," said Brian. "They had solo careers, but they did do that one album together. We were both definitely solo artists. But the group element was fun. It was a different flavor."

And yet the Ill Spoken was never exactly the perfect match. To begin with, Malcolm was closer in age to Brian's younger brother Derek, with whom he shared a real friendship. Malcolm's bond with Brian was tied to their music.

But Brian and Malcolm were also entering two different stages of life. Brian was waving hello to his twenties while Malcolm was still in high school. Heck, Brian hadn't even graduated high school at all, having dropped out at seventeen, and was selling weed to keep his lights on. Now, though, Brian was looking to put that part of his life in the rearview. He was focused, intent on growing up. And he watched dismissively as Malcolm and his friends appeared to be following in his footsteps—footsteps he looked back on with a tinge of regret.

"I was just frustrated," Brian said. "They were such little badass kids, doing things that were risky. And I was trying to calm down from shit like that. They were taking purses. Walking around with guns. Someone shot at someone at one point. You know—stupid shit. I'm older than them, and I'm like—'You're fucking stupid; why do you think you're cool 'cause you have that [gun]?' They just were influenced by stupid shit and they were tryna be the biggest badasses out there."

Sometimes they were simply trying to be badasses; other times, their exploits in juvenile delinquency came down to something more elementary—like money, or rather, the lack of it. Early on, when he needed to pay for studio time, Malcolm's parents footed the bill.

"He would ask his parents for money for studio time," said Will Kalson. "His mom was a legit photographer and she had her own studio; his dad was an architect. He wasn't poor by any means."

But he wanted to get out from under their thumb. "I really wanted to be independent," Malcolm said.[15] So, when he had to make some quick cash to fund his burgeoning rap career, there were ways. Like the time-honored tradition, used by everyone from Jay-Z to Jeezy, of selling drugs.

And though he certainly didn't *need* to do it, he still did it—a choice rife with privilege. For this, he turned to his friend Bill Niels, with whom he'd by now grown much closer, hanging out in the afternoons at Bill's apartment, smoking weed and wasting time. Bill was an aspiring street pharmacist himself; he would become Malcolm's supplier—or so Bill thought.

"It was funny, he really had no concept of selling drugs," Bill said. "I gave him an ounce of weed and he didn't understand that he had to bring back money to me. He definitely didn't do well with that."

To his credit, Malcolm was aware that he absolutely sucked at something most rappers claimed to excel at. He just didn't have the knack for that kind of hustling. "I never knew Malcolm to be shady," Bill said.

But Malcolm and his crew certainly got up to serious mischief. "[M]e and my friends just grew up all around the neighborhood causing trouble," he said. "My childhood was spent getting corrupted by older people."[16]

Like one friend—described by a pal as a "crazy motherfucker"—who would bust into people's homes with his guns drawn, then tie them up and rob them blind. Another friend fired a gun randomly into someone else's house.

"We wreaked havoc," Malcolm said. "We did some horrible things. But I was like the good-hearted person that was like, 'Hey, guys, don't shield stomp that car. They might have some financial problems going on. Don't break that windshield.'"[17]

His words of caution didn't matter. His friends were going to do what they were going to do. And Malcolm was content to hang around with them. At home, his parents disapproved, and things were occasionally tense. For a while, TreeJ was barred from even entering the premises.

"'Hey, we gotta be low key getting you in and out because my mom doesn't really want you—it sounds harsh but—she doesn't really want you over here corrupting me,'" TreeJ remembered Malcolm telling him. "[Karen] thought I was just going there to smoke weed with him. He was still in school. I had dropped out; she thought I was just bullshitting, but I was helping him, so he didn't have to hit record and run over to the mic. Years after, we laughed about it. I was like, 'Karen, come on, there was a time when you didn't even want me at the house' . . . she was like, 'It's not that I didn't want you at the house, I just was worried about him. If I really had known . . .'"

Like TreeJ, Brian sensed that Malcolm's parents weren't entirely on board with what was going on. "I tried at that time to avoid his parents," he said. "I'm sure I was seen as a bad influence. Even though I probably was a good influence, in some ways. I tried to tell him what to steer away from. [But] he already made his own choices; like, what he wanted to do."

As unseemly as his friends appeared to be, Malcolm got a lot from being around them, calling them his "true inspiration."[18] "Those have been the same people that have pushed me since I [*sic*] just started," he said. "When I put the word out that I was gonna be a rapper . . . everyone was just kind of laughing at me. They didn't take me seriously, didn't even listen; they were just like, *There's no way this is gonna happen.* And my homies were the people that stood by me and would go out and be like: *Man, what are you talking about? He's tight.*"[19]

They were also a rich creative source, their activities influencing Malcolm's writing. "Our day to day lives and what we do, that's really where I want to pull music from . . . I just pull it from my life and the people around me," he said.[20]

Before long, Malcolm was becoming more aggressive about chasing his dreams. But while there seemed to be some momentum, there was always the question parents have asked since time immemorial: *But what if this doesn't work out?*

"From my point of view, there was no faith," TreeJ said. "Which is OK. I can't imagine having the belief that your fifteen-year-old wants to pursue a fuckin' rap career."

Perhaps to his parents, who Malcolm described as "pretty cool people,"[21] he needed a plan B because his plan A, being a rapper, was akin to hitting the lottery. After high school, he could always go to college, which seemed like a sensible thing to do. Plus, it literally seemed like hip-hop and the crazy kids he was hanging around with were sending him down the wrong path.

"It was kind of like, why aren't you doing well in school, why do your teachers keep calling me about you writing raps instead of taking tests and doing homework? Like, why are you doing that?" Malcolm recalled. "And I was like—because I really believe that I'm about to be a rapper."[22]

In truth, he was an exceptionally smart kid, but his first two years at Winchester Thurston he was only an average student. John Maione, a performing arts teacher who taught a class in electronic music production, told the *Pittsburgh City Paper* that Malcolm excelled in classes that required actual creativity. He'd bring samples of his music for the other kids to pore over and dissect.

"I remember him as a serious music student," Maione said. "His knowledge, intensity, and seriousness regarding hip-hop and rap music [were] inspiring."[23]

But primarily, school didn't seem to be of much concern. He was a creative kid with grand ambitions, which he wasn't shy about. In the 2008 edition of the school's literary magazine, *Plaid*, he published a poem. Titled "No Excuses for Lovin'," it is little more than a rap refashioned in poetic meter, a bar-by-bar rhyme where each word at the end of a line sounds like the line preceding it—but the poem speaks to the inner thoughts of a young boy at war with himself and many of those around him.

In the poem, he writes that he's awaiting the day when he's "finally driven to insanity/By my family/Who never seemed to be a fan of me." Still, he declares himself "Hip-hop's child," despite feeling confused, in pain, burying his cries in melodies over beats. Meanwhile, his community tells him school is cool and drug users are thugs; he feels so withdrawn, he can't even stand to look at himself.

Coursing through the poem is an underlying sense of—not quite childhood angst, not the anger that powers so many dreamers; rather, discontent, disillusionment, feelings at once unexplainable but ever present. Also, an acknowledgment: Malcolm is being groomed for a certain kind of life, a well-meaning and well-adjusted one, where he is to grow up and make all the right decisions, go to school and get a job, settle down and have some kids, maybe make his home right back in Point Breeze.

But he wants more. In hip-hop there is excitement, freedom, a chance for Malcolm to see all his childhood dreams realized, and he won't give it up. As for that other path, the one kids in Point Breeze had walked since that day William Wilkins set down his roots, he wasn't buying into it.

"They wanna push me down a path but I shall not budge," he writes.

When, after his sophomore year, he transferred from Winchester Thurston, a private school, to Taylor Allderdice—a public school that counted Wiz Khalifa as an alum—this attitude continued driving him. Only then the dial had been cranked to the max.

"By the time I got to 'Dice, I was trying to make music whenever I could," he said.[24]

His other goals were to get high and have sex, things he had greater opportunities to do at Allderdice, a public high school described as "a melting pot for every neighborhood" in the city.[25]

At Allderdice, he said he could "do whatever the fuck *I* wanted," which included sleeping in class, or skipping altogether. "I had teachers that would let me come into their rooms and sleep through other classes," he said.[26]

If he was falling asleep in class, it was because he was often out late at night, recording in the studio—another thing his parents tried tamping down on. After one too many late-night trips out of the house to record with Brian, Karen said she would not give him the code to the burglar alarm; that way, he'd be forced to stay inside.

And when he was at the studio and his whereabouts were known, Karen would still keep tabs on him, calling Tuff Sound to check up. "She was worried that he was smoking cigarettes," said Soy Sos. "She didn't want him smoking cigarettes. I remember she asked me that once; I was like . . . 'I don't know if he's doing that or not.' I mean, I wasn't going to tell."

He got away with a lot, provided his grades didn't suffer. But they were suffering. Graduate and go to college? Malcolm would be lucky if he didn't follow in the footsteps of his friends and simply drop out.

But for now, he was still in school, still rapping, still plugging away with the Ill Spoken. Occasionally, his parents got glimpses of what their son spent all his free time on. A show down in Atlanta over Thanksgiving weekend in 2008 provided Malcolm's father, Mark, an opportunity to tag along and see what all the fuss was about.

"Mark was like—I wanna come, I don't want you going down there with no adults," remembered Kalson, who helped arrange the gig through a promoter, "a really rich kid," whom he knew from back in college. "Malcolm was like sixteen."

Brian flew back from London, where he had briefly gone to stay with a girlfriend studying abroad, to make the gig. From making songs in his mom's attic to traveling overseas for shows, it felt like some real superstar shit. "I was like, 'I'm cuttin' my Europe trip, let's go! Flying to Atlanta,'" Brian said. "It was powerful."

And yet the show turned out to be a whole bunch of nothing. The gig, pegged as a showcase, would introduce the Ill Spoken to Atlanta, fast becoming the new Mecca of hip-hop. But nobody in Atlanta had any idea who the Ill Spoken were. "It was empty as hell," Brian recalled.

"It really wasn't what we had thought it was gonna be," echoed Kalson. "There was basically no one there. It was in this little club, and we ended up just drinking."

But the memory that lasts from that night is that Malcolm was supposed to have been back to the hotel by a certain time. When he wasn't, his dad was on it, blowing up Kalson's phone as the hour grew later.

"I didn't know what to do and I didn't want to pick it up. I said, 'Mac, your dad's calling me' and he was like, 'Well, just pick it up'. So, I finally picked it up. Mark was *really* pissed off. He was paranoid; like, 'Really, guys? You're supposed to be back.' But that was how his dad was. He was laid-back for the most part, but he also was concerned about him at the same time."

Even if the show was primarily a bust, the more things seemed to be happening for Malcolm, the more belief his family seemed to have in what he was doing. In a household where creativity kept the lights on and afforded the family a good, decent life, who would they be if they didn't support his dreams?

"There's no denying that he had a special charisma that he wanted to share with the world," said Brian. "He wanted to do this. He wanted to be, like, a class clown. He was always like, 'Look at me! Look at me! I'm funny.' As a little kid, that's what his energy was. His mother probably pushed him to do what she felt he would want to do."

Now their teenage son had gone from rapping in his bedroom to getting flown out of town for shows. Nobody was in attendance—big deal. It was exciting regardless. Maybe Malcolm's destination wasn't clear yet, but things were happening.

"His mom wasn't sure about the rapper thing, but she knew that he was gonna be famous some way," said Kalson. "She knew that. And that was why she supported him."

Still, he could do more to get his act together. A job could help. It would give Malcolm some structure, maybe teach him some discipline.

"My mom was really on my ass about me being a fuckup, if you will—which, I wasn't even that bad," Malcolm said. "But because I wasn't doing school and I was doing drugs and having sex with girls and . . . whatever."[27]

So he got a job at the Giant Eagle supermarket in Squirrel Hill. It wasn't the hardest of jobs, not the easiest either; he was to be a cashier, the kind of gig that simply put some money in his pocket. It wouldn't make him rich, but the job would prepare him for adult life, teach him to show up on time and be responsible.

Before he began the job, he had a conversation with the manager, to figure out his availability. He was a high school student; how busy could he be? Malcolm told the manager he needed flexibility. If he had something music-related to attend to, he'd have to go. The manager told him that wasn't going to fly; it was either music or cashiering, not both. Reluctantly, Malcolm agreed.

The first day he was scheduled to work, he was intent on showing up. But the more he deliberated, the less it sat right with him. Inevitably, music would conflict with work; besides, it wasn't like this was his dream, working at the supermarket. This wasn't what he wanted to do with his life, wasn't what he was determined to do with his life—in fact, it was the complete opposite of what he hoped to do with his life. Not that he had anything against anyone who cashiered; it just wasn't for him.

Right before he was set to show up, he shot the manager an email, writing to let her know he was not coming. He figured he'd quit before he got fired. Malcolm was a tough, determined kid. He seemed to value and appreciate the merits of hard work. But working a real job was something he could not handle.

"He never worked again," said Bill.

But he did keep busy with other things, some of which arguably impacted him in more instructive ways. Hooked up through a friend, Edward Rawson—who shot the Ill Spoken's first video, "Trying to Get Blazed"—he took a "job" with MLK Mural, a nonprofit Rawson was an advisor for that recruited kids from around Pittsburgh to paint murals.[28]

Kyle Holbrook, a Wilkinsburg native, started MLK Mural in 2002 as a project for the community; it was meant to keep young kids occupied with art as opposed to negative things. Murals could take weeks, sometimes months, to complete, but when finished would feature pops of bright colors and jazzy flourishes that lent a beautified sheen to the city's public spaces. In Wilkinsburg, East Liberty, McKeesport, and elsewhere, street corners that might have once been filled with drug dealers and other sorts of inner-city stragglers became works of art.

When he wasn't helping change the image of his city, Holbrook was at local shows—like the December 2006 album release party at the Brewhouse in Southside for Wiz Khalifa's street album *Show and Prove*, where he painted a mural live on-site.[29] Holbrook seemed to know the 'burgh as well as anyone.

And even though Malcolm hailed from a different part of town, that didn't stop Holbrook from recognizing something undeniable—Malcolm floated through life with palpable ease, becoming fast friends with people who he had met just a moment before.

"I knew as soon as I met him, he was going to be a big star," Holbrook said. "He was a super-humble person, always repped the city."[30]

In their all-too-brief time working together, Holbrook and Malcolm grew close. Malcolm even made a theme song for the nonprofit. But there was no polite way to say it—like drug dealing and school, Malcolm was dreadful at painting. He was so bad at it that, most times, when the kids went out to work on a mural, they'd make sure he didn't even paint.

Instead, Malcolm recalled Holbrook putting a camera in his hand, and telling him to film what the kids were doing instead. That is, until the other kids began giving him the side-eye—like, "Why does the white kid get to film everything and not paint?" So he was given some light work, priming the walls before the real painting began. Still, he didn't do much. It was a job, sort of; more like something to do. He was chilling and hanging out, cracking jokes and, to hear Malcolm tell it, simply "making sure everyone was having a good time."

"I didn't really do shit, to be honest," Malcolm said.[31]

What the program did do was connect him with other aspiring rappers in the city, some of whom would travel to his house and record on the small microphone he had in his bedroom. Sometimes it worked in reverse, like with Paradise Gray. As Paradise the Architect, Gray had, in the late 1980s, been one of the founding members of X-Clan, an Afrocentric hip-hop group that, in 1990, released their landmark debut LP, *To the East, Blackwards*, a modest commercial success that over time has been recognized as one of the best hip-hop albums ever made. After moving to Pittsburgh in 1992, Gray became influential in the local scene,[32] hosting the Pittsburgh Hip-Hop Awards and working with rapper/activist Jasiri X;[33] down with the MLK Mural project, he seemed to think nothing of having a young Malcolm, more than twenty years his junior, to his house to cut a record.

"That's legendary," Malcolm said. "That's X-Clan. It's like, *whoa*."[34]

The gig with MLK Mural eventually ended. Malcolm got out of it what he'd hoped to. "I did it for a little bit to have a job and get on the right path towards what society tells me is the right path," he said, joking—"that's what's really important in life, following what society says you should to do."[35]

Traveling around the city pretending to paint did, however, seem to expose him to parts of Pittsburgh into which he may have otherwise never have ventured. The truth was that, for all the diversity Pittsburghers claimed to have, a 2016 study concluded it was mostly white people who felt that way; people of color saw it as not diverse at all. Another study ranked Pittsburgh[36] among the top five least diverse cities in the entire United States. It's a city in which the character of neighborhoods changes very quickly, as does the makeup of its people.

"Pittsburgh is very segregated by neighborhood," said Brian. "It is, I guess, institutional, the way the city was planned." Soy Sos concurred. "We've created our own diverse thing," he said. "But the city itself is not." Palermo Stone put it more bluntly: "Pittsburgh's so gentrified. You go one block, you'll be in the hood; you go another block, you're in the suburbs. So, you're kinda stuck where you're at and you don't really wanna move around, leave, and do different things."

And yet, through all these early adventures, there remained in Malcolm an unwavering commitment to becoming the thing that he dreamed he could be—a rapper. But to really become one he had to first make inroads on his own, a difficult task as a member of a group where he seemed continuously overruled.

"Because Beedie was the older cat, he would try to impose his will," remembered Franchise. "A certain beat Beedie might want to use, Malcolm would be like, 'Nah, that's a little too happy.' And Beedie—because he's got that big brother thing—would be like, 'No, we don't have a jam like that, so it's almost destined that we have to have a jam like this, bro.' He was more like the aggressor. It's gotta be this way. And Malcolm would just say, 'All right, we'll go with it.'"

But Malcolm was determined. He was not a confrontational person. And getting overruled—he could abide by that, to a degree. Perhaps the disagreements, in the end, made him only want to do his own thing that much more. Little by little, though, he started inching away. And where a conversation over their differences might have helped the group break apart smoothly, he let the music do the work for him instead.

"Malcolm really wanted to start doing some different music," said Palermo Stone. "He wanted to start working with melody a little bit more. He and Brian were close, they were always together; but when the music changed, that's when the friendship started fracturing. That's when the [Ill Spoken's] music really stopped happening. The music stopped being collaborative. When that happens, distance starts growing, because you're not in a studio together all the time."

The end came without an argument or a fight. There was no backstage blowup, the stuff of Hollywood biopics and tell-all memoirs crafted for maximum dramatic effect. In fact, the Ill Spoken never actually broke up. Malcolm just dove headfirst into making his own music, and Brian did the same.

"He was doing what he was doing and I'm sure he had people in his ear like, 'Yo, you don't need this dude,'" Brian said. "But there was never a moment that we were like, 'OK, end of the group.' And there was never a confrontation. He definitely would consistently avoid confrontation. But there was a tension between me and Malcolm. I think we were kind of sick of being in the group together. That's how it felt to me. I don't know. We both were doing solo shit. He was younger; we were butting heads. He was always like a little bro to me; at a certain point, he's gonna wanna stand on his own two."

His first step was finding a studio. There was always Soy Sos—Tuff Sound, after all, was home base for the Ill Spoken—but much of what Malcolm recorded there didn't seem to satisfy him. "We did a couple of demos that were like, more sing-y stuff, guitar, things like that," Soy Sos said. "But I didn't really have the tools as a producer to help him with the beats."

Meanwhile, with Wiz Khalifa's impending success, the whole town was abuzz about ID Labs. So ID Labs is where he went.

He had designs on a new mixtape. He would call it *The Jukebox: Prelude to Class Clown*. If he did it right, he hoped it would garner him the kind of attention that the Ill Spoken had never gotten.

But first, he had to make one major change.

EIGHT

By Malcolm's junior year in high school, he had already made a name for himself. He was the white kid at all the house parties, rapping his little ass off.

"At the parties, he was the only one really rapping," said his friend TreeJ, who was practically attached at the hip to Malcolm at the time. "You know, you'd get your one drunk asshole like *I can freestyle, Mac!*, trying to battle—but you knew Malcolm was good. His freestyling was amazing at this point. And most of the time it was just him doing it."

He was shameless about promoting himself. A CD of his music in hand, he'd play his material at different studios around the city, popping up at spots like Timebomb, a streetwear shop in East Liberty selling clothes and mixtapes that served as a hub for the city's emerging talent. There, he'd rub shoulders with other artists and producers.

When Malcolm brought his first mixtapes into Timebomb, owner Brian Brick, who cut his teeth in the local hip-hop, punk, and graffiti scenes of the eighties and nineties, was immediately supportive—"of course," he said, when Malcolm asked if Timebomb would push it for him. He assumed Brick thought he was a "little clown."

"He ended up being a very vital person in my career in Pittsburgh," Malcolm said. "He's always repped me, always supported everything I did . . . Brick's put a lot of people onto a lot of hip-hop in Pittsburgh."[1]

But even with Brick's support, Malcolm struggled to win people over. For one, he was white. That fact sometimes stopped people in their tracks. Brick told the *Pittsburgh City Paper* that he recalled people coming in the store, seeing the Ill Spoken mixtape, and saying that they should take their faces off the cover—"They're nice," he remembered people commenting, "but if they didn't have themselves on the cover they'd probably sell a lot more because kids wouldn't know that they're white."[2]

Malcolm and Brian were also up against the fact that Pittsburgh was very territorial. Back then, no rapper from Pittsburgh had ever received widespread attention. Every young rapper was peddling a self-released mixtape, but support was limited—sometimes violently so—by the neighborhood you repped.

"Pittsburgh is a hatin' city," Wiz said. "It's hard to be an artist, 'cause you might be from *this* area, and these other people will fuck with you 'cause you're not from *that* area. And if you're from East Hills and you go to Hazelwood and try to sell your CD, it's not gonna happen. You're probably gonna get stomped down and shot."[3]

To make matters worse, Malcolm couldn't even lay claim to a hood. He hailed from Point Breeze, and on its surface, Point Breeze didn't lend itself to the stereotypical hardships that many rappers, at the time, seemed to be escaping from. He smoked weed and hung out with his friends; they got into trouble, but he wasn't looking to escape abject poverty. Point Breeze was the kind of neighborhood hardworking people tried to get into; meanwhile, Malcolm was trying to get out of it.

In a genre where authenticity is—or at the time was—prized, where Malcolm was from created its own set of issues. It was only compounded by the fact that he was white, which didn't make him unique, since there were a number of white rappers, but the relatively vanilla aspects of his background made him an outlier.

"There was a lot of hate on him in the city, for sure," a Pittsburgh source said. "Because there were always white rappers. But they were hood white dudes, really gangsters for real." One group, in particular, fit that mold: The 58s. Comprised of B. White and Mayo (who died in July of 2021), they hailed from McKeesport, in the Mon Valley—about twenty-five minutes south of Pittsburgh—which, according to a 2019 study by the National Council for

Home Safety and Security, was ranked the fourth most-dangerous city in the entire United States.[4] "Their raps are all hustler talk, gangster-type shit," the source said. "And they're really about that life."

Malcolm was friendly with the 58s, but compared to them, he might as well have been from another planet. "He played lacrosse and dressed like a goofy white kid," said Brian. "They all played lacrosse. My brother played lacrosse too. They were all preppier-looking kids, they weren't street-type dudes."

Even if they had been street dudes, there was more to rap than simply rapping words over beats, which, with the proliferation of cheap recording software and sites like Myspace and YouTube, allowed anyone to claim they were a hip-hop artist. But just because you claimed you were a rapper, didn't make it so.

"I knew I wanted to be a rapper," Malcolm said. "I was dedicated. I wrote every day. But there wasn't much I could do. It's not that easy. You can't just be like—I'm a rapper."[5]

● ● ●

Hip-hop is Black music, so it was not odd that Malcolm's credibility, or lack thereof, was an issue. But in hip-hop, credibility has always been an issue.

Concerns date back as far as 1979, when "Rapper's Delight," arguably the first real hit rap record, was recorded by the Sugarhill Gang. Although passed off as an approximation of the then-burgeoning hip-hop culture, the Sugarhill Gang—Michael "Wonder Mike" Wright, Guy "Master Gee" O'Brien, and Henry "Big Bank Hank" Jackson—were really just a group of guys recruited by Sugar Hill Records exec Sylvia Robinson for the express purpose of making a rap song that the label could potentially cash in on.

Compounding things, Big Bank Hank wasn't really a rapper at all; he was a doorman at a nightclub in the Bronx who had once *managed* a rapper—Grandmaster Caz of the Cold Crush Brothers. And according to hip-hop folklore, pressed to come up with lyrics for the song, he borrowed some from Caz and passed them off as his own.[6]

Hank died in 2014, and never copped to cribbing Caz's lyrics, even if the other group members were up front about it. "He didn't write the lyrics,"

Master Gee told journalist Christopher Milan Thomas in 2006. "He's a hell of a performer, totally awesome when it comes to performing lyrics, and his voice is so classy. As far as the lyrics go, he didn't write them. You gotta give credit where credit is due."[7]

But the lyric controversy and the group's inauspicious origin story dogged the Sugarhill Gang for years. There was a strange irony in it, too. "There's this idea that hip-hop has to have street credibility," music critic Oliver Wang once said. "Yet the first big hip-hop song was an inauthentic fabrication."[8]

Nevertheless, that fact has never stopped anyone from playing "Rapper's Delight," and the controversy is a moot point—the song is a bona fide classic. But over time, this tension between reality and fiction, authentic versus inauthentic, real hip-hop against commercial rap, would play out repeatedly against a backdrop where, with just the right song, the right look, the right cosign or affiliation, millions could be made overnight.

Take, for example, gangsta rap. The subgenre no doubt had its roots in street life. But many of the artists who became associated with gangsta rap—whether Ice Cube or Dr. Dre—were not *really* gangsters. Only two of N.W.A's five members could lay claim to being members of the Crips gang (MC Ren and Eazy-E), and neither seemed to wave the flag that proudly.[9] For all of Eazy's tough talk on record, the guy had never written a rap of his own in his life. This isn't to suggest that Eazy-E wasn't a gangster; rather, it's to illustrate that this was show business, after all, with an emphasis on the "show."

That didn't mean rap wasn't based on reality. The more *real* an artist appeared to be, the more points they seemed to score with the audience. And sure, some rappers really were hustlers—ask Jay-Z or Young Jeezy—but much of what passed for credibility in the mainstream rap world was intangible. Credibility had no formula; the audience either bought into the artist or they didn't.

Sometimes, questions about an artist's background and/or integrity hardly impacted them at all. Perhaps most controversially, Rick Ross presented himself as a kind of Miami drug kingpin—this, despite evidence that he had once worked as correctional officer (and thus diametrically oppositional to a drug kingpin).[10] The hip-hop singer Akon made it big with his first hit single, "Locked Up," and titled his second album *Konvicted*, claiming to have spent three years in prison for running an auto theft ring, but *The Smoking*

Gun discovered he had barely spent any time in jail at all.[11] In fact, by the mid-aughts, hip-hop had become so predominant in mainstream culture that it seemed that credibility and authenticity didn't even matter. All that mattered was that an artist made hits.

Which isn't to suggest fabrications couldn't impact a career; selling lies was hard work, and for a white rapper, it was arguably even more challenging. If Malcolm pretended to be someone he was not, the truth might eventually reveal itself, as it often does; moreover, it was exhausting. But if he remained true to himself while somehow proving he was legitimately talented, he would be fine. It was a delicate dance few white rappers had mastered. You could count them on one hand.

There were the Beastie Boys, a trio of upper-middle-class white kids who were among the first artists on Def Jam Records, seen by label head Russell Simmons as key in connecting hip-hop to millions of suburban white teenagers. Produced by Rick Rubin, in 1987 they became the first rappers with a number one album on the *Billboard* charts. Their debut, *Licensed To Ill*, was fun and playful; like much early hip-hop, the songs themselves were extensions of street culture. Group members Mike D, Ad-Rock, and MCA modeled themselves after the rap crews that had come before them, the Treacherous Three, Crash Crew, and Grandmaster Flash and the Furious Five[12]—their music was a blend of rap and rock that was irresistible.

"Right from the start, the Beasties were pretty fly for white guys and they brought a whole new attitude to the look of rap in the seal of hip-hop," said LL Cool J, who was discovered by the Beastie Boys after they played his demo tape for Rick Rubin. "[They] brought their own spirit and flavor to the music, because before the Beasties a lot of rappers were selling ego and forcefulness first and foremost. But the Beasties brought something new, pure, and great to the game. They brought obnoxiousness, they got a tune of fresh humor, and they proved once and for all that rap can come from any street, not just a few. Run-DMC brought rap to the edge of suburbia but the Beasties drove it right to the center."[13]

Much like the Beatles' performance on *The Ed Sullivan Show* in 1964 inspired millions of kids to start rock bands, after the Beastie Boys blew up with "(You Gotta) Fight for Your Right (to Party!)" it seemed like white kids all over the country began rapping. And record labels, eager to make a buck, were more than willing to accommodate them. The goal was simple enough: sign the next great white hope and do what Russell Simmons and Rick Rubin had done with the Beasties at Def Jam.

Then in 1990, a curious thing happened. From ghetto blasters in the most hard-core of housing projects to home stereos in the comfiest, quaintest of suburbs, one song began playing on repeat. It was a real earworm, built around the opening bars of Queen's 1981 hit "Under Pressure."

Undeniably catchy, the song was called "Ice Ice Baby." And the artist behind the tune called himself Vanilla Ice—vanilla, you see, because he was a white dude.

"Ice Ice Baby" became the first rap song to top the *Billboard* Hot 100 (the rock group Blondie technically beat Ice to number one way back in 1981, with their hit song "Rapture," which featured a rap by white lead singer Debbie Harry, though the song is not widely considered a hip-hop record), and with its success, Vanilla Ice was poised to remake rap—music and culture largely born of Black experience—in his white image.

It was easy to see why. His jawline was sharp, his body taut. At six feet tall, his hair was coiffed into a high-top fade, and with baggy clothes draped around his chiseled frame, Vanilla Ice looked like a rapping Ivan Drago. He was a sex symbol, and "Ice Ice Baby" was a simple enough tune; a steady groove, repeatable chorus, kid-friendly (if you weren't paying close attention to the lyrics). Ice was more accessible to pop audiences (read: white audiences), than N.W.A or Public Enemy, whose tracks were brash and abrasive, all pent-up aggression and angst.

The real hip-hop fans, whoever they were, could have their Rakim, A Tribe Called Quest, and N.W.A. Ice could be like Will Smith, who had turned his rap career into *Fresh Prince of Bel-Air* fame; better yet, an MC Hammer, whose comically large pants, frenetic dancing, and uplifting raps had turned him into one of the biggest stars in pop music, complete with global tours, his own Saturday-morning cartoon, and billing as Michael Jackson's heir apparent, the new King of Pop.

But there were drawbacks. As he got increasingly popular, Hammer became the target of much ire, labeled by critics as a sellout of sorts, using cartoonish gimmicks to sell records (as if nobody had ever done that before). Now there was Ice, a rapper whose entire shtick seemed to be the color of his skin. Maybe that wasn't his intention, but you'd be hard-pressed to think it was by accident when the A-side to "Ice Ice Baby" was "Play That Funky Music," with its chorus: "Play that funky music, white boy."

"Say go white boy, go white boy, go!" he shouts on the song. What did he expect people to think?

Like Hammer, Ice was becoming super popular. He seemed fun, friendly, and inoffensive. "The record company cleaned up my image, cleaned up the whole look, and then all of a sudden there's this good-lookin' kid out there, and they made it acceptable for the parents because they saw these kids dancing—oh, it's just a dance song, it's acceptable now and let's find out who he is. Oh, he's wholesome, he's good, and all this," Ice explained in an interview years later.[14]

But it wasn't long before his gimmick began rubbing people the wrong way.

"In a society perceived as indifferent and even hostile to minorities, rappers like KRS-One and Ice Cube are the voice of an increasingly frustrated young [Black] America; Vanilla Ice, on the other hand, offers easily digestible raps about girls, cars and dancing," James Bernard, an editor at the hip-hop magazine *The Source* (and later, founder of *XXL*), wrote in the *New York Times*. "Aficionados know that Vanilla Ice cannot match the cleverness of LL Cool J., the verbal gymnastics of Brand Nubian, the humor of Digital Underground. But Vanilla Ice is white, sexy, palatable in the suburbs, and thus highly marketable."[15]

At the time, Ice seemed to feel that not only was he helping rap music by becoming the face of it—he also had every right to do so. "I'm setting patterns here for other people to come along, bringing rap music into ears that never heard it before or never even considered buying rap music . . . and I'm white," Ice said. "A lot of people don't like that because rap music is [Black]. Blacks did originate it, but rap also belongs to the streets and the street is where I came from."[16]

By late 1990, his debut album *To the Extreme** had sold more than two million copies. "Ice Ice Baby," was still bulletproof on the radio, and all around the world, fans were itching to see Vanilla Ice perform. "A generation of suburbanites was captivated," wrote Michael J. Mooney in the *Miami New Times*.[17]

But something wasn't adding up. "Ice Ice Baby" seemed to have arrived out of nowhere. The track, full of brags and boasts, suggested Ice was stone-cold, raised in the streets. Somehow, he'd risen above it all and lived to tell the tale. The blocks he talks about ("A1A Beachfront Avenue"), the car he rides ("Rolling, in my 5.0"), the jacking he avoids ("trying to get away before the jackers jack"). The songwriting was so vivid, so picturesque. Did Ice really know anything about this stuff, or was it all just a ruse?

Journalists at the *Dallas Morning News* began looking for clues, searching for the true story of who Vanilla Ice actually was. There was a biography, supplied by the record company—a standard document of sorts—which said Ice had been raised on the mean streets of Miami, went to school with Uncle Luke Campbell (of 2 Live Crew fame), was stabbed five times outside of a nightclub, and in his youth rode dirt bikes competitively, winning a number of championships. But much of it only checked out in the abstract; when you looked beneath the surface, Ice appeared to be a poseur.

"All those stories that came out about me not really being from the streets are just a lot of crap," he swatted back. "If you can't see I'm from the streets, then you're blind. How many white people do you know who can dance? How many white people do you know can rap? How many white people you know can beat box? How many white people you know can produce their own rap music?"[18]

Some elements of Ice's biography were, in fact, credible. As a kid he'd split his time between Dallas and Miami. In Dallas, he earned a rep dancing and rapping at his manager Tommy Quon's City Lights nightclub. The only

---

* Although technically released in 1990, an early version of *To the Extreme* hit stores a year earlier. At that time, it was called *Hooked*, and the cover featured Ice, clad in a pink shirt, crouched low on a series of giant ice cubes. When Ice was signed to SBK Records, the label rereleased the album under the new title and dropped two songs from the track list while adding three new ones.

white boy in a predominantly Black scene, Ice was something of an anomaly, though when it came to his actual music there was this—the lyrics to "Ice Ice Baby" were at least partially credited to another songwriter, Mario "Chocolate" Johnson. Until this day, Ice contends he wrote the song himself, composing it in thirty minutes one night in 1988, but back then the mystery of its true origin, and the boasts contained within it, only led to more questions. Maybe Ice *did* make it all up?

"Hey, some things he's said could be embellished," Tommy Quon said at the time. "He's a young guy doing this for the first time."[19] What Quon didn't understand was why his star client's upbringing even mattered. He had discovered Ice dancing and rapping, wowing the Black crowd in his Dallas nightclub City Lights in 1988. It was basic common sense: You didn't need to grow up in a poor, downtrodden environment to be influenced by hip-hop culture.

"Either middle class or lower class, who cares? [Ice's] Miami upbringing could have been well-off, but maybe he chose to go to the street to learn his trade," Quon said. "When he said he's from the ghetto, it may not be true that he grew up in the ghetto—but maybe he spent a lot of time there."[20]

Quon's words fell on deaf ears. This was America in the late eighties and early nineties, where the thought of a white rapper was still a tough pill to swallow. The transgressions of the rock and roll stars of yore remained fresh. How the Beach Boys had allegedly copied Chuck Berry's "Sweet Little Sixteen" for "Surfin' U.S.A.," and how Elvis had been crowned the King of Rock despite seeming to have mined the work of innumerable Black musicians who had come before him. Just as rock had once been the sound of young America, now it was hip-hop. And Vanilla Ice seemed as if he was carrying on tradition, another white dude getting ahead while the Black people who did the real work got left behind.

As 1991 got underway, Vanilla Ice's career continued apace. He toured relentlessly, shot a pair of movies, and even began dating Madonna. But the chattering masses, the undercurrent of criticism that kept coming his way, proved too loud. Accepting a trophy at the American Music Awards, he grew agitated, and shot back: "Those that try to hold the Ice Man down, can kiss my white ass."

The next night, he appeared on *The Arsenio Hall Show*. In late night television, Arsenio's show was insurgent; young, hip, cool, it featured rappers and entertainers who the other late-night hosts, namely Johnny Carson, still hosting *The Tonight Show*, were less likely to book. On any night, it wasn't uncommon to see A Tribe Called Quest or Ice-T holding court on Arsenio's couch, schooling America. Arsenio was a gatekeeper of sorts, and if Ice could win over his audience—well, it'd be a big win.

After a performance, and a brief, unexplained cameo by Public Enemy member Flavor Flav—long before he had become a reality television star, back when Public Enemy was still known for its militant, politically charged music—Ice takes a seat on the couch, dressed in a bedazzled jumpsuit, blond streaks in his spiked hair. Arsenio wastes no time asking him what he meant at the American Music Awards.

"So it's a white rapper being suppressed kind of revenge?" he asks.

Ice responds that his record going to number one has made him an easy target. "They're picking on me," he says. "That's all there is to it."

Arsenio notes the flags in Ice's biography, how the press has called him out for lying or allegedly fabricating his past. But Ice hears none of it. He swears that everything he said is true—he *did* get stabbed almost five times, he *did* almost die, and no, he isn't proud of it.

"I am from the streets," he says. "If you can't see I'm from the streets, then you're blind. Because the majority of white people cannot dance, they don't have much rhythm. It is a fact."

Arsenio then alerts him to what the hip-hop community is saying, citing that KRS-One had said that Ice presents "a distorted mutation of rap."

Ice wants no part of it, says he doesn't know what KRS-One meant. He then argues that some of his supporters believe he's helping to popularize rap music by exposing it to people who might never have listened to it before. "Rap music is here to stay, no matter what color it is," he says. "I'm not the Elvis of rap. I'm Vanilla Ice. I'm not no Elvis Presley."

Arsenio tries unpacking KRS-One's comment, that Black rappers are bothered that some white people weren't buying rap music before Ice began rapping; that is, before they saw a white face, a vanilla face, a face that looked just like theirs, staring back at them on the album cover.

Ice chalks it up to jealousy, says he can't do anything if Black rappers don't like it—white people buying his music, that's not his fault. Anyway, what about Flava Flav; look at him, he isn't a hater.

"Is that why you brought him out, just to show you have a Black supporter?" Arsenio asks.

The crowd boos. Ice tells Arsenio the crowd doesn't like how he's pressing him. Arsenio doesn't care. He's legitimately puzzled as to why he had Flava Flav come out.

"I wanted to show that he's my homeboy and he's in town and I'm kicking it with him," Ice says.

Even if what Ice had said was true, Arsenio didn't seem to be buying it. Here was an authority, someone with a real platform, taking Ice down a peg. A pivotal and damaging moment, Ice's career never seemed to recover. And just as fast as he rose, he quickly began to fall. His credibility in shambles, his gimmick—being white—could only take him so far.

"My being white had something to do with [my success]," he told the *New York Times*. "But not as much as they say it does."[21] Indeed, you couldn't dance or sing along to a skin color. Audiences needed something to move to. But there wasn't much else. And for the immediate future, all Ice had was "Ice Ice Baby," a critically panned movie—*Cool as Ice*—and a cameo in a kids' film, *Ninja Turtles 2: The Secret of the Ooze.*

No doubt, for a brief period, Vanilla Ice was a legit celebrity—but for all the wrong reasons. People didn't love Vanilla Ice. They just loved a song he had made. A one-hit wonder, the answer to a pop culture question on trivia night, that's all he'd ever turn out to be. He spent the nineties hopped up on drugs and alcohol, a cautionary tale. The music business had chewed him up and spit him out.

"I'm sorry," he'd later say. "I have no excuses. I'm sorry for the hairdos, baggy pants, the scandals, the lies, the gangs. And I'm sorry about the music. I was young, manipulated, and I was a puppet."[22]

But the damage was done. If a white rapper was going to make it in a post–Vanilla Ice world, they'd have to show serious skills and tread carefully. The industry, the media, the fans would make that rapper walk through the fire before accepting them. There would be no turning back. For white rappers, Ice left a mess in his wake.

•••

One day in 1995, Wendy Day was booked to speak on a panel at a music conference in Detroit. Day was the founder of Rap Coalition, a nonprofit that helped hip-hop artists navigate the often confusing and sometimes predatory music business. She had worked with 2Pac and Chuck D, and years later would famously broker Cash Money's thirty-million-dollar deal with Universal. But on that day, all she knew was that she was in Chicago when she needed to be in Detroit.

So she rented a car and along with the rapper Rhymefest—who would go on to win a Grammy for cowriting "Jesus Walks" with Kanye West—and drove all the way to the D, a four- to five-hour trip, without stopping. They arrived at the conference in the late afternoon, just in time for Wendy's panel. Not having eaten since she'd left the Windy City, Day was starving. There was a Denny's not far from the Atheneum hotel, the conference site, and the plan was to head in that direction.

But when they exited the theater a cypher was underway. Rhymefest, hungry to prove himself, hopped right in. Day wasn't pressed. She had seen her fair share of cyphers; they were often hit-or-miss. Besides, she was so hungry. Still, she couldn't help but notice a man standing off to the side, not in the cypher but not disinterested in it either. The man, Mark Kemp, caught her attention, and they began talking. He told her about a local magazine he owned, and how he was working with a rapper, this kid who seemed to be getting busy in the cypher.

"As soon as he told me that it was a white rapper, I kind of shut down," Day said. "I knew how difficult it was to get a deal for a white rapper—impossible."[23]

When the cypher ended, Rhymefest came over. "You gotta hear this kid rap," he said. But Day couldn't give any less of a fuck. She took the kid's demo, thought little of it, and shuttled off into the car. Now Day and Rhymefest were speeding down the highway, headed to Denny's. "Let's listen to the tape," Rhymefest implored. But she didn't want to.

"White rappers can't rap," she said. "And there isn't anything I can do for him." She tossed the tape on the car floor.

"That was really foul," Rhymefest said. "You're white, he's white. You know how hard it is when you're white. And you totally discounted him." The car fell silent. Day could feel his eyes on her. The minutes felt like hours as the darkened highway sped by outside her window. Finally, she reached down and picked up the tape. She slid it into the cassette deck. The music came on. Immediately, Day's head began bobbing.

"I got about two minutes into the first song, realized his incredible fucking talent and made a U-turn across the grass to go back to the Atheneum," she said. "When we got there, I [saw him and I] was like—*Get in!*"

Thus began Day's next big project. She was going to help this white rapper she had just met get a deal. His name was Marshall. But he called himself Eminem.

"I knew as soon as people saw his skin color, they would trip," she said. "But if I could get them to hear the music without knowing he was white, the music would suck them in. Then we could figure out what to do from there."

As a music business figure, Day was riding high at the time. Chicago rapper Twista had just inked a deal with Atlantic Records, which she helped broker. Not only did she understand the nuts and bolts of the business, how to negotiate contracts and demand from the labels what she believed the artists deserved, she also had a rep for finding talent. New talent was the lifeblood of the industry; finding talent, developing talent, breaking talent—executives made their careers on this stuff. And Day was helping them with that, so she was hot.

Obtaining a record deal for Eminem should have been a layup. Unlike Vanilla Ice, he not only had the talent, but he also had the backstory. Growing up near 8 Mile Road in Detroit, his life had been particularly hardscrabble. His home was a broken one, and his family was poor and dysfunctional. In the mixed-race neighborhoods he grew up in, he was bullied. He dropped out of high school. He had a daughter he loved with an on-again, off-again girlfriend he hated.

He channeled much of his bleak reality into *Infinite*, an album on which he aped the Brooklyn rapper AZ's vocal tone and rhyme patterns, and which sold very few copies. But Day thought Eminem's talent was undeniable. For months, she passed his music around the industry, slinging CD and tapes to anyone who would take a listen.

"When they found out he was white, they passed," she said. "I got frustrated. I felt like race shouldn't play a role in talent. And I get it. I got a degree in African American studies; I get the whole struggle. I even suggested to Eminem that we make him a little cartoon character that didn't have any race and not let people know that he was white. Then he could pop out after he got [signed] and let people know that. But I just never got anywhere [with him]."

The problem for Eminem wasn't his talent. The problem was Vanilla Ice.

"It damaged the ability for any white rappers to follow behind him," said Day. "They portrayed him to be something that he wasn't. And that wasn't unique to white people—[labels] did that with the rapper Boss, too, who came out as a very hard street rapper from Detroit, then the *Wall Street Journal* did an article about her private school upbringing. But Vanilla Ice really did a lot of damage coming out the way he did. Not only was he white; he was the enemy because he made songs like Hammer. He's dancing around, making bubblegum pop tunes which were offensive to the purists in New York who believed KRS-One was God, Rakim was God, all these people that could actually rap and weren't getting mainstream radio play."

When it came to signing another white rapper, it was no surprise then that record labels were gun-shy about pulling the trigger. Why sign a white rapper when you could sign, literally, anyone else in the world?

But Day was determined. She appreciated that as hip-hop was becoming increasingly commercial, with flashy videos and songs that could double as ads for luxury goods, Eminem was committed to proving he was among the best.

"I just want to be a legitimate MC—that's all I could have ever hoped for—to put food on the table doing what I love to do would be the ultimate goal," Eminem remembered thinking at the time. "I would take different trips to anywhere I could, just trying to make any kind of name, pass out my cassettes."[24]

As part of his quest to become known as a fearless MC, battles were always important to Eminem. He bested many competitors at the famed Hip Hop Shop in Detroit; then there was the 1997 Scribble Jam in Cincinnati, and later that year the Rap Olympics. "Thank God for Wendy Day, because she paid for my plane ticket,"[25] Eminem said. The timing was fortuitous, because he had just been evicted from his Detroit home, returning to the house to find his belongings on the lawn and people from the neighborhood rummaging through his stuff. It felt like his entire future hinged on winning that battle. "The first prize was $500, and I needed that $500. I lost. I was fucking devastated."[26]

But the loss turned out to be a blessing in disguise, because in the crowd that day was a young kid, Dean Geistlinger. He asked Eminem for one of those cassettes he was always handing out; Em tossed him one, not thinking anything of it. How many had he handed out already? Must have been hundreds, and he had very little to show for it. Here he was getting off the stage now, singing for his supper, literally, and not even coming home with the prize. The tape was an EP he had self-released, which differed greatly from *Infinite*—mostly in how aggressive he sounded. The approach was the handiwork of an alter ego he'd created for himself; through the ego, which was separate from who Marshall Mathers really was, he could rap about darker subjects, violent, shocking things like murder and drugs.

"After [*Infinite*] every rhyme I wrote got angrier and angrier," Eminem said. "A lot of it was because of the feedback I got. Motherfuckers was like, 'You're a white boy, what the fuck are you rapping for? Why don't you go into rock & roll?' All that type of shit started pissing me off."[27]

The EP was named *Slim Shady*, after his alter ego, and to his surprise it wound up in the hands of Interscope Records chief Jimmy Iovine, for whom Geistlinger was interning. In the thick of helping famed gangsta rap pioneer Dr. Dre launch his new label, Aftermath, Iovine was in a peculiar position. Dre had experienced tremendous success: first with N.W.A, then as a solo artist, and finally, as a producer crafting hits for Snoop Dogg and 2Pac.

One day Dre was visiting Iovine at his house. Dre was looking for a new artist to work with, but he never had much luck finding talent through demo tapes; he discovered Snoop Dogg through his stepbrother Warren G, and the streets of Los Angeles were filled with rappers. Gangsta rap, though, had become stale, and Dre was looking to do something new. As soon as he heard Eminem's tape, he gave Iovine one command: "Find him. Now."[28]

"My gut told me Eminem was the artist I'm supposed to be working with right now,"[29] Dre said. He didn't care that Eminem was white. Still, Dre was just one man. He had people around him, other executives who needed to buy in. And Eminem was a hard sell. "It's like seeing a Black guy doing country [and] western," Dre said.[30]

"Everyone was telling [Dr. Dre] don't fuck with him," Eminem recalled.[31]

"I didn't know how many racists I had around me," Dre said. "Everybody around me, the so-called execs and what have you, were all against it. The records I had done at the time, they didn't work—they wanted me out the building. And then I come up with Eminem, this white boy. My general manager had this eight by ten picture and was like, Dre, this boy's got blue eyes, what are we doing?"[32]

All that seemed to matter to Dre was that Eminem had talent. That was it. Did it hurt that he was white? Certainly, because there was no blueprint for white rappers to follow. And in the industry Dre was ice-cold, having misfired with a compilation album (*Dr. Dre Presents . . . the Aftermath*) and bungling the production on the debut album from rap supergroup The Firm (made up of Nas, Foxy Brown, AZ, and Cormega).

One of the architects of gangsta rap working with a white rapper would be controversial, and controversy had its perks. Dre learned that in the late eighties, when N.W.A's "Fuck Tha Police" drew the FBI's ire, who wrote the group a letter objecting to the lyrics; then, concerned parent groups campaigned to have the song banned, and promoters tried dissuading the group from performing it. Which only made N.W.A that much more notorious—and arguably led to more record sales.

Then there was his protégé Snoop Dogg. In 1993, Snoop held promise, but just as Snoop's career was taking off, he and his bodyguard were charged with first-degree murder in the death of gang member Philip Woldemariam. Though he was eventually acquitted of the charges, it was not before flipping the negative attention into a hit single seemingly inspired by the events—"Murder Was the Case" (followed by an eighteen-minute short film and subsequent soundtrack that became the third highest-selling album of 1994).[33]

Finally, having been shot, imprisoned on a rape charge, and later embroiled in a personal dispute with the Notorious B.I.G.—kicking off the East Coast vs. West Coast rap beef—2Pac was seen by some as damaged goods, too loose of a cannon to take a flier on. But that didn't stop Dre (and then-partner Suge Knight) from bailing him out of prison, signing him to Death Row Records, and producing "California Love," which, with its *Mad Max*-inspired music video playing on MTV nearly nonstop, quickly shot to number one on the charts (and stayed there for eight weeks).

Where there was smoke, there was fire, and Dre seemed to know that. But in the end, you couldn't sell headlines at a Sam Goody. Music went in the ears, not the eyes; if his records weren't up to par, if he wasn't a real MC, if all the shock and awe tactics he would later employ to create controversy only ever amounted to controversy itself, nothing Eminem did would have mattered.

"We weren't looking for a white controversial rapper," said Jimmy Iovine. "We were looking for great."[34]

• • •

Malcolm was not Vanilla Ice or Eminem. When Ice broke into the rap game, Malcolm hadn't even been born yet. As for Eminem, Malcolm was a fan, as many people were. But he wasn't obsessed with him.

"I think people assume that that was how I got into rap—by the way of like, *The Marshall Mathers LP*," he said. "I had some good moments with that when I was younger, but like didn't really understand the genius of Em until I was, like, fifteen, sixteen."[35]

As an album, *The Marshall Mathers LP* mixed Eminem's trademark shock and awe with slick commentary. A song like "Kim," for example, finds our hero killing his significant other and stuffing her in the trunk of his car (not the first time he'd rapped about that subject); meanwhile, "The Real Slim Shady" explores the media's double standards; "The Way I Am" touches on childhood angst and the Columbine school shooting, for which he, along with Marilyn Manson, received blame.

By some estimates the album sold as many as twenty-one million copies. It was among the most commercially successful records of all time. But it was released in the year 2000, when Malcolm was all of eight years old; therefore, even if Eminem's cultural influence was impossible to ignore, it was unlikely to have had a defining impact on him.

What Eminem did provide, however, was an opportunity. The music industry was like any other industry; once something became successful, others sought to copy it, only with slight differences. For white rappers, a door that had once been shut was suddenly open.

Bubba Sparxxx was a white rapper, a protégé of the producer Timbaland, signed to Interscope Records, the same label that had broken Eminem. And just as Dre had cosigned a white rapper, providing him a platform, so, too, had Timbaland vouched for Sparxxx.

"There are distinct similarities between Sparxxx and Eminem," a writer for the *Independent* posited in 2001. "For a start, they are both white and come with a unique rapping style. They both originate from a white-trash background—Eminem was brought up in a run-down district of east Detroit, Sparxxx in a house at the end of a dirt track in the Deep South."[36]

But short of the strip club jam "Ms. New Booty," Sparxxx's hillbilly persona remained an anathema, and thus he never really caught on. Less circumspect was Paul Wall, who hailed from Houston, and after years of independent grind with rap partner Chamillionaire, hit it big in 2004 when he was featured, along with Slim Thug, on Mike Jones's single "Still Tippin.'" With lyrics like "What it do, it's Paul Wall, I'm the people's champ," and the meme-ready "I got the Internet going nuts," Wall introduced himself with a flurry; a year later he'd top the charts with *The Peoples Champ*, and become known behind the scenes for his work with jeweler Johnny "TV Johnny" Dang for supplying grillz—gold teeth, that is—to the entertainment industry's elite.

"Earlier, white rappers were just on the super storytelling, very poetic . . . Paul Wall, to the culture, is so important and crazy because he was a white dude that was just like, 'I'm just a cool ass white dude, so I'mma rap,' Malcolm said. "It wasn't, 'I know I'm not supposed to be here, so let me get really next-level.'"[37]

In fact, at the time Wall was just one of many H-Town rappers introducing Texas culture to the world. There was also Big Hawk, Lil Flip, Lil Keke, Trae Tha Truth, and Z-Ro, to say nothing of elder statesmen like Scarface and UGK. Fans were taken with their songs; they celebrated grills, candy-painted cars, and the Texas lifestyle, unique to that part of the country. But crucially, one of its biggest exports was lean, a recreational drug created by mixing prescription-strength cough syrup with a soft drink like Sprite; when sipped, it was the perfect complement to a rap subgenre called "chopped and screwed."

Popularized by DJ Screw—and to a larger extent his crew the Screwed Up Click—a chopped-and-screwed mixtape featured ordinary elements, like cuts, scratches, and blends. But the tracks would be slowed to half speed, pitched down until the lyrics and beats resembled a haunting, hypnotic drawl. Combined with lean, the effects were intoxicating.

"The first thing [people] think of when they hear Screw's name, or Screw music in general, is the syrup sippin'," Screwed Up Click member E.S.G. told the *Guardian*. "That's just the culture down here and a way of life."[38]

Sometimes called "syrup," "sizzurp," or "drank," and later seen in the hands of artists like Lil Wayne and Future, lean had been long celebrated in southern hip-hop culture. "Sippin' on Some Syrup," a Three 6 Mafia collaboration with UGK and Project Pat released in 1999, might as well have been considered lean's unofficial anthem, though the sometimes-tragic effects of lean were barely acknowledged. In fact, for all he did to popularize Screw music and lean, in November of 2000 the man himself, DJ Screw, was found dead on the floor of a toilet stall in his studio, an ice cream wrapper in hand. The cause: an overdose of lean mixed with Valium and PCP.[39] He was only twenty-nine.

"A lot of people were sad about losing him," said Bun B. "He was a local hero. He wasn't just a DJ or a musical icon, he was a hero. He gave a lot of guys careers, followings. People still care for their families because of DJ Screw."[40]

That lean had taken the life of someone so legendary did not stop artists from embracing it. Some rappers in the Texas scene swore it off, only to get back on; but by then its influence was already being felt all over the country, showing up in places as far-flung as New York. When Cam'ron and Jim Jones launched a cognac-infused liqueur in 2004 dubbed Sizzurp—promoted with a mixtape featuring a young Kanye West, among other artists—it felt like lean had reached critical mass (notwithstanding the fact that Sizzurp, the brand, did not contain any actual lean).[41]

Screw's death remained a cautionary tale. But it wasn't until seven years later that lean's tragic effects became widely known. That was when UGK's Pimp C, a veritable hip-hop legend, who had famously rapped on "Sippin' on Some Syrup," was found in his room at the Mondrian Hotel. Kneeling on his bed in a praying position, surrounded by blood, the thirty-three-year-old was dead.[42] His death was attributed to an accidental overdose caused by the effects of lean with a preexisting medical condition, sleep apnea.

That all of this was happening in the culture was likely not lost on Malcolm. He was a student of the game, paying attention to its many facets, the way it ebbed and flowed. Whether consciously or unconsciously, he was aware that hip-hop and drug culture went hand in hand; rappers rhymed about drugs—selling them, doing them, the works—and he was also aware that there were few white rappers of real notoriety, though it wasn't inconceivable to be a white dude who rapped. The underground was filled with white rappers; it wasn't like being white ever stopped anyone from spitting a few bars.

And while he couldn't deny the obvious, that Point Breeze was affluent, liberal, safe—in some ways a throwback to the Norman Rockwell vision of what an American neighborhood could be—he also couldn't deny a rare quality that Pittsburgh had: You walked a few blocks and that safety evaporated.

"It's very deceiving that Malcolm lived in Point Breeze," said a friend from Woodland Hills. "Point Breeze is nice as shit, but you walk two blocks to the left, across Penn Avenue, and it's fuckin' Homewood, and Homewood is horrible. It's crazy. So, he could have been in school with all rich-ass kids, but he'd go home and be influenced by some real-ass shit. Which is probably why he wanted to be a rapper. He was around this shit. You get influenced by this stuff."

Malcolm himself acknowledged as much. In his interview on MTV's *When I Was 17*, he said Point Breeze's central locale made most people dub it the "best neighborhood in Pittsburgh," putting him a stone's throw away from everything in the city—from the grandest of houses to the toughest of housing projects. Because of this, he could rub elbows with people from all walks of life, not just rich kids or poor kids or white kids or black kids—but everyone.

"I was able to hang out with everybody," he said. "It was a great place. It was safe but also too safe. Sometimes shit popped off."[43]

Still, if you listened to Malcolm's early music, saw him at Timebomb, at a show at the Shadow Lounge, or simply in the street, you'd see this new image he was projecting—his pants hanging low, his fitted cap tilted, and hear how he'd talk to his homies and wonder . . .

"Being a white dude in this, it's like—you're white, you know what it is," one pal said. "People look at you and ask: *Are you trying to be something other than what you are?* They're always knocking you down a peg."

Malcolm didn't seem to care, though. He was white, and there was nothing he could do about it. Would it help him? Maybe. Would it hurt him? Maybe. But it wasn't like there were a ton of white rappers to point to and say, *If he can do it, so can I.* His modus operandi was rather simple.

"If I'm honest, you can't tell me shit," he said. "You really gonna be mad at a kid who loves music and talks about his life? Whoever wants to listen, can listen. I think that's what's most important—authenticity. As long as you're being real with yourself and who you are. It's all about being authentic to who you are. Even outside of your music. It's a lot about your music, but it's a lot about who you are. If people don't fuck with you as a person, they have a hard time getting into your music, because when you're speaking to them, they don't really want to listen."[44]

If it sometimes seemed that Malcolm was putting on airs, that he was acting Black—as if all Black people acted a certain way—that just may have been who he really was. His Woodland Hills pal dubbed him his "light-skin homie," because of all the Black mannerisms he seemed to have adopted—like his obsessive need to "get fresh," and the dutiful care he paid to his hygiene, not even wanting to be seen outside unless his hair was trimmed into the perfect temple fade.

Another thing—his taste in music. Malcolm's palate was expansive and all-encompassing. He was just as familiar with the music many white people liked as he was with the music many Black people liked. He knew the kind of songs that drunk white folks sang along to at karaoke; he also knew deep cuts that went off at the cookout. He was really inclined toward, really in tune, almost intuitively, with Black culture, according to friends.

Still, not everyone was sold. First impressions were everything, and Malcolm didn't always make the best one. There was that name, Easy Mac—you heard it and, even if you dug his music, it was possible you'd cringe.

What did Easy Mac represent? What did it say? In truth, Easy Mac was the kind of name you chose when you didn't know what to call yourself, or when you did know what to call yourself, and you seemingly didn't care how you were perceived, or were under the impression, somehow, that the perception was a positive one.

His friend Jimmy Murton actually came up with the name. It was like Eazy-E—except, well, it was Easy Mac.

"It was more like a joke," Malcolm said. "It stuck because it was like—Ha! A little white kid named Easy Mac, look at him rap! You couldn't forget the kid named Easy Mac."[45]

The name stuck until he connected with Quentin "Q" Cuff, a journalism major at Pittsburgh's Point Park University. When he wasn't studying, Q busied himself interviewing rappers for a local media outlet covering music and lifestyle called *Jenesis* magazine and Point Park University's student newspaper, the *Globe*.

For Q, one particular interview proved instructive; it was with the rapper Asher Roth, who was from Morristown, PA, and as a white rapper himself, had become one of the music industry's most promising new artists. His 2008 Gangsta Grillz mixtape *The Greenhouse Effect Vol. 1* attracted tremendous buzz.

The interview went swimmingly. But after the interview was over, and Q had gone on his merry way, his phone rang. On the other end was Roth's manager, a young upstart with a small list of clients, among them a Canadian teen with the last name Bieber.

Scooter Braun seemed to be impressed by Q's hip-hop knowledge and asked him if he could help talk up the new song Roth was hoping would put him on the charts.

So Q went to work spreading the word about "I Love College," Roth's ode to sleeping late, beer pong, and red Solo cups. And when the song began rising in the charts in early 2009, peaking at number twelve on the Hot 100, he seemed to be inspired to get into the music business himself, switching his major to arts and entertainment.[46]

His timing was fortuitous. Some months earlier, Malcolm was at a party at Central Catholic High School when a girl spilled a beer on him. His shirt was ruined. And Q, who was at the party, told him not to worry—he had an extra shirt in the car, and ran out to get it. Q didn't know Malcolm at the time, but he did look familiar; Q had his ear to the streets and the Internet, and he was certain he'd seen this kid before.

"He was known in the local Pittsburgh area for freestyling in public," Q told the website AudioKorner.com. "I always saw him. He'd go on Facebook forums and battle people. I heard about him battling kids after school, and freestyling at parties."[47]

Battles, especially, were bringing Malcolm more attention. Local rapper Misdemeanor challenged him directly—five hundred dollars for whoever came out on top. And they met in a parking lot, where they went verse for verse. "My swagger mean, so fresh and so clean, in a flash getting change like a vending machine," Malcolm rapped. Misdemeanor was crushed.

At the Pittsburgh Indoor Sports Arena in the summer of 2008, where the Ill Spoken were opening for Soulja Boy, Malcolm and Q reconnected. Malcolm felt Q had his finger on the pulse, and they made plans to hang out. The first time they got together, they spent hours listening to rap records and discussing life. And from then on, whatever Malcolm needed done, Q would attempt to do.

"It didn't initially start with him being a manager," Malcolm said. "He just wanted to be involved. We just started talking and building and then I realized that he would be a good person for [a managerial] position."[48]

And it was when Q began getting more involved that the issue of Malcolm's rap name came back up. Q felt he needed a more serious name. Rappers were increasingly thinking of themselves as brands. To be a big brand, you had to have a big name. Miller was a family name, the first name of Malcolm's older brother, and the maiden name of his maternal grandmother. Mac was a nickname, the name his grandfather had called him his whole life. The more he said the two words together, the more they made sense.

"It's a family name, but it just sounds really good after Mac," he said. "Mac Miller—that sounds cool."[49]

Brian liked the name immediately. The pair had by then begun their permanent hiatus. "Mac Miller is obviously ready to be in the lexicon of pop culture," Brian said. "Easy Mac is not. It's like that old-timey, showbiz-y name. That's what he was going for."

"His goal is to make Mac Miller a brand . . ." Q said. "He's shooting to be an icon."[50]

His first project under the new name was *The Jukebox: Prelude to Class Clown*. He cut most of the songs at ID Labs, where he initially worked with engineer Josh Everette. Like Wiz before him, Malcolm had entered ID Labs as a paying client. But after a while he impressed upon E. Dan and the crew that he had a little more going for himself. The battles were one thing, but the mixtape seemed to be connecting with many of the young kids in the Pittsburgh area.

The Jukebox dropped in June of 2009. Kalson, technically still his manager—working in tandem with Q—rented out the Shadow Lounge for its release party.

"It was a pretty small room," said Kalson. "But it was filled with people. There had to be close to two hundred people. It was dope."

The Shadow Lounge's owner, Justin Strong, was taken aback. A 1996 graduate of Taylor Allderdice, he got his start with house parties in the late nineties, dubbing his crib at 305 Meyran Avenue in South Oakland "The 305 Spot," before opening the Shadow Lounge in East Liberty in 2000. When the venue opened its doors, the neighborhood was desolate, having been on the decline for decades.

"All of the businesses were vacant at the time; there was nothing but I think a Bell Telephone," Timebomb's Brian Brick told the *Pittsburgh City Paper*. "It was really the first revival of the art community as a whole."[51]

In the interim, the spot had become increasingly popular. Whether you rapped, sang, played an instrument, or wrote poetry, the Shadow Lounge welcomed you.

"[T]hey had the open mic on Friday nights," a poet, Nikki Allen, told the *Post-Gazette*. "They had a live band and everyone from poets to emcees to singers to upright bassists would throw down on that stage."[52]

Mondays were jazz night, Tuesday was the "Steel City Poetry Jam," another night was specifically a hip-hop open mic with a live band; all races and genders were welcome, so it became the place to be. "From the other owners to the staff, we were living it," Strong said. "There'd be cyphers onstage, where the bartenders leave the bar and jump onstage. The doorman would be like, 'Yo hold my spot, I'm on the open mic list next.'"

The lounge was among the first local venues to have Malcolm grace its stage, and he'd made numerous appearances there before, in June of 2009, partaking in Rhyme Calisthenics, a freestyle competition built around spinning a game show wheel—described as "[p]art '8 Mile,' part 'Wheel of Fortune,'"[53]— and placing in the final four.

Strong was fourteen years older than Malcolm and his personal tastes fell more to hip-hop from the nineties. "If it was up to me I'd just be booking De La Soul and Camp Lo," he said. But while the Shadow Lounge was mostly for people twenty-one and older, Malcolm got in despite his age, which led to some awkward moments, like the time, Strong recalled, when he was ". . . yelling at him for having a bottle of Hennessy in the greenroom."[54] Every time Malcolm showed up at the Shadow Lounge, though, more people seemed to come, and Strong took note.

"They would say—hey, we want to do a release or an event, and it was packed with young folks and young women," Strong said. "If you know hip-hop, that sometimes does not happen. What a purist would call more hip-hop than most, usually doesn't attract a lot of women. I was like, 'Yo, this like a social scene.' If I was their age, even if I didn't like the music, I'm coming. Mac Miller's performing? Yeah, I'll be there, I'll be there."[55]

As for the music itself, *The Jukebox* picked up where the Ill Spoken's *How High* left off. Freed of jockeying with his partner for attention, Mac could rhyme about whatever he wanted: like how his music defied categorization. "I sound like old, I sound like new, I sound like me, I sound like you," he raps on "Sound Like."

Elsewhere, he gets his bars off on "PA Hustla," while paying homage to his hero Big L by rhyming over the same beat he had rapped on during a freestyle with Jay-Z in 1995 (Milkbone's "Keep It Real"). "A Night in the Studio" is a first-person story about, literally, his night in the studio—complete with a mock phone call from his mom asking when he's coming home, reminding him he has school. A particularly strong cut is "Keep Me Alive," about the bad things he and friends have done, and acknowledging his relatively atypical upbringing.

Among the mixtapes most heartfelt songs is "What Up Cousin (R.I.P. Nick)," a letter of sorts, updating his cousin on his life. "They say my style ain't different . . . all those people is just hatin' 'cause they don't know how to love theyself," he raps.

Joining forces with one of the hottest rappers in the streets at that time, Max B, there's "Chow Line," an Ill Spoken song the group had released a year earlier, which Malcolm re-released because, well, why not? "Max B charged us a thousand dollars," Brian recalled of the rapper (who shortly afterward was sentenced to seventy-five years in prison for conspiracy to commit murder and robbery). "And he was awaiting trial at the time. It was worth it though. He was a trendsetter. That got us some traction, for sure."

Another highlight: "So Far to Go," a freestyle over one of J Dilla's most-loved beats,* a syrupy, feel-good track that finds Malcolm resplendent, celebrating his love for hip-hop, his love for life, and reminding us how far he still has to go.

Finally, "Got a Clue" provides the biggest peek into a part of Malcolm's life that, in later years, he was never particularly open about. It's an ode to a woman he's taken with, a portrait of someone head over heels for a girl he believes to be his soul mate.

In the song, the girl stands at a distance, though, hardly impressed. Here Malcolm is the proverbial mack, kicking game, hoping to land a number; maybe, if he's lucky, it'll lead to something more. Perhaps a relationship, at least a little sex. But she isn't easy. She wants him to work for it.

The song's music video was shot by Ian Wolfson—who would become, in his early videos, Malcolm's go-to collaborator—and the concept is simple: a girl walks by Malcolm while he's hanging out with Q; he begins trying to get her attention, and the video follows them as they enjoy each other's company. They parade around town, Malcolm rapping to her while sitting on playground swings, her eyes ablaze under a red umbrella. In the end, though, it's little more than a daydream; the girl he spotted ends up cruising right by.

The girl in the video was Nomi Leasure. Malcolm had known her since the eighth grade.[56] She described herself as a "a weird curly haired girl [whose] Barbie [dolls'] lives were so complex they could have been studied by Freud,"[57]

---

* The instrumental to "So Far to Go," by Common ft. D'Angelo, released on Dilla's 2006 LP *The Shining* as well as Common's 2007 LP *Finding Forever*.

and had gone to Pittsburgh's high school for the performing and creative arts (CAPA), where she took an interest in theater, landing starring roles in plays like *The Secret Garden* and competing in Shakespeare contests. At the end of Malcolm's junior year of high school, she was a year older than him, due to leave soon for Philadelphia, where she'd be attending college at Temple University. Malcolm was taken with her from the very start.

"Things were picking up, girls were coming around who never came around before; girls that used to play him would be like, 'Oh, Mac,'" said Palermo Stone. "And then Nomi came around. He loved her immediately. He just shut everything else down. Once he met Nomi—that's exactly what he wanted—and he just kind of locked into her."

Even with *The Jukebox* out, Malcolm was working obsessively at ID Labs, where he'd settled into a comfortable groove.* There, he was joined by a rotating cast of characters, like Stone, TreeJ, Q, Bill Niels, and Will Kalson. Nomi would come, too, often with friends, and they'd hang out, contributing their energy and soaking up the vibes.

The studio cost money, though. Forty dollars an hour, three hundred dollars for an eight-hour block of time, and mixing fees that ran between seventy-five to one hundred fifty dollars per song. Individual beats could be purchased for as little as twenty-five dollars—and two hundred fifty dollars could get you as many as fifteen (three hundred dollars would get you sixteen beats or more).[58] Day after day, it added up. Malcolm's parents often picked up the tab.

"They would give money for the studio and tell Q, 'Don't let Mac know you got that from me,'" said Stone. "He never wanted help."

Sometimes Malcolm and his friends would pull off scams to pay for the studio. "We was doing a lot of silly shit to get the money," said Stone. "TreeJ would sell fake weed to this white kid. Like, oregano in a bag. He would bag up an ounce and charge him. We tried pawning shit, or going to house parties, grabbing shit, and taking it to the studio. Like a flat-screen TV that we found at a party. The parents are away, the kids throw a party, and we'd just go there, take some shit, and leave. They can't tell their parents because their parents

---

* "Only ones with ID Labs tatted, that's E. Dan and Me," Miller would rap in a guest verse on Choo Jackson's "HD," released in 2015.

didn't know they was having a party. And Mac, there was a really good energy about him, so he would just be rapping and bullshitting and we'd be in the back trying to get some shit off so we could get some studio time."

"I was just hittin' licks," said TreeJ. "Like, this is me going back to my fuckin' Hill District days. Whatever we needed to keep us fucking going—ecstasy, pills, shrooms, whatever the fuck we needed. Selling it and doing it."

Much of Malcolm's early material at ID Labs was recorded by Josh Everette, but he also befriended another engineer, Jeremy Kolousek, who would come to be known as the producer Big Jerm. Jerm had actually met Miller before he had ever set foot inside the studio. It was when he was still calling himself Easy Mac, hitting up people he wanted to work with on Myspace— his profile was Myspace.com/mcomiflows—hoping they'd write him back.

"He just said he wanted a beat," Jerm recalled. He thought nothing of the request. Jerm had been putting in work with Wiz Khalifa and Boaz (another artist who would later sign to Rostrum). He was accustomed to rappers asking him for beats, and was happy to supply them—so long as they paid.[59]

"When you're kind of fresh [as a producer], you don't wanna go too hard and be demanding," he said. "In Pittsburgh, you have to understand, the market is not like New York, where you selling somebody a beat is gonna mean people are gonna hear it or anything; most of the time, the people I'd worked with in Pittsburgh were like, drug dealers. Not to air anybody out, but that's just what it is. It's dudes who kind of rap on the side or whatever, so I would just take what I could get."

But Malcolm was willing to pay. For two hundred dollars, he got Jerm to sample "Just My Imagination (Running Away with Me)," a number one hit for the Temptations in 1971, which he was determined to flip into a fantasy of his own. Over Jerm's soulful beat, Malcolm kicks a rap about his fantasy version of life, complete with a king-size bed, a swarm of women, clothes, jewelry, money, cars, mansions, and more; in short, the makings of the average aspirational rap tune, although with Malcolm it seemed as if the track served as a kind of audio vision board—this is what he imagined for himself, and one day, if he kept working, he would have it.

"And then that was the beginning of us doing *The High Life*," Jerm said of Malcolm's next mixtape. "We just kept doing stuff. He was so persistent—like,

I used to think he was annoying back then. From there, it led to us forming a friendship."

By then, Jerm had taken over the main engineering duties at ID Labs, due to a car accident that Josh Everette had been in, and so most of the recording duties for Malcolm's sessions fell to him. Money was tight, so Malcolm would come in with his raps prewritten.

"Palermo Stone had his own setup in East Pittsburgh," said Franchise. "So what Malcolm would do is—he'd come over and demo a lot of his tracks at Palermo Stone's. Bill Niels [also] had an apartment where [he] would record at, on the third floor."

At ID Labs, he'd record the songs he demoed as fast as he could. In the company of others, he did not overanalyze his own creations. He was simply determined to get shit done. "I like to be able to record it right after I write it," Malcolm said. "Because you're never as excited about a verse as when you first write it."[60]

And day after day, he'd hole up in the studio, a relatively small, nondescript building—by some estimates, not more than seven hundred square feet—where the back room served as an "A" room, which E. Dan worked out of in daylight hours, and where Jerm arrived in the evenings, getting his sessions going around seven P.M., then running them into the wee hours of the morning. It was hardly a fancy place, but it served its purpose.

"I wouldn't say it was a nice studio or anything like that," said Jerm. "We did what we could with it, and it worked out."

Meanwhile, Malcolm was making a strong impression on Jerm, who saw in him some of the very same things that E. Dan had once seen in Wiz Khalifa. "There was a charisma, just a natural kind of thing," Jerm said. "Wiz and Malcolm, they didn't have to try too hard. And work ethic too. In Pittsburgh back then, a lot of people wanted to do their one song and do a video. With those two, they looked at it like more of a career, even when they were younger."

But in the time Malcolm was working on his craft, turning himself from Easy Mac, a guy who simply liked to rap, into Mac Miller, a more serious artist, it was the fortunes of another artist rising elsewhere at the same time that would have the most lasting impact on his young career.

NINE

Rostrum Records thought it had hit it big. Wiz Khalifa's buzz hadn't yet reached a fever pitch, but Warner Bros. had seen enough. In June of 2007, Wiz signed a deal with Warner, with Rostrum managing and serving as the production company.

It wasn't the most complex of arrangements; labels were in the business of signing talent, and Wiz showed promise.

"Warner heard about me and took some interest," Wiz said. "I went out there, and they heard a bunch of my new stuff and figured they wanted to do it. And we got it right."[1]

Warner was excited about Wiz. One music executive remembered bumping into Tick, the A&R rep who signed him, at an industry event. The exec had just gotten an artist he represented—Jean Grae—a deal at Warner too. He was hoping to get Tick involved.

"I just signed Wiz Khalifa," Tick demurred. "He's gonna be a big star."

As for Wiz, he celebrated the signing with a party in late July at the Deja Vu Lounge in Pittsburgh's Strip District. The next night he appeared at the WAMO Summer Jam at the Mellon Arena, performing alongside Mario, Pretty Ricky, DJ Unk, Lil Scrappy, and others.

The show was co-headlined by Jeezy and Lil Wayne. A palpable buzz filled the arena. One of the city's very own had just signed with a major label.

Though a neophyte next to the seasoned veterans with whom he was sharing the stage, Wiz held his own. But it was clear that he was a little out of his depth.

Reviewing the show in the *Pittsburgh Post-Gazette*, Cody McDevitt wrote: "He is more of a storytelling rapper than a catch-phrasey one. His lyrics shined through on 'Pittsburgh Sound' and 'Damn Thing.' On other songs though, the loud background beats often overshadowed his voice—and the stories he had written."[2]

The review was slightly prophetic. Talk of a record deal made it seem as if Wiz's pockets were overflowing with advance money. But that wasn't exactly the case.

"We ended up getting a singles deal," said Arthur Pitt. "It was wack."

Pegged in the low five figures, the deal was typical for its time. The major record labels were struggling to adapt to a changing music business, one in which piracy was rampant,* and where selling singles—one song, as opposed to an entire album—was a winning strategy.†

It was a business model that lent itself to one-hit wonders. Whether it was Yung Joc ("It's Going Down"); Dem Franchize Boyz ("Lean Wit It, Rock Wit It"); Huey ("Pop, Lock It & Drop It"); the Shop Boyz ("Party Like a Rockstar"); Jibbs ("Chain Hang Low"); Mims ("This Is Why I'm Hot"); D4L ("Laffy Taffy")—even, for that matter, Soulja Boy, who had gone viral with "Crank That (Soulja Boy)" (and its Superman-inspired dance)—it seemed the priority was to sign artists who could sell a million downloads of one song before moving on to the next flash in the pan.

It was no wonder then that Nas had just declared: "Hip-hop is dead." But Wiz seemed to think of himself differently. If given the chance, he felt he could make a lasting impact. Rostrum didn't bet the farm on him just so he could have a viral hit and disappear. So he dropped a buzz record, "Youngin on His Grind," then followed it up with the mixtape *Prince of the City 2*.

---

* By 2008, the IFPI, a recording industry trade group, estimated that for every legitimate download, there were twenty that were illegal—ninety-five percent of the market was then effectively stolen. (www.eff.org/wp/riaa-v-people-five-years-later)

† In the span of one year—2006 to 2007—album sales dropped fifteen percent, according to performance rights agency BMI. Meanwhile, digital downloads increased from 581.9 million to 844.2—a forty-five percent surge. Before that, ringtones, which grew alongside the download business, grew from 245 million dollars in 2004 to 600 million dollars in 2006.

On the mixtape, Wiz is still finding his footing—his voice is not fully developed, and on some songs he belts his rhymes with a stylized emphasis, a little unsure of who he is. There are positives though. On other songs he sounds comfortable. At ease. There is a reflexive "Uh-huh," which he ad-libs, soon to be a trademark. The beats are bottom-heavy, the bounce Southern; the rhymes are East Coast–accented, studied and bold. Listening to *Prince of the City 2*, one senses that Wiz is from both everywhere and nowhere. He is a pure talent in search of a sound to call home.

". . . Being from Pittsburgh, you have room to make up your own sound," Wiz said. "People don't have expectations. We're not as East Coast in Pittsburgh as people are in Philly, so our vibe is just a little bit different. We're a little bit more country, more Midwest in general. We have a different way about us when it comes down to music. The beats are really melodic and musical, but they're still really heavy. They just ride out, almost like down South mixed with West Coast."[3]

The buzzy single and mixtape were appetizers meant to prepare listeners for the main meal, a proper single released in 2008 called "Say Yeah," built around a sample of Alice Deejay's "Better Off Alone," a Eurotrance hit that had cycled through its usefulness, from chic dance clubs to a staple at weddings and on Carnival cruises.

Repurposing the song was the whole thing; the original track was so familiar that, within earshot of Wiz's version, you'd stick around and listen. Warner Bros. loved it. "It was a rap song mixed with a techno beat, they never heard that wave before, never heard those two together," Wiz said. "So they were like—let's make a million songs like this!"[4]

And yet "Say Yeah" was not reinventing the wheel. Beating him by a few months, in September of 2007, Kanye West dropped *Graduation*; buoyed by "Stronger," built around a Daft Punk sample, it also put a recognizable dance tune behind a hip-hop song. To better effect, Kanye was . . . Kanye, while Wiz was still largely unknown. Nevertheless, "Say Yeah" was a modest success, going gold with more than five hundred thousand copies sold. It proved Wiz could make hits.

"It was really me just trying to make the biggest music possible," Wiz said. "I have my side, where I can make big songs. But I also have my underground side, where I can really rap and make mixtapes. So I was more or less trying to move towards writing bigger songs."[5]

Whatever success the song had, it wasn't enough. Warner, once excited about Wiz, was now circumspect. Wiz wanted to release a major label album. ID Labs had become Rostrum's home base, and Wiz stayed in the studio. But Warner wouldn't give the project a green light.

"There was no lane for me there," Wiz said. "Because there was nobody who had really done what I was doing—where it was rap and pop-type shit. It was either you were rap, or you were just corny pop. There was no mixture of the two, so they didn't really understand it."[6]

Benjy Grinberg, too, was frustrated. "[When] we signed to Warner Bros.—you would think that's when it really popped off, but it didn't really," he said. "[I]t just wasn't clicking."[7]

The morale at Rostrum was low. They had begun developing other artists from Pittsburgh, buzzy street rappers like S Money and Boaz, who they hoped Warner might become interested in. With Wiz, they already had their foot in the door. But they were finding that the major label system was a corporate industry not unlike any other, with myriad bureaucracies and red tape.

"The last year at Warner Bros. was pretty rough," said Artie. "It wasn't a good look. We were just stuck there. And no one cared."

Eventually, they lost their patience.

"We asked to get let go," Benjy said. "We thought we could do more being independent, being freer."[8]

On July 16, 2009, Rostrum announced that Wiz had left Warner Bros. In a press release, they cited constant delays by Warner to release Wiz's debut album, teasing upcoming indie projects from him like a mixtape with New Orleans rapper Curren$y called *How Fly*, and a cross-country tour to begin the next fall.

"We feel that this 'divorce' is the best thing for both parties at this juncture and we appreciate the leniency Warner has shown with our release," Benjy said in the announcement. "We are excited to be independent again."

It was a good time to be independent. By then, the new tool for breaking artists was the Internet. Blogs, with links to free, downloadable music, updated multiple times per day, had become the de facto promotional tool.

In hip-hop, much of the new music was being broken via a collection of music sites that dubbed themselves the New Music Cartel: *NahRight*, *2DOPEBOYZ*, *OnSMASH*, *YouHeardThatNew*, *Xclusives Zone*, *DaJaz1*, and *MissInfo*. There were others, too, but these sites were the authorities on dope music. Every day, you'd find a steady stream of the latest music—not just from major artists like Kanye West or Lil Wayne, but also artists in mid-career like Cam'ron, and underground darlings like Sean Price.

The blogs needed new content. That was their draw. No matter when you looked at them, there would be something new to check out. Artists who were nimble, worked fast, and produced a lot of content were rewarded.

"We were all fans of the music, and we were just working together to do our best to make sure the music we thought was the best at the time was going to get the proper spotlight," said Kevin Hofman, owner of *OnSMASH*. "Because the music we thought of as the best at the time, those artists didn't have a proven sales history or any singles history."

One of the artists blogs had begun to champion was Wiz. He always had fresh material, and most of it was good.

"Every time we'd put something out, I'd give it to all the blogs," said Artie. "We just kept doing stuff and promoting stuff. We still weren't making money. But I started studying the data behind Wiz's downloads. I'd look at the zShare link and—holy fuck—he'd have, like, fifty thousand downloads."

It helped that they no longer had Warner slowing them down.

"When we got off Warner Bros., we just hit the ground running," Benjy said.[9]

With things heating up, Benjy was approached by a small, New York–based label called iHipHop. A sister company to indie label Babygrande Records, storied for its work in the underground hip-hop scene, its catalog was filled with music by the likes of Jedi Mind Tricks, Hi-Tek, and any number of random Wu-Tang affiliates. iHipHop was a new venture; headed by Chuck Wilson, the label's goal was to traffic in "cool" music.

"What I took it as was something that would be cool for the younger generation, that wasn't necessarily the backpack, gangsta, shoot-'em-up-type shit," said Ruddy Rock, an A&R rep for the label.[10] "iHipHop was more for the motherfuckers who wear Dunks, more stylish—we were coming out of that whole backpack, hoodie era, army pants and fatigue style of music. I'm like, I got the guy to sign—Wiz Khalifa."

Ruddy had been a fan of Wiz's for some time. There was something intangible about him, an energy. "He was like Snoop Dogg for a young generation," Ruddy said. "He always kept a joint in his mouth. You know, you'd never really see him upset, and his music is never really upset. But at that time, I think it was just a relatability—he was a cool-ass motherfucker, man. He was *Doggystyle* for young ni**as."

And Wiz was also growing increasingly popular, even if Warner Bros. had failed to see it. By then, he was performing one-off shows around the country—fashion shows, college shows, Carnegie Mellon, Penn State, Point Park, Pitt, IUP—anywhere he could get a gig. In lieu of radio play, shows were the best way to develop a fan base. "In a lot of cases we treat our rappers like indie rock bands," Benjy said. "It's like, 'Get in the van, and let's go!'"[11]

But Ruddy was seeing a lot of what Arthur Pitt was seeing—real data, hard numbers. When you looked deeper, you saw that something was happening.

"This was the time of Cash Money bling bling, Lil Wayne and Baby, the last wave of 50 Cent, last of the big era rap, and this was also the last days of Myspace," Ruddy said. "If you was up on Myspace looking for artists back then—it was the song plays. Wiz was getting like eighty-five thousand plays a day. Mind you, Myspace is on its last legs. So I'm like, there's a wave here. It was just super cool. He was this kid who wasn't trying to be a thug. He was just being himself."

In the summer of 2009, Ruddy went to see Wiz perform at the Williamsburg, Brooklyn, waterfront. The show was mobbed, and Wiz tore the place down; fans knew every word to his songs, and these were tracks that were only available on mixtapes.

After the show, Ruddy made a beeline for Wiz's trailer. What he saw when he got there floored him. "At the security check, we walk up and there's maybe eleven kids just going ham—they're waiting to see Wiz. I remember seeing that being like, 'Whoa, what's going on?' I'd never seen nothing like that. We were coming from straight thug rap, where after the show ain't nobody lined up to take no pictures, they lined up to rob you. This was different. This was a youth movement. These kids were different."

The pitch to release an album was simple—blogs were helping artists get discovered, but blogs had their limitations. "Artists were propelling from the blogs, but then, some artists were also becoming [pigeonholed as] blog artists," Ruddy said. With a proper album, Wiz would get more than just a day's worth of mentions on all the blogs; he'd get marketing, promotion, PR, the works. iHipHop offered Rostrum a deal said to be worth about fifty thousand dollars.

On November 24, 2009, through iHipHop, Wiz released an album called *Deal or No Deal*. He celebrated it with a show, hosted by radio personality Angela Yee and blogger Combat Jack, at the Highline Ballroom in New York.

"It's a span of a couple months, when there's the eleven kids lined up for autographs," Ruddy recalled. "Now, we're walking from the iHipHop office on Twenty-Fifth Street and we get to the block of the Highline. We walk in closer to the venue and I'm just seeing ruckus. I'm seeing pandemonium. This shit is crazy. This is like some WWF shit. The closer I get, I see white kids wilding; security carrying out young white kids. Ni**as is yelling 'Wiz!' They're going crazy. Mind you, Wiz isn't even there yet. I'm like, what the fuck is going on here? That moment showed me the youth wave. Rap was all old ni**as drinking beers and shit like that. It was rap ni**as screwing you, rap ni**as coming through with their posses and their entourages; it wasn't this kind of energy at all. This was fake IDs, kids making out, little kid shit. Walking through the venue to go backstage, seeing the way these kids were anticipating him, it was like, whoa, a star is born."[12]

The entire music industry took notice. "For an indie artist to sell out the Highline was a big deal," said Artie Pitt.

"Having booked hip-hop in New York for twenty years, I know the crowd that usually comes, and that definitely wasn't it," veteran booking agent Peter Schwartz told *Billboard*. "There were clearly a lot of kids there from New Jersey and Long Island. It wasn't the sort of city-jaded, seen-it-all hip-hop kids who tend to stand there. They were going ballistic, they knew every word, and they were very young, too. I was looking at him thinking, 'Picture him with the Bamboozle [music festival] crowd; the reach this guy could have.'"[13]

Though *Deal or No Deal* did not initially sell many copies—a few thousand in its first week—sales were down across the industry, and the project was still pivotal. It showed that Wiz, having been dropped from Warner Bros., could sell records, he could sell tickets; most importantly, it showed that his fans, the Taylor Gang, were a real movement.

"The night *Deal or No Deal* was released, we were just watching the iTunes numbers," Ruddy said. "We were also watching the numbers on Twitter. It was like crowdsourcing. A lot of the campaign was Wiz Khalifa himself, riling up the fan base through his Twitter. His fans, at the time, wanted to see him win. They were in on something that no one was in on."

It helped that the album was filled with bangers, many displaying the casual cool that Ruddy, as well as Wiz's fans, found so irresistible. All around Wiz, too, was a kinetic energy, a buzz. This kid was going places. Everyone could hear it, see it, and feel it.

"Wiz had a chip on his shoulder," said Ruddy. "He felt a certain way about Warner Bros. and how that situation ended. And that's what *Deal or No Deal* was about really; that's what the single's about, 'This Plane,' you're gonna miss this plane, he was referring to himself as the plane, and Warner Bros., that's who was gonna miss the plane. He was definitely determined to prove somebody wrong. They all were—Artie, Benjy, all them ni**as."

•••

While Wiz Khalifa was in New York tearing down stages, Malcolm was back in Pittsburgh, stuck in high school.

"By the time he was a senior," said Will Kalson, "he was already well-known."

The Jukebox had gotten him some local attention over the summer, but he wasn't resting on his laurels. He was already hard at work on his next project.

In the rare moments when he wasn't writing rhymes, he was online, trying to find new ways to engage with his fan base, a small but growing contingent who had heard about him on Myspace, seen his music posted on the blogs, or connected with him at one of his shows.

On October 15, 2009, he made his first post on his new blog, listentomac .blogspot.com, writing that he had taken to blogging to keep fans updated: "Go tell your friends!," he wrote. "Yours Truly, Mac Miller."

The idea of an artist writing their own blog posts, speaking directly to their fans, or whomever else happened to land on their website, was not a new idea. While he was in prison, Mobb Deep member Prodigy maintained a candid and at times hilarious blog at HNIC2.com; and Kanye West was known to post pictures and stream-of-consciousness rants, much like the ones he'd later become famous for, on his site KanyeUniversity.com.

Blogging was popular. And even relatively unproven artists were getting in on it: J. Cole maintained a blog at dreamvillain.blogspot.com, and Drake wrote posts at OctobersVeryOwn.blogspot.com. Then there was Mac, who was now typing away, trying to find his crowd.

He didn't waste time with getting to the promo. The next post, written a day later, was a leak from the new mixtape he was working on. The song was called "Pen Game"; the mixtape, *The High Life*. It featured Brooklyn rapper Skyzoo, an underground favorite, and was circulated on all the blogs—Malcolm made sure to shout out *2DOPEBOYZ*, which had helped him get the record moving.

His next post, written a whole seven minutes later, included the cover of *The Jukebox: Prelude to Class Clown*, with a link to where the mixtape could be heard. Already, Malcolm was cultivating a mythology about himself, writing his present while referencing his past, pointing back at what he'd done so as to help new listeners understand where he was going.

Included in the post were also links to videos he'd shot, which sat on a YouTube channel with a very identifiable name. It was called TreeJTV.

"That's what I really brought to the equation," said TreeJ. "I was like—yo, we need to set something up where like we just pump everything through it. It's almost like a book. You can start from the very fucking beginning. And then work your way all the way up. Because I did realize what was about to crack off. I was like, if we jump on this and start smackin' 'em, we'd be the first people to do that. Obviously not the first, because the shit was online, but we just gotta pump it. Like, 'Bro, all we have to do is push one thing and they go there.'"

What TreeJ was creating was a hub, a space where updates on Malcolm could be found, and where, if he continuously worked, he would always have new content. It was a big leap, but it was a must, because between Myspace, Facebook, and Twitter, there was a lot to keep up with.

"Every single night, we'd sit on AIM and be messaging each other, I'd be on the Hill, he'd be in Point Breeze, and I'd go on Myspace, and I would go through people's pages. I wouldn't copy and paste, I would write a personal message for each fuckin' person. And be like, 'Yo, Ashley, check out this new Easy Mac blazay-blah.' They feel like they're talking to this person. 'He's taking out time to talk to me. Maybe, let me see, and listen for ten seconds. You know, and if it sounds all right, I'll listen to thirty. And if I fuck with it I'll listen to it.'"

Many nights, Malcolm would be at home writing raps, TreeJ would be at home sending Myspace messages, and the whole while the two would be talking over AOL Instant Messenger, discussing the big dreams they had. Everything was in their grasp, it seemed—all they had to do was go and get it.

"The first person ever to hit us back on Myspace was Lil B. Officially. In the very early Myspace days. Because I was hitting people up, asking for drops," TreeJ said, referring to the common practice of a DJ, artist, or otherwise famous person recording a personal message in support of someone, which could then be inserted over a song on a mixtape or in a video. "I hit him up like, 'Check out blazay-blazay if I could get a drop for our YouTube channel, here's the script. And he messaged back like—fuck, I can't remember exactly what he said—but it was just amazing. It wasn't like, some bullshit. I just thought, 'Oh, all right, cool. I'ma hit everyone up.'"

Not everyone responded. But Snoop Dogg, Bow Wow, and a few others got back to him with supportive messages. For Malcolm, a kid living in the middle of nowhere, it was a big deal. It was only a matter of time, it seemed, before everyone knew who he was.

A few days after launching the blog, Malcolm took a trip to Temple University. Nomi, who was still nominally his girlfriend, had gone there for college. Malcolm was in town visiting her, though he didn't say as much on the blog. The trip was good, restorative in ways, for he had spent so much time in the studio that it often felt as if he didn't have much of a life outside of music.

"For the first time in awhile i went out and jus had fun," he wrote. He said he'd been so consumed with working on music, that he'd let it slip what it felt like to just get drunk and be a kid. Again, he shouted out the blogs *2DOPEBOYZ* and *NahRight*—noting that "Pen Game," the track with Brooklyn rapper Skyzoo, whom he had connected with on Myspace,[14] was his first song to receive support from any major sites. "It's nice that motherfuckers are finally taking notice," he said. "But, it's a shame i need a feature to get noticed."[15]

As he saw it, the music he made on his own was good enough. He had even made a song called "The Blog Is Hot," cleverly weaving in shout-outs to all the influential blogs and rap websites, large and small. The list touched on everyone, including RapMullet, AllHipHop, HipHopGame, HipHopUpdate, 2DOPEBOYZ, OnSmash, DCtoBC, NahRight, and many more.

But until he had a song featuring someone with more renown, someone whose music was frequently posted on the blogs—like Skyzoo—it didn't seem that anyone really cared to post his music. He was realizing, early on, that there was a game he had to play. The music industry was all about who you were standing next to.

College was also a major question. He was in his senior year of high school, and had his sights set on joining Nomi at Temple when he graduated—that was if he went to college at all. See, while Asher Roth was busy singing college's praises, Malcolm was wondering if the whole experience might be overrated. He had performed at some colleges, and he'd visited colleges. Often, he came away unconvinced.

"I'm at a point in my career where i often question the topic of college," he wrote. "Will i apply and try to get in right out of high school? Will i take a year to grind super hard? Will I keep my life on the 'safe route'? I really don't know."[16] For the moment, he was doing what brought him joy—and that was making music that came from his heart. If he continued to do that, he felt that everything he was worried about it would ultimately resolve itself.

He closed that particular post with words of encouragement for the handful of people who might have been reading: "Dream of bigger and better things for yourself."

With graduation looming, Malcolm was enjoying his journey into music, but the question of commitment—what to commit to, exactly—was weighing on him heavily. Even the trip to Temple made him question his moves.

At the end of the weekend, he was contemplating a full-time move to Philadelphia, while also wondering about travel. The way he saw it, traveling for shows was work, but traveling just to travel, see places, experience new things, that was something not everyone got the chance to do. And he wanted to do more of it. The more he experienced, the more he'd have to write about it. In the post, he seems slightly confused, writing as much to his audience as, it seemed, to himself, closing with: "even if I don't know where I'm going and I don't know where I'm headed . . . I'm never lost."[17]

The pressing issue for Malcolm in that moment—October of 2009—was *The High Life*, a mixtape he hoped would garner the kind of attention that could land him in a much better spot. Not just a kid rapping for cool points on the Internet. Not just known among the local high school crowd. And not just a kid who could put on a great show at nearby colleges. If getting signed outright wasn't a goal, the main thing he was out for was the thing he always craved: respect.

He wanted the mixtape to get the credit he felt it deserved, and said he was the most focused he'd ever been. All he wanted was an ear and a fair shake. "I jus hope people stop worrying about the fact that I'm white and just listen," he wrote. He was also clear: he and his team were on the cusp of greatness—get down with us now, not later, when it'll be too late.[18]

But by the end of that month, he seemed down—not lacking direction, but wanting so very badly to break out of the small world he seemed to inhabit. Pittsburgh, he wrote, was limiting; there was nothing for anyone his age to do. At seventeen, he was already bored of clubs and bars. "I'm not hating I'm just searching for something more for the next couple years of my life," he wrote. "I want to travel. Not just to NYC, but to other countries. I won't feel my life is complete until i can say i've seen the world. Hopefully, that happens."[19]

Another post, titled "Memories Don't Live like People Do . . ." (perhaps a nod to "Travellin' Man '09," a song from *The High Life* over the instrumental to Mos Def and DJ Honda's 1998 track of the same name, and partially inspired by Beenie Man's 1995 hit "Memories") deals with death. Its fundamental concern is legacy; how, when a person dies, what they've accumulated is rarely spoken of. In the end, all we have are memories.

"The Majority of lives lost in this world are sudden . . . any day could be our last. What will you do to leave your positive lasting memory in this world?" the post read.[20]

• • •

The High Life was released on December 16, 2009, just a few weeks shy of Wiz Khalifa's performance at the Highline Ballroom. Only a few months had passed since Malcolm's previous release, but he had shown tremendous growth.

"I was still trying to figure out who I was [on *The Jukebox*]," he told the *Pittsburgh Post-Gazette*. "When you're a young kid and you're trying to rap you listen to the radio and you don't know what you want to talk about. I didn't know what I wanted to talk about. I just wanted to tell people I could rap."[21]

Palermo Stone saw these incremental changes as they were happening. Shows, at which he served as Malcolm's hype man, were becoming more numerous. Around town, he was recognized with more frequency. And in the studio, working exclusively with producer Big Jerm, he was exploring more of his sound.

"He was growing into his own identity," Stone said. "It was a maturation mode. This was a calculated thing, like—'All right, I gotta be Mac Miller.'"

His determination to be that next big rapper out of Pittsburgh was contagious.

"It was so hopeful and his energy was just crazy," said Stone. "It was really infectious, man. I never met anybody before or after him that believed as much in himself as he did. He just felt like he was in uncharted territory, like he was changing the world."

It was hard to argue that he wasn't. He would get on Ustream—an app where you could broadcast live from your phone—and have thousands of kids watching him freestyle. "Whoever was in the shot with him would just say words, and he would freestyle for half an hour, forty minutes, an hour—so people would start telling other people they had to get on this Ustream," remembers Stone. "So now he's getting fans from Ustream before he even really had songs that people were connected to. He was the white dude on Ustream that knew how to freestyle. It started building so fast."

Part of the speed with which he was embraced by listeners had to do with his command of social media. Whether it was Myspace, Facebook, or Ustream—wherever people were, he made it is his business to be there. More than simple promotional tools, these platforms were ways for him to uniquely express himself. All his video content was uploaded to TreeJTV, and he was early to Twitter, where he accumulated followers at a rapid clip.

Social media helped him in more professional ways too. With Ustream, for example, he could analyze the data to see where people were watching. Then he could have Q, who had worked as a party promoter in college—the Fab 5 is what he and his partners called their company—hit up promoters in those areas, in search of shows.

"He was getting paid a couple hundred bucks to go travel and do shit," said Stone. "It was just wild; the energy was so pure. He just didn't give a fuck."

Still in high school but barely attending classes, he had moved out of his parents' house into an apartment across the street from Taylor Allderdice that—according to friends—he sublet with Nomi, home from her first year at college, and her sister. The rent he allegedly paid for with an inheritance he'd received after his grandfather passed away, and whatever small amounts he earned from music.[22]

"He had an apartment and we were just traveling the country, trying to make rent," said Stone. "It was just an amazing time, man. He knew what he wanted and there was no telling him any different. [What people said] didn't matter at all to him."

Booking gigs was a team effort, though, so in addition to Q, there was also Will Kalson. He was still in school at Indiana University, plugged into a network of college promoters who brought shows to campuses for students who spent weekends juggling red Solo cups. These kids were always in search of new ways to channel their pent-up energy. And they loved Malcolm.

"It was this college ring that we were doing at the time, that white artists were able to get into," said Stone. The ring would welcome not only Malcolm, but also collegiate-friendly white rappers like Chris Webby, Sammy Adams, Hoodie Allen, and countless others. "Asher Roth and things like that were paving the way," Stone said. "College radio, college shows; we fit right into that mold and it just made sense. Mac would just ride with whatever was working."

One of the shows Kalson landed was at Indiana University's Little 500, a week of parties, concerts, and all-out revelry that takes over the streets of Bloomington each year. In 2009, Wiz was slated to perform, as well as DJ Unk and Young Jeezy; Malcolm slipped in as an opening act and got his friends together to drive seven hours from Pittsburgh to Indiana.

Stone recalled: "Mac had this song that he had really never put out called, 'White People Drunk Dance.' It was just some college shit, some drunk kid shit, and it was a hit. He would do it at shows locally and everyone loved it. We did it there and it just went off. And there was a specific part in the show where Mac wanted a cigarette real bad, but didn't have a lighter. He waved to some dude in the front row that was smoking a cigarette to give him a lighter. The dude threw a lighter and a cigarette onstage—Mac caught it! The whole crowd went crazy."

Mac left the stage thinking nobody could top his performance. He had killed it. Tore the place down. "We had probably one of the best shows we ever had," Stone said. "But then Wiz came out and stole the whole show, standing on speakers and shit. I think it made Mac realize we had to go harder."

By then, Malcolm was on Rostrum's radar. He had been brought to the attention of Arthur Pitt by DJ Shef, who was down with Boaz (another Rostrum artist). Impressed by what he heard and saw, Artie sent Malcolm a message on Twitter: "You have a gift."[23]

Malcolm was geeked. Back when he was fifteen, he'd sent demos to Rostrum; the label didn't respond, though he chalked it up to him simply not being good enough. Still, he looked up to Wiz and loved the moves the label was making. To get on their radar was big.[24]

"I loved that Mac was from Pittsburgh, that he was from my neighborhood—Point Breeze—and that he went to Allderdice," said Arthur Pitt. "His lyricism jumped out at me and I don't like white rappers. I didn't then and I don't now, still. But I didn't think there was anything corny about him. He was a deep-thinking, intelligent human being. Wise beyond his years. He had these YouTube freestyles where he'd step up to the mic, light a cigarette, and rap. It was dope to me. I liked his swagger. It was raw. He was just himself, man."

Despite their significant age difference, the two bonded quickly. And when Malcolm was gearing up for *The High Life*'s release, he asked Artie if he could pay him to mount a small PR campaign. Artie thought: "This dude is so good, I feel like I could make him famous." So he told Malcolm something even he couldn't believe he was saying: "I'll do it for free."

And Artie got to work, sending Mac's material to all the music outlets that had, in the previous few years, been showing strong support for Wiz. "He couldn't believe that he was on *XXL*'s [website]." Artie recalled. "He was like, freaking out."

Some of Malcolm's wide-eyed enthusiasm can best be seen in the video for "Live Free," a jazzy track for which the visuals were shot during a short trip with his crew to the Big Apple. In the clip, the gangly group of childhood friends—Malcolm, TreeJay, Q, and Bill Niels—are seen exiting Penn Station, traveling east to Chinatown, along the way hitting up bars and gazing at the bright lights of the big city, the world beyond Pittsburgh laid out before them.

"New York was tight because it was one of the first few times that we went up there," said TreeJ. "That was like such an epic-ass time; it was like all the homies up there. Though the video only showed like four people, there was still more people. It was just fun."

The carefree feel of "Live Free" could be gleaned from the song and the video, but the good vibes came with some caveats—it was around then that some of Malcolm's friends began dabbling with more creative ways of being free.

"I remember I brought an Oxy with me up to New York," said Bill. "That weekend was about the last weekend that I ever went without doing Oxys for a long time. I snorted it, did it, and I'll never forget that because when I got back to Pittsburgh, I started doing them every day. I kind of made that decision when I was up there; I was like 'I fuckin' love these things.'"

Malcolm didn't partake. At most, he smoked weed and cigarettes. He drank recreationally. Before long, though, it seemed everyone around him was into one substance or another.

But there was simply too much at stake for Malcolm to get involved with hard drugs. "Live Free" and *The High Life* mixtape had garnered a positive response; his small but devoted fans were taken with the project's aspirational tone, soulful production ("Finer Things"), and stoner-boy theme ("Riding High"). That Malcolm leaned into his young age, played up the fact that he was still in high school ("Class President"), and was just another kid on the Internet like his listeners ("Another Night"), helped him connect with young fans—they saw parallels between his life and theirs. He would also break the fourth wall and talk directly to his imagined audience, as he does on the mixtape's closer "Thanks for Coming Out," creating an intimate, tight bond between him and the listener.

You would hear a project like *The High Life* and feel like you were on a journey with Malcolm as he was growing up, the narrator writing a memoir of his life through music in real time, the mixtape like a journal or a blog set to hip-hop beats. Interest in Malcolm kept growing. A collab with Wiz Khalifa, "Cruise Control," seemed an acknowledgment from the 'burgh's biggest artist that Malcolm, who was putting in almost as much time at ID Labs as he was, might be next to blow.

"Wiz was paying attention to him . . ." Artie said. "One night, Wiz, Mac, and Benjy were at the studio and they decided to do a song together. That was really the first time Wiz did a verse for a younger person in Pittsburgh."[25]

"[Working together] was dope, especially coming up at that time," Wiz recalled. "There wasn't that much light on Pittsburgh, so we were both really, really underground, but on the come-up at the same time in our own way. It was really cool to both be heavyweight contenders but still local."[26]

At the time, Benjy was back living in Pittsburgh, and Malcolm's presence at ID Labs began piquing his interest in working with him in a more official capacity, as opposed to the freelance/no-pay basis arrangement Artie had proposed for *The High Life*.

"When I was recording with Wiz at ID Labs, Mac would be there recording as well," Benjy said. "And over the course of time I would give Mac advice and guidance from afar. We weren't working closely together, but I would give him a little hand along the way."[27]

Rostrum was experiencing its own success, releasing Wiz's mixtape *Kush & Orange Juice* to wide acclaim that April, becoming a Twitter trending topic, back when doing so was a rare feat.[28] Malcolm had certainly taken notice of this and was in search of his next move. The traditional route for any aspiring artist was a record deal. Rostrum was a local label, and Wiz was a local artist. The energy was definitely with Rostrum in that moment.

But Malcolm was trying other options. He had already fallen in with New York Jets cornerback Darrelle Revis, a Pennsylvania native and former star at the University of Pittsburgh, who was older than Malcolm but immediately recognized his talent.

The minute he popped Malcolm's CD in his car stereo, he was shocked—he couldn't believe that there was a high school kid, a Caucasian no less, who sounded that good. He took him for a Black person, he said. He was determined to meet him.[29]

In his spare time, Revis played drums and sang, but he didn't have any real experience in the music business, and he was still early in his NFL career. What he did have was resources, which he put to use—less than five grand, total—funding some of Malcolm's studio sessions. One of those sessions even led to a collaboration called "Friday Night Lights" (with Revis adopting the moniker Mr. Manhattan), inspired by Pittsburgh's house party culture.

The track with Revis hipped a few people to Malcolm who had otherwise never paid him any mind—like Greg Fleming, a college student from Mount Pleasant, Pennsylvania, who ran a popular website for Wiz Khalifa fans called That New Khalifa. Fleming was a ravenous hip-hop fan, and he had extra love for artists from Pittsburgh, but when *The High Life* came out, he deliberately avoided it. The only song he listened to was "Cruise Control," because Wiz was on it, and he thought: *Oh, another white boy trying to pay more established artists to collaborate with them.*

"The Internet, it's so easy to hate someone before you like [them]; so at the time, I'd see another white kid rapping from Pittsburgh, and make a bad assumption and just say, 'Oh, this kid sucks,'" Fleming said. But two months later, Mac released a song with Darrelle Revis. Darrelle Revis is from Pittsburgh, he went to Pitt, and he's one of my favorite NFL players—so I'm like, I'm gonna listen to this song. And I remember thinking, wow, this kid Mac Miller is incredible. From that moment on, every movement he made, I was completely hooked onto."[30]

While Fleming was turning his new interest in Mac Miller into an actual website—MacMiller.org, complete with message boards where kids could discuss his new shit—Malcolm was counting on Revis to help open some real doors for him. After *The High Life*, he was already at work on a new project, a mixtape he felt would speak for his generation. He was supremely confident in the work, and felt something positive would come from it: bigger shows, maybe even a real record deal.

Revis and his business manager at the time, John Geiger, seemed to believe Malcolm was ready to leap into the big leagues. He had a huge online following, with most videos topping a million views; more importantly, he approached music the way Revis approached football. He'd watch him work tirelessly in the studio, cranking out ten songs in four or five hours, barely pausing for a break. It was the kind of effort he'd brought to his football career.

Revis and Geiger felt they had a star on their hands. And in the early summer of 2010, they set up a meeting for Malcolm at Sony Music. He was to meet with Barry Weiss, one of the music industry's most accomplished executives—twenty years earlier, Weiss had famously signed A Tribe Called Quest to Jive Records and Mac was a huge fan of the group; he had "Beats, Rhymes, and Life" tattooed on his forearm. Weiss also had experience dealing with white rappers, inking a deal with a not-yet-famous Kid Rock in his hip-hop days. He was now the company chairman and held considerable influence, with the power to sign Malcolm on the spot. Like Revis waiting for his name to be called at the NFL draft, Malcolm's life could have changed in an instant.

Malcolm was excited about the opportunity. It wasn't about the money a record deal could yield; more so, it was about the chance to have his artistry, which he worked so hard on, reach a wider audience.

So Malcolm drove from Pittsburgh to New York with his friends to take the meeting. Outside Sony, he huddled with Revis, and discussed strategy. They hoped to walk out of the meeting with a deal. Revis likened it to being a ballplayer, how an agent might tell him they were fighting for that big check. You kept your hopes high, but never knew if you'd get it.

Walking into the meeting, Malcolm brought the music that he was working on for his next project—he was calling it *KIDS*. Weiss listened closely. He wasn't unimpressed, but in the end, he told him he didn't hear a single.

Revis tried explaining to Weiss how big his YouTube following was. But nobody else in the meeting seemed convinced that being popular on YouTube really mattered.

In the end, Sony turned Malcolm down. They never outwardly told him they weren't interested, but he could take a hint. He walked out of the meeting that day with his head hanging low.

Outside the label, he and his crew huddled with Revis again. A bunch of young kids with book bags strapped to their backs as the world went on around them. Malcolm wanted to know—what's the next move? Revis, who was helping out unofficially, told him he wasn't really sure.

Malcolm returned to Pittsburgh and shortly afterward told Revis he was having discussions with Rostrum Records. He had grown closer with Benjy and Artie and was convinced that based on the success they were having with Wiz, they were the label he needed to be with.

Revis was understanding; their arrangement was informal—and his number one priority was football. Still, he wanted to know what Malcolm was going to do with *KIDS*.

"I'm dropping it next month," Malcolm said.

The next month, *KIDS* dropped. And it blew up.

TEN

A boy and a young girl sit on a bed. They passionately kiss, their eyes closed, lips smacking. They are otherwise naked, the boy stripped to his boxers, girl to her bra and panties.

"You know what I wanna do," he says.

"Yeah," she replies.

He stares into her eyes, rubs her neck, pushes back her hair.

"What do I wanna do?"

"You wanna fuck me."

The cat-and-mouse game continues, the boy pressuring the girl. *Let's have sex.* Eventually, her head goes back against the pillow, her eyes closed; she moans while he pumps, pumps, and pumps.

Then a voice-over: "Virgins. I love them. No diseases, no loose-as-a-goose pussy, no skank. No nothing. Just pure pleasure."

Cut to the boy, Telly, exiting the girl's house.

"You fucked her?" his friend Casper asks. "I knew you fucked her, I was out here for like two hours. That girl was twelve. You hit that shit up?"

"Man, who am I—I'm the motherfucking virgin surgeon. . . . That girl can fuck. . . . Halfway through, I was thinking, this girl's no virgin, no virgin can fuck like this."

Malcolm McCormick saw *Kids* when he was in the eighth grade. He was fascinated by the film's cinema verité style, how it captured young people in downtown New York at their craziest, sans any Hollywood phoniness.

Not everyone was as enthralled. When the movie came out in 1995, the *Washington Post* called it "child pornography disguised as a cautionary documentary."[1] *Time Out New York* said it was ". . . relentlessly sordid, the view of these pubescent hedonists so hermetic, that the film-makers' 'honesty' seems exploitative and sensational."[2] And the *Los Angeles Times* trashed it, writing: "Those who have the stamina will be treated to weed smoking, gay bashing, throwing up, thieving and brawling, food fights and a general weakness for getting stoned and creating a mess . . . *Kids* is more tedious than titillating, one of those cinematic irritations more interesting to read about than to see."[3]

But Malcolm saw something in the movie that he identified with. Maybe the movie was exploitative, maybe it was child pornography, maybe it was everything the critics said it was. But to him, *Kids* captured kids for how they really were.

"There's so many movies about kids and that age," he said. "Like Disney movies. All that shit to me is just bullshit—bubblegum bullshit. *Kids*, the movie, that is real shit."[4]

This was deliberate. "I wanted to present the way kids see things," director Larry Clark said. "But without all this baggage, this morality that these old middle-aged Hollywood guys bring to it. You know, living for the moment . . . Man, I just have to see this concert and I've just got to smoke this joint, go to this party. They're living in the moment not thinking about anything beyond that and that's what I wanted to catch. And I wanted the viewer to feel like you're there with them, you can be there fucking, smoking dope, having sex, you can be there in the movie and have it all too. . . . in my movie, it starts in the day and goes through the night and ends with the morning light—but it's just another day. These kids will get up and life will go on."[5]

To that end, in the movie the characters smoke, drink, skateboard, and fuck. Malcolm seemed to look around himself and think, *Aren't me and my friends doing all the same things?* They weren't quite as extreme; they weren't hunting virgins, and certainly they weren't raping them and passing around

HIV, as in the movie's climax. But hanging out and getting into mischief, even if it's not literally the same thing, didn't *feel* all that dissimilar.

"When I was younger, I saw that, and I just remember thinking: Damn, these are some crazy ass kids," he said. "Not that my life is that crazy, twisted and disturbed—but I saw that that's like . . . real."[6]

There was something to the concept. Thus far, his fan base was growing, but he hadn't yet made a singular statement. *The High Life* proved he could actually rap. But to really make a name for himself, he had to do something definitive, something that set him apart. Up-and-coming rappers were everywhere. Many could rap well. That wasn't enough.

But what did Mac Miller *really* represent?

He began to imagine a project with the energy of *Kids* infused into it. Film and music were different mediums, of course, and whereas the kids in *Kids* were of a pre-Internet generation, with fewer opportunities and even lower expectations, Malcolm felt his generation, raised on *Harry Potter* and *Lord of the Rings*, Outkast and Jay-Z, *Mean Girls* and *Freaky Friday*, *The Hills*, *Laguna Beach*, Paris Hilton, Kim Kardashian, *Jersey Shore*, *The Sopranos*, *Entourage*, *Curb Your Enthusiasm*, Myspace, Facebook, Twitter, copious amounts of Internet porn and mixtapes, mixtapes, and more mixtapes, was stifled in other ways. Told from birth to follow their dreams, it sometimes felt as if that was only lip service. One day, they'd have to settle, just like everyone else did, for a completely and totally average life. How depressing.

"That's what Malcolm had in front of him," said Will Kalson. "He could go this way and play lacrosse, be a good student, go to college and do that shit. Or, he could go this way and rap, smoke weed, and have fun doing shit he probably shouldn't be doing. And that's the way he went."

In the spring of 2010, Malcolm graduated from Taylor Allderdice High School. At the end of the year, he was voted "Most Likely to Become a Rapper" and "Most Likely to Be Famous."[7] His parents threw him a small party in their backyard (in attendance: TreeJ, Bill, Jimmy, Q and Q's then-girlfriend). They even made him a sign that read: CONGRATULATIONS TO OUR GRADUATE AKA MAC MILLER.

But as soon as Malcolm finished school, he began thinking about where he was headed next. And it sure wasn't college. He had built incredible momentum in his music career, traveling for shows and beginning to get paid for performances. Music was starting to feel less like a hobby and more like a job. Still, there was much to prove. And as he hit the studio that summer, he kept coming back to *Kids*.

"You watch that movie and you really feel those kids aren't actors," he said. "You just feel like it's a documentary . . . I wanted to do that through music."[8]

Until then, there hadn't yet been a modern youth movement in hip-hop. When you saw a teenage rapper, they were more likely to crank that soulja boy, teach you how to dougie, or swag surf. Older artists were still about the trappings of the old hip-hop music business—money, glitz, glamour. In the Internet age, it sometimes felt as if these artists came from separate planets.

Malcolm's new mixtape would be different. It would embody the spirit of an everyday kid. It wouldn't project a fantasy—OK, maybe a little fantasy, it was music after all—but it would take the listener on a journey into the life of someone just like them. Mac Miller wasn't some blinged-out rap star popping bottles in the club; Mac Miller was just a kid who drove a Civic, "Justin Bieber meets Jadakiss" (as he'd declare on the cut "Get Em Up").

"Kids are just some kids," Malcolm said. "So, that's what I wanted my mixtape [*KIDS*] to do. I wanted to tell it from a perspective of a real ass, regular ass kid. And that's what that movie did; show the point of view from a group of people who don't really have a voice as much anymore. People just have their assumptions about kids at that age, and they just kind of leave it at that. No one ever steps out and says, this is what some real ass kids do."[9]

KIDS was preceded by a trio of videos—"Nikes on My Feet," "La La La La" and "Kool Aid and Frozen Pizza," which grew interest in the project. The videos followed a basic formula: an emphasis on Malcolm and his friends running amok in Pittsburgh's East End. They would smoke weed, hang out, and kick it to girls. Everyday things, because, you see, Mac Miller is just like you.

What the videos lacked in technical wizardry, they made up for in charm. On camera, Malcolm was a ball of energy, his passion practically leaping off the screen. "Kool Aid and Frozen Pizza" attracted the most attention. In it, Malcolm rapped over the instrumental to Lord Finesse's 1995 cult hit "Hip 2 Da Game."

Boom bap hip-hop was not trendy, so its throwback vibe was welcomed by many; some fans, however, were turned off, and made their opinions known via dismissive comments on Twitter, noting how tasteless the song seemed. Who was this young kid—a white kid, no less—jocking a bona fide hip-hop classic made by a guy who never got much mainstream attention, seemingly pretending the beat was his? It didn't help that many of the blogs posting the video failed to mention Finesse (the writers behind the posts likely too young to have known who Finesse was in the first place).

In the end, it didn't really matter. The blowback was minimal; this was just the way things were now, and the video was racking up hundreds of thousands of views. If the industry hadn't paid attention before, they certainly would now.

"That's what really led me to appreciate him—because there's always a generational disconnect," said the producer Just Blaze. "Every generation, it gets more increasingly intense where the current generation doesn't really want to pay attention or acknowledge what came before. Around that time, it had almost become cool to not acknowledge the previous generation. And when I was younger, the cool thing to do was go digging in the crates and find out what came before, so you could apply it to what you're doing now. He was doing the same thing that I was doing when I was younger. As opposed to being like—'Fuck the old guys'—he was like, 'Let me go back and find out who these guys were; let me go back and do my research.' That is really what I appreciated about him more so than anything else."[10]

Malcolm was a serious student of hip-hop culture. He often spent hours digging through old YouTube clips in search of inspiration. He was also aided by his older brother and friends, who schooled him on music from before his time. And the videos looked basic because they were.

TreeJ carried a boom box in the "Kool Aid and Frozen Pizza" video—a striking image that may have helped it go viral. "It was just like a normal day when we were hanging out," he said. Nothing was planned. He picked up the boom box because it was there. Just as easily, one of Malcolm's other friends could have done it. "Either way, we were going to link up. There was no big set or anything. The early videos, I'd shoot them on Handicam. He'd be like, 'Yo, whatchu doing?,' 'Alright, nothing,' 'Alright, I'm taking the whip, I'ma scoop you, we're going to shoot a video,' boom, 'Cool.'"

KIDS signaled a change for Malcolm. It was, as far as he was concerned, his first real project. It wasn't an album, because it had freestyles on it, but he treated it like one. And for good reason, because between getting turned down by Sony and graduating high school, his conversations with Benjy Grinberg began occurring more frequently.

"We sat down one day, he played me some of the songs that were to become *KIDS*, and that's when I was like, 'Maybe, I should pay more attention to this,'" Benjy said. "He's getting even better at his craft, and he's really growing exponentially from the last project. It really piqued my interest in actually wanting to work with him."[11]

By then, Rostrum had come a long way. They were still an indie label, but they were going places. Wiz was hotter than he'd ever been; after his performance at the Highline Ballroom in 2009, an A&R executive at Atlantic Records—Zvi Edelman—wanted to sign him. For Wiz and Rostrum, it'd be a trip back to the majors; this time on different terms. No singles deal, no bullshit.

"Everything happened pretty fast," said Artie Pitt. "Wiz got more popular when he got off Warner Bros. Atlantic approached us in November 2009 when *Deal or No Deal* came out. They made a move right away. And *Kush & Orange Juice* came out the next spring [of 2010]. I met for lunch with Zvi and we talked. More of the business stuff was with Benjy. Then there was a signing party—a toast with champagne in [chairman and COO] Julie Greenwald's office at Atlantic. And then we were on Atlantic."

But there was still a negotiation period, months of back-and-forth between Wiz, Rostrum, and Atlantic. In that time, Malcolm and Rostrum grew closer, with both parties mutually interested in working with each other. "He wanted to sign with us," said Artie. "He'd send me music and I helped him with *The High Life*. But nothing happened for a long time."

It didn't matter if Malcolm wanted to sign with Rostrum; before anything could get done, the label would first have to win over Mac's mother. The company had potential, but Karen allegedly had concerns, as any mother would. TreeJ, Will, Q—he'd been hanging with those guys for years. But a bunch of older men were different.

So she did her due diligence. According to Artie, she called one of his friends who, years earlier, had been Malcolm's babysitter. She peppered the friend with questions. When the friend told Artie about her concerns, he called her right up and asked her to lunch.

Instead, Karen invited Artie over for tea. It was a rudimentary conversation, with Artie simply telling Karen about his experience in the music industry, his background, where he saw Malcolm going, why he believed in him, and life itself. "It was a really a cool conversation," Artie recalled. "She was very friendly. Very warm."

In the end, Artie made his pitch, told her what Rostrum could do for Malcolm. She listened intently. She didn't seem completely sold—not on Rostrum, or Malcolm's prospects.

"I'm not sure she was convinced that Mac would become, like, worldwide famous," Artie said. But some of her apprehensiveness may have been due to a lack of clarity on how the music business worked. She was also concerned about his safety.

"Malcolm's mom, she's a cool woman; she's hip, she gets it," Artie said. "She knew young kids party a lot, that shit gets dangerous. So she was worried about that. She asked me: 'What is he gonna do, just go on the road?' I told her, 'No, you get a booking agent and a tour manager, everything's organized.'"

She eventually warmed to the idea of Malcolm working with Rostrum. But then came the question—was the deal a good one?

According to Malcolm's pals, the offer was a 360 deal. A 360 deal was a type of contract with its roots dating back to the Motown era, when it was typical for a label to underwrite an artist's career in exchange for a cut of everything—record sales, merchandise, endorsements, and touring income. For many years, 360 deals were out of fashion for they were seen as disadvantageous for the artist. But in the early aughts, as smaller, more nimble independent labels began taking on the hard work that major labels once did—marketing, public relations, tour support (and the associated financial burden)—they were becoming more common.

In addition to the 360 structure of the contract, the deal came with little to no advance money. Malcolm said it was roughly a thousand dollars,[12] nothing that would change his life once he signed on the dotted line.

Still, there were upsides. Wiz's deal with Atlantic hadn't been announced yet, but he was fast becoming one of the most-buzzed-about rappers in the game. MTV crowned him their "Hottest Breakthrough MC of 2010"[13] (beating out Nicki Minaj, J. Cole, Travis Porter, and Diggy Simmons), and *Kush & Orange Juice* was closing in on a quarter million downloads, making it, at the time, DatPiff.com's most popular mixtape ever.

So Rostrum had tremendous momentum, and there was the hometown connection. "It was Pittsburgh—it just felt like home," Palermo Stone said, describing the deal as more of a development situation than a traditional record contract. "It *felt* very independent."

Franchise saw synergies between Malcolm, Benjy, and Artie—they were all from the same area in Pittsburgh, all had gone to Taylor Allderdice, and all were fans of the same music. "It was almost like them working with their little brother," he said. "They were keeping stuff in-house, keeping [Malcolm] in good hands."

But not everyone in Malcolm's corner was sold. Many of his friends had invested their time and energy into getting Malcolm's career off the ground. It felt like Rostrum was muscling in on their territory.

"At first, I was kind of against it. Q was kind of against it. I guess we just felt that we could keep the buzz going ourselves," said Kalson. "The momentum was already there, he was going to blow up regardless. With or without them, Mac would have been huge. And I don't think Benjy would take credit for his career. But I also don't think it would have mattered whether or not he signed with Rostrum. 'Nikes on My Feet' had already taken off without their help."

In the end, the decision was Malcolm's to make. And when he wanted something, it seemed he couldn't be shaken.

"He wanted to sign with Rostrum," said Kalson. "He felt like it was the right team for him. At this point Rostrum was already established. He really looked up to Wiz, he looked up to Benjy, and he loved Artie."

So they shook hands, agreed in principle. On July 21, 2010, Rostrum Records emailed a press release:

ROSTRUM RECORDS SIGNS MAC MILLER, PREPS "KIDS."

The press release noted Malcolm's previous mixtapes, the following he'd cultivated, and that he'd done it all while still in high school.

"We're very excited to be working with Mac," said Benjy. "His talent, musicianship, and charisma are inspiring, and we're looking forward to helping him reach new levels in his career."

"It was only right to do this with my family," Malcolm said in the press release. "It's a good situation here at Rostrum, I love the team around me and I'm prepared for a very bright future."[14]

• • •

Bill Niels remembers the day like it was yesterday. Larry Clark, the director of *Kids*, the movie, had originally become famous for *Tulsa*, a photo book documenting his friends' experiences with drugs. Inspired, Bill got into photography himself; whenever he could, he would snap pictures of Malcolm and their friends. He thought nothing of it, it was just something to do.

"I bought a camera around 2009, and I just started taking pictures, street photos, and stuff like that," he said. "Mac liked to keep to himself. Then he'd bust out— 'Hey, I'm putting out this mixtape with Rostrum.' He wouldn't talk too much about what he was doing, he would just do shit."

One day in the summer of 2010, Malcolm did exactly that. "Let's go down to Allderdice Field," he said. "Let's go take some pictures."

Bill shrugged—why not—and they headed out. He knew that Malcolm wanted to shoot a mixtape cover, but he didn't know he'd be the one taking the photos. Or that they'd get taken on this day.

When they got down to Allderdice Field, Malcolm sat on the bleachers. TreeJay, Q, and Jimmy Murton stood behind him, looking away. The boom box from "Kool-Aid and Frozen Pizza" lay to Malcolm's immediate right. He looked directly at the camera with his backpack on and hat turned back. Bill was nervous; it was his Supreme hat that Mac was wearing, and he didn't want Malcolm to fuck it up.

"He was sweating in my favorite Supreme cap," he said. "We were the only dudes in the city rocking shit like that, and we just had this original, New York style."

It was overcast that day, the sky gray. It wasn't the best light for photography, but the beauty of street photography was that imperfection could make for beautiful mistakes. He turned the flash on, was all set to jump in the picture, and as he was about to set the timer, he thought—*Let me just snap the shot.*

At home, he made some minor tweaks, then sent the photos to Malcolm. One of the photos was striking, the light from the camera's flash giving Malcolm's young face a warm, effervescent glow. An hour later, Malcolm sent Bill a text: "Congratulations, bro, you just shot the cover of *KIDS*."

KIDS stands for Kickin Incredibly Dope Shit—the point of the mixtape was, after all, to display Malcolm's quickly sharpening rap skills. The content is joyful and fun, because at the time, Malcolm's life was joyful and fun. Mobb Deep rapper Prodigy once famously rapped that he "put his lifetime in between the paper's lines,"[15] and that was what Malcolm was doing.

"I'm going to parties, so I'm rapping about my life," he said. "My life wasn't complex at that point. I'm getting high. I want to be a superstar. I want to make music for the rest of my life. And I love what I do. That's not a bad message."[16]

But while much of *KIDS* concerns itself with having a good time, it has its personal moments. "Poppy," a song on which Malcolm writes a letter to his grandfather, Milton "Mickey" Weiss—telling him all the things he wishes he could have said—is of particular importance: He made the song a mere twenty-four hours after his grandfather's death.

Malcolm and his grandfather were close. As an infant, Weiss had come to America from Czechoslovakia; upon arriving in Pittsburgh, he was sent to an orphanage. Nevertheless, he was—according to Malcolm—self-sufficient by the age of thirteen, hopping a ride on the back of the bus every day to get to work. He would later serve in World War II, rising to the rank of drill sergeant; returning to Pittsburgh, he opened a sporting goods store which eventually evolved into a big chain. "He was a real inspiration to me," Malcolm told the *Boston Globe*. "He came here with absolutely nothing."[17]

In the studio working on "Poppy," he fought back tears while recording his vocals. Nobody at ID Labs had ever seen him this way; Malcolm was always the happy kid, smiling and cracking jokes.

"Everyone just kind of stopped for a second like—damn, this is some real shit," Malcolm said. But the song challenged him, made him commit certain feelings and thoughts to the beat that, were it a year earlier, he might have totally scrapped, for fear of being judged too harshly. "It was definitely a bit of growth for me, it was hard to get that song out."[18]

No matter how difficult the sessions were, Malcolm remained confident. Something positive would come from *KIDS*, he knew it. Just as he had done with Ustream, the more he put out, the more he got back, and in turn, the larger his movement grew. The key, in the end, was to simply continue doing things; to get help when necessary—that was what Rostrum was for—but to not wait on anyone to make his future happen. To be a fly on the wall in the sessions, you could just feel that history was being made.

The song that really clinched it was "Knock Knock." Built around a sample of Linda Scott's "I've Told Every Little Star," a top ten hit in 1961, the song flips the original's AM radio–style production, turning it into an up-tempo banger—*West Side Story* meets Westside Connection. It was made during one of Malcolm's first sessions with producer/engineer E. Dan, who had now gotten involved due to Rostrum's ability to pay him his rate. Malcolm found the sample, brought it to the studio, and E. Dan immediately began building a beat around it.

Malcolm started writing. He was inspired. He quickly came up with the verses, followed by a chorus, and, after that, a bridge: "One, two, three, four / Some crazy-ass kids gonna knock up on your door, so let 'em in, let 'em in, let 'em in."

"E. Dan, being so smart, was like, 'Nah, you should switch it, you should do "Knock, Knock" as the hook and the other part as the bridge, it plays better,'" remembered Palermo Stone.

The song was good, everyone agreed, but it could be better. It was composed in a minor key; what if that wasn't the case?

"We should put this in major chords, it's gonna make the girls like it," Stone recalled E. Dan saying. "Once we switched it to major chords and played it back, that shit just changed."

It was that extra attention to detail, experimenting just to see what it might yield, that led Malcolm and his crew to believe something truly special was happening.

"We all knew in that moment that it made the song incredible," said Stone. "And that *KIDS* was gonna do what it was gonna do."

Then suddenly it was August 12; *KIDS* was due out the next day, and Malcolm was in New York. He had begun making frequent trips there; Artie would set up magazine interviews, radio appearances—the ball was rolling. So there he was, at Shade 45, for DJ Statik Selektah's *Showoff* radio show.

"Artie was trying to get me to work [as a producer] with Wiz years before he blew up, back when he was on Warner Bros.," said Statik. "I wasn't feeling the music I heard from him. So, I told him he could buy a beat. Boaz, who was another artist on Rostrum, was buying beats off of me, and Wiz could do the same thing. Artie said he wouldn't do it. That Wiz was making a lot of noise. Fast-forward, Wiz Khalifa drops *Kush & Orange Juice*. I hear it and immediately think, OK, he's found a sound. So then I was working on my own album, and I hit Artie up. *What's up with Wiz*, I said, *I want to get him on my album*. He says to me, 'You snooze, you lose. But check out this kid. We just signed him. His name's Mac Miller.'"[19]

Statik went to his computer, pulled up "Nikes on My Feet." Old-school vibe, good lyrics, cool video. Sold. *Bring him up to the show*, he told Artie. So Malcolm came up to the show, spit a freestyle, and Statik was impressed. So impressed that he wanted to do more than just have him on the show.

"Come to my crib tomorrow," he told Malcolm.

But Malcolm couldn't come. He had to go back to Pittsburgh for the record release party at Timebomb.

"I'm coming back," Malcolm said.

And Statik thought—*Right, whatever*. Who would drive from New York to Pittsburgh and back in a twenty-four-hour period? It was six and a half hours each way.

But Malcolm was determined. At eleven o'clock that night, with Will Kalson behind the wheel of Malcolm's Honda Civic, they left New York, pushing the car west on what Artie and Benjy used to call the "suicide drive," a four-hundred-mile trek through a vast stretch of American nothingness so boring it felt like death.

Toward the end of the drive, with the sun rising in the east behind them, a problem arose—the engine was making noise. "I'm like—oh fuck, this is bad," Kalson recalled. "I've been driving all night. I'm like, 'Yo, bro, the car's like . . . the shit's like, smoking. He said, 'Dude, just keep going. I don't care about the car, we just gotta make it for the release party. I'll get a new engine or something.'"

By a stroke of luck, they made it back to Pittsburgh with the car intact, crashed for a few hours, then went to the release event at Timebomb. After signing copies of the mixtape for fans, they hopped right back into a car—this time, it was Kalson's mother's station wagon.

"He went to Pittsburgh, and then he came right back," said Statik Selektah. "When I see shit like that in an artist, I think, this dude is probably gonna make it. Because they're doing crazy moves. A lot of cats would have been like, I ain't going to Pittsburgh and coming back."

The plan, once Malcolm was back in Statik's Brooklyn basement, was to cut a song with rapper Termanalogy, an underground MC with a fierce, tongue-twisting flow. Malcolm said he was a fan, so Statik called him right up, told him to drive down from where he lived in Lawrenceville, Massachusetts. But Statik's recollection was that Term was reluctant. It was a four-hour drive. And he didn't know who Mac Miller was. *Trust me, bro, this kid is gonna blow up,* Statik told him. So Term hopped in the car and drove straight down. Statik just sat there, waiting for both rappers to arrive, and chatted with Rob Markman, an editor from *XXL* magazine, who was visiting.

According to Statik, Markman told him it was unlikely Malcolm would make the magazine's annual Freshmen Class list—he just wasn't hot enough. But Statik said he was wrong, that Malcolm would.

Then Malcolm arrived. And Term arrived shortly after him. Again, Term became reluctant. But then Statik threw on the instrumental to Eric B. and Rakim's "Paid in Full" and the two got to rapping. Malcolm wasn't what Term expected—he was legitimately dope, not just some white kid who had somehow gotten himself hot on the Internet.

They made plans to do a real song. But again, Malcolm needed a rain check. There was a show in the city. He had to be there. So he left, and Statik recalled Term turning to him, saying: "Ahh, he ain't coming back." "He's coming back," Statik told him. "Watch." And three hours later, he came back. With his whole crew. And he and Term recorded their collab "82–92."

Markman watched it all. And before he left, Statik remembered him saying, "As far as the Freshmen list, yeah, you're probably right."

"Part of the thing that made Mac such a star was not even his lyrical rapping or any of that," Statik said. "It was just his smile, man. The kid can really make you happy just by smiling."

...

When it came to the release of *KIDS*, even though Rostrum was now involved, Malcolm still felt it was crucial that the people who had supported him from the beginning—his "day ones"—got to hear it first. So on the day of the release, August 13, 2010, he hopped on the platform that had served him best so far, Ustream, and teased its imminent arrival.[20]

"If you're in Pittsburgh, I'll be at Timebomb today at three o'clock with all hard copies," Malcolm said. "You can come in and get it right from me—ten bucks. It's gonna be a collector's item, I'm telling you."

Then he posted a Sendspace link to the file—"Mac Miller _ K.I.D.S.zip"—and let out a cheer.

KIDS was live, out there in the world. Within hours, the project was met with applause from Malcolm's longtime fans. For those new to Mac Miller, it was a welcome to his universe. Steeped in old-school charm, *KIDS* is infused with the exuberant energy of a reclusive stoner reared on nineties-era hip-hop, contemporary pop, and indie rock. The mixture sounds as if the kid who seemed to always be cutting class to get high with his friends had poured his every thought into a mixtape. That it came on the heels of his high school graduation felt apropos. *KIDS* was Malcolm's shot at really making it, and he threw everything he had into its creation.

In the process, he became a hero to kids who saw themselves represented in the music.

"I think it is important to remember that he raps for the youth," wrote Nora Wahlbrink, at the time a fourteen-year-old, in response to a particularly negative takedown of Malcolm published by the *Washington Post*. "I don't always want music to be teaching me something and have some intense deeper meaning. . . . [H]e reveals the life of an average teenager through music we like to hear. He represents the hope of following your dreams and doing something you love, and the idea that no matter what happens in your life, everything will be okay . . . [H]e gives us pride in being kids."[21]

From the title to the cover art to the material itself, it seemed Malcolm had hit the target right where he'd placed it. "It was about being positive and being happy, having a good time," he said in an interview with HardKnockTV. He felt that people from his generation would relate, and that people who were older might hear its throwback vibe and be reminded of their youth. The feeling of being a kid, he believed, was universal—you held on to that feeling no matter how old you were.[22]

Seemingly overnight, it felt as if Malcolm had made the leap from a nominally known aspiring rapper with a few mixtapes floating around on the Internet to a bona fide artist, complete with a real fan base hanging on his every move.

For Rostrum, it was a revelation, how quickly Malcolm seemed to take off. "With Wiz it took years and years," said Arthur Pitt. "But when we dropped *KIDS*, everyone was talking about it. And people were hating on him like crazy—that's always a good sign."

The hate was at least partially because Malcolm was white. He was also from Pittsburgh, which, apart from Wiz, had no real hip-hop profile. And there wasn't a cosign; collaborating and being on the same label as Wiz certainly made people pay attention—he acknowledged, for that matter, that their collab, "Cruise Control," had brought him much-needed exposure[23]—but it was hardly a Dr. Dre–Eminem relationship, where it appeared one artist was completely under the other's wing.

Still, there was more love than hate, and Malcolm got to experience both the week after *KIDS* was released, when he came to New York for a round of press. That Monday, August 16, there was a party at a Moroccan-themed SoHo lounge called Sway, which *New York* magazine had once dubbed "the definitive late-nineties lounge."[24] Still popping in the aughts, it caught a second wind with its Morrissey-themed Sunday night parties, and was the kind of place Lindsay Lohan would randomly pop into for a guest DJ set, and relatively unknown artists—like a pre-fame Lady Gaga—would have to ask to get their records played.

Monday nights, promoted by DJ Roxy Cottontail, were also the stuff of local legend, filled with music industry insiders and assorted cultural taste-makers. There, it was not uncommon to bump into Kid Cudi at the bar or Mark Ronson by the bathroom, drink with Fool's Gold Records' founders Dust La Rock, A-Trak, and Nick Catchdubs, or catch early performances by the likes of LMFAO, Spank Rock, and M.I.A. Even the kids from *Kids*, like Chloë Sevigny and skateboarder Harold Hunter (before he died of a cocaine-induced heart attack in 2006) were regulars.[25]

"Sway on Monday night during that time period, was the hottest shit in the streets," said Ruddy Rock. "It'd be jam-packed, lines outside, completely mobbed, can't-get-in type of shit. That's where New York City culture on the downtown scene was pretty much coming from. The mixture of skateboarders, hip-hop underground mothafuckers, DJs, Diplo, Mad Decent, Santigold, Ninjasonik. It was the place to be for creatives. It was a melting pot."

That night, Seth Zaplin, a promoter who was friends with Benjy, texted him a random invite. "It's funny, I remember before I invited him, I was like 'Benjy could totally be in fucking Pittsburgh right now, but whatever,'" Zaplin said. "He hit me back and was like, 'Hey, not only am I in New York, but Mac Miller's here.' And I was like, 'Yo! Let's get him to perform tonight!'"[26]

Malcolm arrived at Sway with Artie and his friends in tow; his pals were too young, though, and had to wait outside. The spot wasn't large; it fit two hundred people at capacity. But that night it was packed. So packed, in fact, that some of Malcolm's competition was also there. A group called Team Facelift—whom *Time Out New York* once called "endearing white-dork rappers,"[27] and which included future Internet personality the Fat Jew—stood not far from where Malcolm was posted up, on a couch against a wall next to the DJ booth.

"They was upset on some white boy shit," said Ruddy Rock. "They were totally against that young white rap shit. And he was the new white boy in town."[28]

Team Facelift was so bothered by Malcolm that one of its members picked up a drink and threw it at him. The drink didn't land, but for a moment Malcolm just sat there stunned. Here he was, not old enough to even buy a drink, and he had other white rappers throwing drinks at him.

"He was kind of shook," said Ruddy. "He was a young kid. He was in an environment he'd never seen before. But he wasn't running scared."[29]

No, Malcolm was primed and ready. He was in New York, and New York, tough as it was, wasn't going to get him off his game. "He was battling grown men when he was a teenager," said Artie Pitt. "He was a pretty fearless kid."[30]

He just knew that come two A.M., he would grab the microphone and do what he'd come to do. Not many people in the crowd that night knew who he was. But fifteen years after the movie had come out, it felt like these were the kids that *Kids* was actually about. And now, Malcolm was right there with them.

"New York works fast," said Zaplin. "And if an influencer like a Roxy Cottontail puts a flier out at noon,[31] there's going to be some level of anticipation for it at two A.M. And that's what it was."

The whole performance lasted all of fifteen minutes. He did two songs, maybe two and a half.

"You could tell he was just getting started, and performing at Sway—for any artist at any level—is a little awkward and intimidating," said Zaplin. "You're performing on a couch. You're literally in there with the people. It's a couch. There's bottle service two inches away from you. It's a real awkward environment, but it goes up."[32]

The most important thing was that none of it got to him. Whether it was the drink thrown in his direction, his boys getting denied entry, or the crazy crowd that didn't know what to expect from a teenager who looked like he got lost trying to find the Chinatown bus back to the suburbs, he smiled through it all.

"He's like a little white kid from Pittsburgh, in a bar in New York City," said Zaplin. "But he still got up there. And he did it."[33]

ELEVEN

The road to *Blue Slide Park* was paved with good intentions.

For the better part of a year, Malcolm had been touring and releasing music. This flurry of activity began after *KIDS* dropped and continued through the start of 2011, when he began his first real tour—the Incredibly Dope Tour.

KIDS had been a tremendous success, downloaded thousands of times, while the counts on his YouTube videos numbered in the millions. *Vibe* magazine dubbed the mixtape one of the eight best of its kind in 2010; *XXL* included it in its top fifty, and said: "Imagine the damage this kid will be doing once he's of drinking age."[1]

Mac Miller was like a boulder rolling down a hill; anything he did—a song, a video, a show, a tweet, anything!—increased his momentum. The fans were his engine. They hung on his every word as if he were delivering the Sermon on the Mount. And he was just being himself.

"It was just like, hey guys, I'm me, and this is me making music, and you guys can like it or not," he said. "It wasn't something I had to do too much for. I didn't have to chase after fans. I kind of just kept it real and they'd tell their friends. That's how it really grew."[2]

On the road, he realized how big he actually was. The Incredibly Dope Tour started on January 13, 2011, at the Epicentre concert hall in San Diego. The whole crew flew in. Q was the manager, TreeJ was the hype man, Clockwork was the DJ, Will Kalson was the driver and sold merch, and Jimmy was . . . well, he was Malcolm's best friend.[3]

"We flew into LA and I picked up a Sprinter van," remembered Will. "We drove down to San Diego the next day and started the tour. Benjy was there. Casey Veggies was the opening act. And the show was pretty dope. Then we just went up the coast, man. And it was like the best time in our lives. Even though Mac wasn't even of drinking age yet, we would have Hennessy and shit like that on the rider. The venues would provide it. And we would drink, party with the girls, do the shit that young people do on tour. It was great. We got to see the whole country. It was just like, a really fun tour. It was the best tour."

They traveled from California, up to Oregon, across the coast into British Columbia, then back down through Washington, Utah, Colorado, the Southwest, the Midwest, and finally Pennsylvania, for a closeout gig at Club 27 in Philadelphia, and every night the shows were packed.

But touring was a grind. The pace was relentless. You were in a city one night, out the next morning; in the interim, all you did was drive.

"At first it was kind of shocking, how rough it was," Malcolm said. "It's awesome, but at the same time you live in a van. You don't move until you hit the stage. That's your movement for 24 hours a day. And it's hard to explain never staying in the same place longer than 13 hours, but it is a bitch. That was a big surprise to me. I thought it was gonna be—*oh tour, man!*—just chilling, party all the time, you're never tired, you have unlimited energy. Fuck that, I be tired as fuck."[4]

While onstage he did his best to appear cocky and confident—a rap star in the making, oozing swag—behind the scenes he was anything but. "He would get really nervous before shows," Will Kalson recalled. "Definitely, early on, I remember him having to throw up before the show or having to take a shit. That's kind of gross, but he would get nervous. He really wanted to just do a good job. He wanted to make everyone happy. And he took that really seriously."

One example: a show, some years later, in New Jersey, where the sound was on the fritz. "His mic kept cutting out and he was pissed," said Kalson. "He came off stage and he punched the wall really hard and he ended up getting a boxer's fracture. He fucked his hand up, we were able to get the mics working;

he went out and finished the set, then he went to the hospital. He was very dedicated to his craft."

But no matter how challenging the road was—and no matter how far he was from Nomi, who was back in school at Temple University in Philadelphia—Malcolm did love it. Girls were throwing themselves at him, and he was eager to indulge them. One time, at a show in Minnesota, a girl in the crowd pretended to be injured; when the EMTs came and brought her backstage, she leapt up off the stretcher and ran onto the stage to grab him.[5]

Another time, in Rhode Island, a potential threesome with two girls proved a test of his resolve when one of his hometown friends, hired to work security, got so drunk and high that he barged into the room he was sharing with Malcolm just as he was about to get it on. Frustrated, Malcolm kicked him out and locked the door—at which point the security guy, a white dude, hurled the N-word at Malcolm.

"Mac was super pissed," Kalson recalled. TreeJ had been standing right there the whole time, and here this Pittsburgh bruiser, a real "Yinzer" (as locals are sometimes called), felt it was his right to use a racial slur. He'd also, in a fit of rage, tossed a Hennessy bottle down the hall, getting the whole crew kicked out of the hotel. Malcolm got rid of that security guy shortly after.

For the most part, though, touring was fun, and even when it wasn't, Malcolm found ways to make the best of it. To wit, in February of 2011, when the Steelers played the Packers in Super Bowl XLV, and he was on the road in Oregon, he thought nothing of tweeting to his hundreds of thousands of followers that he needed somewhere to watch the game.

"These random fans were like, 'Come watch it at our house!'," Clockwork recalled. So they drove right over. "This girl answers it, and there was like two guys in there, and they were just like, 'Oh, you really came?! What the fuck, man! We got like mad chips and shit! You guys hungry?' They was in awe that Mac was in their crib."

He did this a lot back then. "People knew him, but he wasn't a superstar," Clockwork said. "That's another reason why I fucked with him—because he acted like he wasn't famous, like he wasn't the star of the whole show. So he would just tweet out, 'I'm tryna go to somebody's crib tonight.' 'Where can we party?' And we'd just go to somebody's crib and tell mad people to come."[6]

The concerts, the partying, the fans—this was what he had been working for all along. One show down, on to the next, each show a slight improvement on the last. What a far cry it was from his life back in Pittsburgh, where he lived in a dumpy apartment in South Oakland, splitting his twelve-hundred-dollar monthly rent with TreeJ, Bill Niels, and Q.

This was the dream. And everybody around him knew it. "It was probably the best winter of Mac's life," said Bill Niels.

But it also around this time that some changes began to occur inside Malcolm's inner circle. Ever since he'd met Q, Malcolm had deferred to him as his manager. Between him, TreeJ, and Will Kalson, they covered a lot of ground—they were his "team." Now, though, Rostrum was exerting more influence, operating not only as the record label but also the management company.

Benjy had significantly more experience—he had worked for L.A. Reid, and there was all Rostrum had done for Wiz. Surely Benjy and Artie could do more than Q and Will alone; besides, Malcolm was already signed to the label. Sort of.

"He was signed to Rostrum with the word 'signed' in quotation marks," said a lawyer with knowledge of the deal. "That's who he was running with. That's what everybody thought. But there was no ink on paper. There was concern about—you know, Benjy's the manager and he's the label. Everybody does that now. That's like the Scooter Braun model. But that's a lot of eggs to put in one basket."

When an artist signed to a company that took on the duties of both a manager and label, there was inherent conflict of interest; what was best for the artist was not always what was best for the label, and vice versa. And when problems arose, the artist would have nobody to advocate for them, because the management would effectively be operating against own self-interest. It was an arrangement that on paper made little sense but was and still is typical.

The lawyer described Malcolm's deal as a "fairly standard" production deal, where the label profited from whatever the artist did, and had the right to furnish the artist's services—in the form of records, merchandise, and so forth—to a bigger record label, a *major* record label, if and when that opportunity presented itself. It was no different from the kind of deal Wiz Khalifa had originally signed with Rostrum; now, Wiz was on Atlantic, with

Rostrum managing, and "Black and Yellow," his first big single, was inching its way up the charts.

"Given their track record, at that moment, with Wiz, it wasn't a terrible situation," said the lawyer. "If you have momentum already, and somebody's been putting time into your career without the agreement, and they've made that commitment to you, there's something to be said about doing that deal. What are you gonna do, you gonna go back to square one? Start again when somebody's already invested in it? And you're having success?"

Malcolm seemed inclined to agree. He had always wanted to be on Rostrum, and he'd have probably signed the contract the minute it got put in front of him, but because he had people in his corner raising red flags about the deal—and more specifically, whether Benjy was the right guy to guide his career—he dragged his feet. For months, the contract went unsigned. To its credit, Rostrum went to work for him anyway.

One of the label's goals was landing Malcolm a spot on *XXL*'s coveted Freshman Cover. In 2010, the buzz surrounding Wiz earned him a spot alongside Nipsey Hu$$le, OJ Da Juiceman, Pill, J. Cole, Freddie Gibbs, Jay Rock, Fashawn, Donnis, and Big Sean. Now, Artie was working overtime to make the same thing happen for Malcolm.

"Freshmen is trying to predict the future," said *XXL*'s editor in chief Vanessa Satten. "It's trying to predict, over the next year, who's hot right now, and who's going to get bigger. Are you going to be a star? How are you going to be a star? How are people going to tap into you? It's not just always music hype; it's how you're going to try to be a star long term. And what star power do you have to keep a career going."

In Malcolm, *XXL* saw the makings of someone who could one day be big. He seemed to already be on his way, and Rostrum, like Top Dawg Entertainment—the label home to Jay Rock and Kendrick Lamar—was one of the industry's hottest new labels. Most importantly, the team at *XXL* were fans of Malcolm's music. "Some white kid from Pittsburgh doing boom bap rap stuff—his shit was catered to the nineties," said Rondell Conway, a former editor. "But that was his appeal. That was his story. Now, I'm from Brooklyn, I love my city, but I'm realistic about hip-hop. It was a different person doing that kind of music. With Mac, I was hearing stories about his upbringing in

Pittsburgh, not his upbringing in Queens, Staten Island, or the Bronx. So there was an added layer to it. I could relate to it musically, but what he was talking about was new. This was the first time I'm hearing this version of it; it sounded phenomenal to me."[7]

So *XXL* picked him. And there he was at Industria in NYC shooting the *XXL* cover alongside Kendrick Lamar, Lil B, Meek Mill, YG, Big K.R.I.T., Cyhi The Prynce, Lil Twist, YelaWolf, Fred the Godson, and Diggy Simmons. "Lil B was probably the biggest star at the time, and his energy in the room was huge—Mac was the only person who could match that energy and buzz," said Conway. "Now, if you get in a room full of rappers, everybody's on guard, everybody's all tough. But Mac wasn't pretentious, like 'I gotta be a rapper, I gotta be a star in the room, and not say anything to people.' Whether you were on staff, the dude getting the coffee, the woman ironing clothes, or the woman doing makeup, he'd talk to you no matter who you were. He was just authentic."

XXL believed Malcolm was going to be a star—and, as with every Freshman Cover, their credibility was on the line. And now he was standing among other artists who might also one day be stars, winning them over. Artie knew this would bring Malcolm's career to another level. But he was taken aback when, right after the shoot, talk turned to the Rostrum contract.

"Mac was waiting to get on the subway after the *XXL* thing," he recalled. "He was all fired up. It was a great day and he was like, 'Why should I sign with you guys for five albums?' and I was like, 'I don't know, bud.' I wasn't mad at him, I was surprised. He was asking questions. I tried to be as honest as I could. I cared about him a lot."

Five albums was a lot of music, Artie conceded that, but the ball was really rolling now. Anyway, Malcolm told him he was going to sign. And then he just didn't. At least not for a while. Rostrum was content to leave things as they were; Wiz's first real hit song, "Black and Yellow," was climbing up the charts and had become the anthem for the Steelers as they went on to the Super Bowl. They were one of the hottest labels in music. Malcolm would be a fool to let them do all this work and not sign.

Then the Incredibly Dope Tour landed in New York City for a show at the Highline Ballroom, the very same spot that had altered the trajectory of Wiz Khalifa's career. The lines again snaked around the block, and inside the young kids went crazy as they nursed their beers and grinded up on one another while Malcolm and his crew tore the stage to shreds.

"It was an absolute zoo," said HOT 97 DJ Peter Rosenberg.[8]

Clad in a black MOST DOPE T-shirt (the logo styled like the lettering from the *Do the Right Thing* movie poster), Malcolm darted back and forth and bounced off his feet as the crowd rapped along. It looked like a polished show, and it was, but it was a team effort, rehearsed well in advance and perfected over the many nights Malcolm had already been on the road.

He was flanked by Jimmy and Q, backed by DJ Clockwork, while videographer Ian "Rex Arrow" Wolfson caught footage of the show from behind. The X factor was TreeJ, whose energy was contagious. He split the stage with Malcolm, whipping from one side to the other, the perfect hype man. "All I knew from my end was, if he's [on the stage] over there, I gotta be over here," TreeJ said. "Whichever way he goes, I gotta go the other way; he picks where he wants to go. And don't get in front of him. It always looked good."

Which is putting it mildly. At times, TreeJ would jump off the DJ booth, leap over Malcolm's back and interact directly with the crowd, extending his hands to slap palms with the fans. "TreeJ was doing fucking three-sixties off my fucking DJ booth," Clockwork said. "He would jump up on that shit and do a three-sixty, bro. And be high off of thirty blunts. TreeJ was like the best hype man. Ever."

With the whole Most Dope crew onstage, it was hard not to get swept up in the energy of it all. And scattered among the kids were bigwigs from all the major labels, eager to see what all the fuss was about. Some seemed wholly convinced—like Avery Lipman, the president of Republic Records, whom Artie recalled saying that Mac Miller was "the future of music." Meanwhile, Karen watched from the balcony, beaming as her son made it big in the Big Apple.

"She was super proud of him," said Artie. "It's New York City. The place is fucking packed. And there's music executives all over the place. It just felt big."

It was fun. It was work, but it didn't feel like work. Even when he did twelve hours of press before the show—interviews and photo shoots—and he was visibly tired, he didn't complain. Then more press after the show; interviews, handshakes, smiling for this one, a picture with that one, and the fans, he couldn't forget about the fans. This was it, though. This is what Malcolm had signed up for. He was in the game now. It was time to play ball.

That night, on March 11, 2011, at one o'clock in the morning, in his hotel room with Benjy by his side, Malcolm officially signed with Rostrum Records. His next mixtape, *Best Day Ever*, was due out later in the day, and just as he'd done with *KIDS*, he went on Ustream to give the link to his fans directly. A Corona in his palm, he said: "Everybody who's been here since the beginning; whoever's been here since *Mackin Ain't Easy*, since *The Jukebox*, since *The High Life*, anyone who's been here since *KIDS*, anyone that's been here since yesterday, anyone that's been here since this Ustream—basically, everybody—I want to thank you guys, we're making history tonight, for real. I remember I did Ustreams and had five people. We got twenty thousand people in here. It's pretty crazy."[9]

In the middle of the stream, he received a text. "Holy fuck," Benjy Grinberg wrote. "You're famous."[10]

And Malcolm really was. *Best Day Ever* dropped just weeks after the *XXL* Freshman Cover was unveiled; hype for Malcolm was at an all-time high, but his main concern was continuing to drop music that spoke to what his life was like at that particular time. To continue being himself. "My life is so dope," he declares on the title track, its chorus proclaiming: "No matter where life takes me, find me with a smile . . ."

The upbeat vibes continue throughout. "Life Ain't Easy" is about overcoming adversity ("I know, that life is nothing easy / one day I'ma change the world and they'll finally believe me"), while "Wake Up" is all about seizing the moment ("I came to get fucked up, I came to get wild/you came to prepare for the future, I live for right now"). Vibes in the studio were extremely positive. It was not uncommon for Bill Niels, Will Kalson, Jimmy Murton—even Benjy Grinberg himself—to get in the booth and shout out ad-libs on a track (like on the song "Get Up").[11]

And Malcolm was branching out, working with new producers, like Just Blaze. "He came through the studio, and what I remember most was hanging out and chopping it up, him telling me about himself, how he grew up and what he grew up listening to," said Just. "The one thing that tripped me out was his song references. It was all stuff that was around either before he was born or when he was so young that it was surprising that somebody his age would understand it. I was amazed by that; like, 'How do you even know this song?'"[12]

They didn't cut any records at first, but whenever Malcolm was in New York, Just would give him free reign at his Harlem studio, Stadium Red. One day, Malcolm came by to play him *Best Day Ever*. When he heard "All Around the World," he immediately thought it sounded familiar. "I was like—I actually know the dude they sampled on the record. It was 'Heartbreaker' by MSTRKRFT, which was a Canadian EDM duo, JFK and Al-P. I knew Al-P fairly well, and was actually good friends with JFK, who wrote that record randomly in his living room one night; a year later, he has this hit record with John Legend, and I was kind of around for all that."

He told Malcolm he could not only get the sample cleared but could also get the files from the original recording. "If you go back and listen to 'Heartbreaker,' there's two different piano riffs that alternate throughout the song, but in the MSTRKRFT version that got released, only one of those piano riffs is isolated. When Malcolm cut the demo of 'All Around the World,' they just sampled the intro. I loved the idea, but it felt repetitive."

He got the files from MSTRKRFT, and went to work, careful to preserve the demo's original feel, but now able to incorporate elements that added much-needed variety to the record. The MSTRKRFT song was a popular tune in the indie dance world, and the reworked version flipped it into a celebratory hip-hop jam, complete with skittering drums and brassy swells. It proved a fan favorite, showing Malcolm could make big songs with the industry's elite.

Another track of note is "I'll Be There"—a dedication to his mom. "See, I was six years old with a dream, when my moms told me I could do anything," he raps over a syrupy piano melody. It features a guest vocal from Phonte Coleman. As a member of North Carolina trio Little Brother, Phonte was and still is a cult hero, one of the few artists who can lay claim to being one of your favorite rapper's favorite rappers.

Phonte ignored most feature requests. But he loved Malcolm's take on Lord Finesse's "Hip to the Game," and knew that he had been collaborating with Little Brother affiliate Rapsody and that producer 9th Wonder, a man with impossibly high standards, was a fan.

"He's not trying to be anything he's not, which is a bad epidemic in Hip-Hop," 9th Wonder said. "You got a whole lot of ni**as lying. Doing things, and being things that they're not because they think that gets them somewhere. Mac Miller is totally opposite."[13]

When 9th passed Malcolm Phonte's number, he received a text. "Everything was through text, it was a very millennial thing," said Phonte. "He sent me the song; now, the guys who produced it, their names was Beanz N Kornbread, and when I listened to the track it sounded very much like 'Be Real Black for Me' by Donny Hathaway and Roberta Flack. It was a church chord kind of progression, a gospel progression. The original joint had them singing the reference for the hook. Mac wanted me to make it bigger, make it what it was, add more harmonies, make it more full."

Now, even though he didn't take on many features, when he did do them, Phonte often charged a fee. Back in 2007, when an up-and-coming Canadian rapper named Drake asked him to appear on his mixtape *Comeback Season*, it was a similar arrangement. He told Drake he had to pay. But with Malcolm, he did it on the arm. "I just looked at it like, 'Hey, this kid is reaching out to me, he knows the music, he knows who I am, obviously has a love and respect for the art, and so, hitting me for a verse or a hook, cool, don't even trip, I got you.' It was a paying-it-forward kind of thing. And I liked the song. That was the main thing."

The big selling point was that it was about Malcolm's mom. "I don't know if it's the deepest song ever, but it is a 'mom song,'" Phonte said. "And the hip-hop tradition of the 'mom song' is kind of unexplored. I don't think a lot of people really look at [moms] that intensely. There's a lot of 'fuck dad' songs, but not a lot of really good 'mom songs.' I thought that was interesting. In retrospect, it holds more weight. I think about his mother listening to the song."

But there was one song on *Best Day Ever* that seemed to be a cut above the rest. It had a different bop than anything else. The producer—Sap—had made it one night at ID Labs, after a nine-hour train ride from his home in Delaware. When he walked into the studio, he found Malcolm sitting at the computer, smoking, and drinking Hennessy. Sap immediately took out his laptop and started flipping through samples. One caught Malcolm's ear.

"Yo, what's that?" Malcolm said.

It was "Vesuvius" by singer-songwriter Sufjan Stevens.

"And I just thought—OK, let's make something new," Sap recalled. "It took twenty minutes. And as I was creating, he was writing."

"Gonna take over the world when I'm on my Donald Trump shit, look at all this money, ain't that some shit," Malcolm rapped out loud, geeking over the beat.

At the time, Malcolm didn't think twice. Trump was a real estate mogul who had parlayed his success into a reality TV show called *The Apprentice.* Because he was super wealthy, and not afraid to show it, rappers loved Trump. And Malcolm wasn't even the only rapper in that moment to make a song inspired by him—Big Sean, too, had a Donald Trump song.

"Donald Trump was somebody you looked up to—a businessman, a boss," said Sap. "We just thought it was dope. We didn't really think nothing too much of it. I played it for my parents when I got back from Pittsburgh. They were like, 'All right, yeah, that's cool.' We ain't have no idea what that shit was gonna turn into."

Neither did anyone else. Big Jerm had recorded it; to him, it was just another record. TreeJ liked it, but saw it through the lens of all the other music Malcolm was recording. "This is one of the better ones [he'd] been making recently," he recalled thinking. "I didn't know it was gonna be a crazy hit song." Perhaps the only one who could see the future was Sufjan Stevens, who cleared the sample for free (because if the song blew up, he'd make money from the publishing on it).[14]

But "Donald Trump" was something. The track had a bounce to it, the sample building to a crescendo before the beat dropped. At shows, "Nikes on My Feet" went off, and so did "Kool Aid and Frozen Pizza," but "Donald Trump" just made everyone lose their minds.

"I can't even tell you how incredible the impact was of that song," said Greg Fleming, who by this point was running numerous Mac Miller fan pages. "You couldn't go anywhere—bars or parties—without hearing that song. DJs would have to play it every hour at the bars when we were in college. It was nuts; people would just go crazy whenever 'Donald Trump' came on."

The song was so hot that, even though it never got promoted to radio, some DJs took it upon themselves to give it spins; it broke into the Hot 100 at number seventy-five—a respectable showing for an independent record in a pre-streaming music business. That July, when the video had surpassed sixteen million views, Trump began tweeting about Malcolm and the song.

Malcolm was excited about Trump's acknowledgment.[15] That he was getting attention from The Donald was remarkable. It wasn't every day that Trump was tweeting about rappers, though when he made the track Trump was kind of an afterthought. "It's funny because the Donald Trump thing came at the end," he said. "I never really thought about [how he'd react] because I never really thought about it reaching that level."[16]

A month later, the love affair between Malcolm and Trump reached new heights. "This kid is the new Eminem," Trump said in a video. "Everyone says he's fantastic . . . the Donald Trump song just hit over twenty million. That's not so bad. I'm very proud of that."[17]

"To have Trump making videos about the shit, that was crazy," said Sap. "Obviously he don't listen to rap music, but that was pretty dope."

Malcolm was becoming more famous. But when he was home he remained low-key, living with his friends in an old town house in South Oakland, right near the University of Pittsburgh.

"It was a fun house," said Will Kalson. "A good house for a bunch of young dudes to live at together. Everyone had their rooms and that was our home base when we first started touring. We would meet there, or meet at Mac's parents' house. That was a good time in life—when he was living there. Everyone was pretty happy. Stuff was going really well."

Life was simple. It was the road or the studio. When he wasn't working, he hung out with Nomi.

His friends weren't that fortunate. Bill Niels didn't really have a job to do, so he hung back when the crew hit the road. He needed to make rent, so he started selling drugs. And the house was empty. With nothing to really occupy his time, he began doing drugs. He had dabbled for years, but now he was really going hard. Malcolm didn't approve. At least not at first.

"Mac was the young kid, so us moving in together and what happened in that house would kind of shape what would happen for a couple years to come," said Bill. "He didn't do [hard] drugs. He said in his song 'Loud'—*I'll never fuck with that yay* . . .' And he didn't do drugs . . . for a while. I was the only one. I was doing pills. That was one thing I was into; benzos and Oxys. Mac wasn't cool with that."

One day when Malcolm was home from touring, he started arguing with Bill.

"I hear you in there doing pills all the time."

And what could Bill say?

It was true, he was doing pills in there all the time. And then, gradually, so were many of his other friends. It was only natural, it seemed, that with his friends doing drugs, Malcolm would start doing them too.

"I woke up late one day, at two or three in the afternoon, and the whole house was rolling on molly," said Bill. "Mac was sitting there smoking a cigarette, on his computer, writing to a beat. I see all these crystals next to him, I'm like, 'What the fuck is that?' He says: 'It's molly.' I had never done molly before. I did a lot of drugs up to that point—I snorted heroin for the first time when I was like sixteen—but I'd never done molly. Mac gave me a rock and I just swallowed it."

It was recreational use. And on the road, drugs were hard to turn down. No matter what city Malcolm landed in, some kind of party favor was there to indulge in. At an after-party in Massachusetts, Statik Selektah ran into him, asked what he was up to. He was surprised when Malcolm told him he'd been sniffing cocaine and doing pills.

"I was kind of disappointed when he said that because that's not a thing, especially in hip-hop, someone's quick to say," Statik said. "Out of everything, it wasn't like, 'Yeah, I've been getting drunk.' He was like, 'Yeah, I've been fucking with the shit.' It hit me in a certain way."

Then there was a show in Houston where Mac linked up with rapper Bun B before the concert. They rode around the city, went to see hip-hop landmarks like the DJ Screw shop and the Fifth Ward, where Rap-A-Lot Records was started, and had fried chicken at Frenchy's. Malcolm was fascinated.

"Mac had a very wide-eyed view of the world," Bun said. "He was very interested in like what it was like working with Pimp C, Pimp as a person as opposed to an artist, but then also the Houston sound, the Screwed Up Click, DJ Screw, Swisha House."

But that wasn't all he wanted to know about. "He was very interested in syrup and stuff like that," Bun said. "People come to Houston looking for that. I don't come in like, 'Oh, you want some syrup? Oh, you want some drank? Here ya go!'"

Bun kept it real about the risks. He had lost Pimp C to syrup—prescription-strength cough medicine with promethazine and codeine in it—and had put his days using the drug behind him. He told Malcolm what was at stake. "Look, this isn't just a fad, this isn't just a very passive thing; this is a very real drug, it has very serious addictive possibilities," he said. "So, I'm not just gonna tell you that you drink it and it's cool and all of that. You gotta be very careful with it because you can become easily addicted to it. Everybody wants to try it [in Houston], it's part of the nostalgia of the environment."

In the end, Malcolm's curiosities won out. "You can already tell that that's what he had on his mind and that's what he was gonna do," Bun said. "He and his crew had it on their mind that when they got to Houston, they wanted to try the syrup. Like, most people go to LA, they wanna smoke chronic. That's just a part of the experience, and there's really no way of necessarily talking people out of it. Just like when your parents tell you not to do something; you hear what your parents say, you understand what they mean, but if you have it on your mind to do it, you're just going to do it when they're not around. You're going to hide that behavior."

None of it appeared to have an effect on Malcolm. "He was just in this experimental phase," said Will Kalson. Things were moving fast, every experience was new. And there was lots to do. New music to release—*Best Day Ever*, followed by an EP, *On and On and Beyond*. That spring and summer he was opening for Wiz Khalifa. These were big shows, eight thousand people a night for a guy who had once performed to empty rooms. It was quite the leap. And it was physically draining.

"I don't know how I'm alive," he said after a concert back then. "I'm low key dying on stage, but nobody knows."[18]

•••

Malcolm wanted to make an album. The mixtapes were cool, they were *like* albums, but they weren't albums.

Everywhere he went, he tried to record songs. "He was always trying to do music," said Kalson. "He was never not creative. And I can't really think of a time being around him where he wasn't trying to go make music."

Big Jerm flew out to meet up on tour stops, setting up equipment inside his hotel rooms. And some recordings got done. But it wasn't until he came off the road and settled in at ID Labs that Mac began work on his studio debut.

He titled the record *Blue Slide Park*. It was named for a spot near his home where he spent time as a child. Metaphorically, it was an entry point: a small section of Frick Park—the deeper one got into the woods, the more things they discovered. He wanted the album to feel like that. Only, the park represented his life.

"It's a journey," Malcolm said. "From the beginning, you walk up to the park, almost like you get what you see; you know, it's a park. But as you get into the album, you're kind of walking through and it gets deeper, and it takes you places you didn't expect to go. As you're traveling through, everything opens up and you start discovering things about yourself that you didn't even think you could."[19]

The sound of the record, too, was supposed to match the concept—upbeat, loose, and young. "He's really centered around the idea of keeping this fun," ID Labs producer E. Dan said. "He uses 'playground' as an adjective—'Let's keep it playground,' or 'Make it more playground.'"[20]

Malcolm talked up the album a lot—it was due out November 8, 2011—but told people not to expect anything from it. "That's the worst thing you can do," he said. "If you expect something and it's not what you expected, then it's going to make you not enjoy it as much . . . Don't expect anything. Just expect sounds to come from the speaker when you put the CD in. And those sounds will have a melody, and it will be a song."[21]

Fans were ready for it, though. The big thing at the time was iTunes preorders. And to promote it, he told his fans that when he hit certain numbers of preorders, they'd get a reward. Twenty-five thousand preorders and he'd release the title track; fifty thousand and he'd donate fifty grand to the Make-A-Wish Foundation; a hundred thousand, he'd release the whole album early.

"We're independent, wanted to do something different," he said. "We can do whatever we want. There's no major label. If I wanted to be like hey, the album's gonna come out right now—if I called Benjy up and was like let's release the album right now, he'd be like are you sure . . . then we would do it.

Which is why Rostrum is awesome. Because I have a lot of control over what happens in my career."[22]

People bought multiple copies, juicing the numbers. And he committed to making the donation even if he didn't break the fifty thousand mark. "I want to give back," he said. "It's not about the money. It's about accomplishing things. If they can rally up and put that money in my pocket, I'm gonna give it right back. No matter what, it's all gonna be gravy."[23]

A week before the album dropped, it leaked online. Early reviews were mixed. A sampling of the comments on the HipHopHeads Reddit forum reveal fans pegging *Blue Slide Park* as a decent pop rap album, but as a hip-hop record, a hard pass.[24] "Just listen to Mike Stud,"* one commenter wrote. Ouch.

Malcolm wasn't initially fazed by the criticism. The album was number one on iTunes, even with the leak. And he celebrated its release with a sold-out concert at the House of Blues in Hollywood. "This is the most important day of my life," he said from the stage. "Everywhere I go, people always try to categorize me. They try to tell me what my purpose is. They say Mac Miller, ah man, all he raps about is girls, weed, and alcohol. That's what they say. First of all, where are all these people that have a problem with girls, weed, and alcohol? Like, damn, that's your problem . . . I'm sorry, man, I smoke a lot of weed, drink a lot of alcohol, and fuck a lot of girls. I'm just trying to express myself. That's what they said—they said if you're gonna make music, be honest and express yourself."

The crowd ate it up. He ran through his mixtape cuts. He ran through songs from *Blue Slide Park*. Midway, he jammed on guitar, covering Weezer, 2Pac, and Oasis. He thanked his parents, and performed "Poppy," crying his eyes out at the end. He closed with "Donald Trump," and everyone went ape shit.

Blue Slide Park debuted at number one on the *Billboard* 200 album chart—the first independent record to do so in more than fifteen years.

And to think, it had all started in Malcolm's bedroom.

---

* Mike Stud is a former college baseball player turned rapper who, at the time, occupied a similar milieu as Mac Miller.

TWELVE

Malcolm was depressed.

It was December 8, the day before the last show on the Blue Slide Park Tour. He'd played the venue, Stage AE, a year earlier, opening for Wiz Khalifa. Back then, boos and cheers greeted him. The crowd was not yet completely sold on the young rapper.

Now he was back, a different artist, a different man. There was *KIDS*, then the videos with millions of YouTube views, *Best Day Ever*, "Donald Trump," the *On and On and Beyond* EP, the mixtape *I Love Life, Thank You*—better still, more than two hundred shows and a number one album, *Blue Slide Park*, under his belt.

Nobody could fuck with Malcolm. Or so he thought.

In the weeks after *Blue Slide Park* was released, reviews began trickling out. Some were good. But many were bad. Really bad.

In a review for *XXL*, Neil Martinez-Belkin wrote: ". . . the jury is still out whether he'll pursue an artistic vision, or ride out the Jonas Brothers–esque commercial appeal."

Chuck Eddy at *Rolling Stone* said: "White rapper from the Rust Belt conquers the world—sound familiar? Pittsburgh's Mac Miller, the Wiz Khalifa labelmate whose debut LP has already topped the album charts, is no Marshall Mathers."

And Phillip Mlynar at *SPIN* derided the record completely, writing: ". . . Mac Miller's *Blue Slide Park* suggests what would happen if the cast of Glee tried to make a rap album."

Each review stung in its own way, but then there was the granddaddy of them all—Pitchfork's.

"When I started out, it was about really laying into people who really deserved it," the site's founder, Ryan Schreiber, told the *Washington Post*.[1] "If it gets sacrificed or tempered at all for the sake of not offending somebody, then what we do sort of loses its value. . . . That's so the opposite of what criticism is supposed to be."

By the time Malcolm was ascendant, the site was, according to the *New York Times*, "the most prominent brand in online music journalism." So Malcolm sat there, captivated, reading their review of *Blue Slide Park*.

And Pitchfork absolutely hated it.

"The reason Miller's mass of fans follow him is not because of his music, at least not completely," Jordan Sargent wrote in his review. "It's because he looks just like them, because they can see themselves up on the stage behind him, if not next to him."

Pitchfork was rejecting not only Malcolm's music, but the very idea of Malcolm himself.

"He is an outsider, but he brings no outsider's perspective to his music," the review continued. ". . . [He's mostly just a crushingly bland, more intolerable version of Wiz Khalifa without the chops, desire, or pocketbook for enjoyable singles."

If you were white, Sargent argued—a "frat rapper," as Malcolm had been dubbed—you could co-opt hip-hop's attitude and slang, saw off its rough edges, and cash in with a young, ostensibly white, pop-leaning audience who didn't know any better.

The album's final score: 1.0.

Malcolm was distraught. To him, *Blue Slide Park* wasn't just an album, it was home. And Pitchfork had taken a flamethrower to it.

"That fucked him up," Arthur Pitt recalled. "I had twenty missed calls from him when that came out. He got really down on himself."

How could Pitchfork have gotten him so wrong? Malcolm was white. That was plain as day. And sure, his audience was young kids who maybe weren't up on the latest and greatest in underground rap. But he was more than a frat rapper.

If only they'd seen the pilgrimage he'd taken months earlier to HeadQCourterz, the former home of D&D Studios in New York, seeking counsel from DJ Premier, the legendary producer who had cut songs there with many of the very same rappers Malcolm aspired to be like.

"Nas was in here?"

"Yeah," Premier said.

"What about Big L?"

"Yup."

"Biggie was in here?"

"Stood right there," Premier said.

"Jay-Z?"

"Yes, sir."

"Who else?"

"Man, Limp Bitzkit has been in there."

Malcolm cocked his head.

"Fred Durst was in here?"

"He was."

"But Big L was definitely in here?"

"We did 'Da Enemy' right there," Premier said.

Then Malcolm starting rapping the lyrics to "Da Enemy," from D.I.T.C.'s self-titled 2000 album, right in front of him.

"Can I stand in the vocal booth and just feel the energy?"

Premier told him he could, and stepped out. *When I return*, he thought, *Malcolm will be in the lounge watching TV*. But five minutes went by, ten minutes, fifteen minutes—back into the studio he went, and there Malcolm was, right where he'd left him, standing in the booth, surrounded by darkness.

His eyes closed, head to the sky, he said: "I want to absorb all the energy of the MCs who have been in here."

Of the artists Premier had met, not a single one had done what Malcolm did. *This dude is cool*, Premier thought. And the pair began smoking and drinking, talking hip-hop. The next thing they knew it was six in the morning, and Premier turned to his MPC beat machine, began programming a track.

Malcolm ran into the booth, the same booth in which Jay-Z, Biggie, Big L—and, yes, Fred Durst—had once stood.[2]

"Face the Facts," their one song together, was never sold; its home was to have been a mixtape Malcolm was working on with DJ Jazzy Jeff called *'92 Til Infinity*,[3] set to feature production from Premier, Jeff, Pete Rock, 9th Wonder, and others. *This* was who Malcolm really was. Frat rapper? Wow. If only Pitchfork knew.

"They killed him in that review," said DJ Clockwork. "It was a personal attack. They were just trying to get him out of there, like, let's not listen to this kid. They boxed him in—'frat rap'—and that really, really fucked with him. It definitely fucked him up."

"They were bullying him," Artie said. "It was disgusting."

Ritz Reynolds, the Philly-based producer behind three cuts on *Blue Slide Park*, felt the album was unfairly panned. Via email, he worked with Malcolm on "Best Day Ever," then met him at the Roots Picnic in June 2011, playing as a supporting act, along with Esperanza Spalding, Little Dragon and Yelawolf, among others, on a bill headlined by Nas, his labelmate Wiz Khalifa, and the Roots themselves. The crème de la crème of urban cool, the Roots Picnic was a gig he'd have never landed if he was merely a poseur.

"That was a big deal," Reynolds said. "The first four or five Roots Picnics, I was there every year, I always had passes, and it was just an amazing day in Philly. The Roots have always been my childhood favorites, and the Roots Picnic would always have amazing people."[4]

At the picnic, Malcolm told Reynolds he'd recorded to a piece of ambient music he'd previously emailed. "Wait till you hear this, wait till you hear this one," he said. The song was "Missed Calls," one of the more commercial-leaning tracks on *Blue Slide Park*. Malcolm thought it could be a real hit.

"It was about his girl, Nomi—she was always really cool, and Malcolm and her, they just had a great ease to them," he said. "And he killed it. There was a long video, it was pretty cinematic. I remember when they put it out, it was the number one trending topic worldwide on Twitter. It was like, 'Oh shit.'"

The song finds Malcolm narrating a conversation between a man and woman—presumably him and Nomi—as the man chases his dreams. It's a syrupy ode that could have slid into any pop playlist; from another rapper, it might have been celebrated by critics for its introspection, but they had a hard time buying it from Malcolm.

"Malcolm was dope. I mean, he was, like, really talented, man—he clearly could rap his ass off," Reynolds said. "But it was some bullshit, the criticism he got. Music criticism is so important, but sometimes, it's like, you're criticizing a nineteen-year-old. There was some really dope stuff on *Blue Slide Park*."

And yet even he could understand the slights. "There was this one track on *Blue Slide Park*—'Up All Night'—where he's just like, drink, drink, drink, drink, drink. It's some shit about drinking," Reynolds said. "That song alone probably helped put him into that frat pack. And, whatever, he was white."

His skin color, it seemed, was only part of the problem. In hip-hop, it was one thing to be white, it was another thing to lean all the way into it.

"Asher Roth had his one hit around the time *Blue Slide Park* came out—I wanna say maybe a year or a year and a half before," Pitchfork's Sargent said today, in retrospect. "So I think my interest in it, at the time, was like, 'Oh, there's something in this "frat rap" genre that's blowing up for real.'"

Sargent wasn't overly familiar with Malcolm before *Blue Slide Park*. But he had trouble connecting the LP's commercial success with, what he felt, was its staggering mediocrity. It had to be that he was a white dude selling mediocre white rap to white kids who didn't know any better. For that, taking him down a peg was almost like an act of social justice.

"I mean, he clearly can rap," Sargent said. "But I would still say it's a bad album. People were kind of connecting to the realness of it; if you were someone who looks like Mac Miller or grew up like Mac Miller, it was approachable, relatable, in that sense."

Forbes journalist Zach O'Malley Greenburg, however, felt that was exactly the genius of *Blue Slide Park*, and Malcolm more generally. He felt the record was a celebration of "suburban ennui," which captured "a world of endless adolescent possibility." In Malcolm, there was no Gen-X angst, no machine he seemed to be raging against. This was fine because, for many people, this was, well . . . the world.[5]

"That's precisely what makes Miller's music so appealing to many middle class high school and college aged students," O'Malley Greenburg wrote.

"They grew up on hip-hop, but the music's content didn't always mirror their experience. In Miller, however, there's a bit more with which to identify."[6]

Regardless, the Pitchfork review left a stank on Malcolm. Before it, Malcolm had moved through the music business relatively unchecked; he was not unlike any other random American white dude, free to go and do as he pleased. He had faced challenges, sure, but nothing like the most credible music outlet in the world questioning his very existence.

"He was just super upset," Artie said. "I had many duties with him, but my main duty was to make sure his image was good and his music was connecting with people. He was mad at me. He was professional and tactful. But he let me know, like, professionally. He was like, 'How could this happen? What the fuck is this? What can we do?' We were flying high at that time. We were unfuckingstoppable. And I had no answers."

Compounded by the review was something else. A problem that crept up unannounced, and presented itself one night, long before the Pitchfork review had been published, back when *Blue Slide Park* was set to drop, and Malcolm was sitting in Benjy's car.

"He had a cup of lean," said Artie. "Lean was a popular drug, but it kills people. I'd see artists do it while we were touring, they were like junkies to me, nodding off and pouring into the cup. I didn't like it. I never liked being around anyone on lean. He liked it, though. He told me that it helped relax him and calm his nerves and he was under a lot of pressure. I don't know. Maybe he could have done different things. He tried. We got out and Benjy was like, 'Dude, don't ever bring that shit in my car.'"

Malcolm had always been a good kid. And Rostrum was artist-friendly. The label didn't want to police its artists.

"I knew he liked to experiment," Artie said. "I experimented when I was younger and I'm not a huge fan of telling an artist what they can and can't do if they're not self-destructing. To me, he wasn't self-destructing."

But neither Benjy nor Artie approved of his lean use. And according to Artie, Malcolm didn't like that Benjy had tried disciplining him.

"He just didn't want to be told what to do," Artie said.

The interaction created some awkward tension that seemed to linger. The night *Blue Slide Park* came out, at the Mondrian Hotel, Malcolm watched with Rostrum and friends as the album shot to number one on the iTunes chart.

Afterward, Artie went to Malcolm's room and knocked on the door. Malcolm opened it halfway, told Artie he'd get with him later.

Inside, he was with his lawyer. And yeah, he had a number one album, which was great, but he was also upset. *Billboard* had run a cover story on him that week. Why, he wanted to know, were Benjy and Artie featured so prominently in it?

"I feel like people started getting in his ear around then," Artie said. "It went from party, party, party, sold-out shows, *Blue Slide Park*'s the first number one independent album released in a million years, to nobody could even make good eye contact. He was probably looking at when the contract was gonna end."

•••

Malcolm brought 2011 to a close on a high note, sharing a bill with Demi Lovato, Selena Gomez, Jason Derulo, and J. Cole for a nationally televised New Year's Eve concert on MTV.

For the performance, he turned to one of *Blue Slide Park*'s throwback-style singles—"Party on Fifth Ave.," a rework of Mark the 45 King's "The 900 Number" (made popular by DJ Kool with "Let Me Clear My Throat").

The song was popular and spoke to how Malcolm's confidence in his own ideas could prove beneficial. Back when he was making the song at ID Labs, making something out of "The 900 Number" struck everyone as too silly to merit serious effort.

"He was bugging us to work on this record. It was this energy like a little brother or something—*do this, do this*—and you're just like, little brother, leave me alone, I don't want to do this," the producer Ritz Reynolds recalled. "But when he wanted something, he just did it. He was hell-bent on chopping that shit. He made the beat, which was always great about Mac—he was an outgoing music creator that had his hands on everything. So he was in a room by himself, and everyone was just like, 'What are you doing?' And slowly, this son of a bitch started pulling it together. It was funny—it turned out to be like a single, and it was like a gold or a platinum record."

When he made it, Malcolm liked the song. The music video found Malcolm and his friends styled as old men wreaking havoc in and around Pittsburgh. Fun-loving and harmless, "Party on Fifth Ave." presented Malcolm as a hip-hop artist for the PG-rated set. But looking back, he could see how it might give off the wrong impression.

"I was an easy target—if you listen to 'Party on Fifth Ave.,' you're gonna think that I'm a little, fucking . . . whatever," he said.[7]

That version of himself, the halfway serious, child-friendly one, was a version he wanted to put in the rearview.

"He was on a mission to prove himself," Artie said. "He told me he was working on a project that would change everyone's mind about him. He called it *Macadelic*."

Macadelic would be a radical departure from *Blue Slide Park*. Beats would go harder. Rhymes would be sharper. He would dig deeper, talk about real things, not just what he thought his fans wanted to hear. And he would collaborate. On board: Lil Wayne, Juicy J, Cam'ron, Kendrick Lamar, Joey Bada$$, and others.

The idea of collaborating with more well-established artists was a new wrinkle. He had learned, back when he was trying to get his music posted on rap blogs, that hip-hop was very much like a high school cafeteria—it was all about the table you were sitting at.

At a glance, it could seem as if he were sitting all by himself. *Blue Slide Park* had no features, *Best Day Ever* was light on them, too, as was *KIDS*. He had begun to collaborate more on the mixtape *I Love Life, Thank You*, pulling in Sir Michael Rocks (of the Cool Kids), Bun B, and Talib Kweli (whom he connected with through Clockwork, a former DJ for Kweli's group Reflection Eternal).

"He called me to be on a song with him; he was studying what we were doing in that Rawkus era," Kweli wrote in an Instagram post, referencing the underground rap label that, in the nineties and early 2000s, had put out records by him, Mos Def, and even (posthumously) Big L.[8]

It was on soulful songs like "Family First"—with Kweli—where he would pen some of his most poignant lyrics to date, addressing his critics, detail issues with Nomi, and weigh in on the distance growing between him and his family. "It's hard when I can't even find the time to call my mom / And she thinks I'm goin' Hollywood, I guess she probably should . . ." he raps.

A similar energy was what he was hoping to capture on *Macadelic*; collaborate, but do it in a way that felt authentic to who he was. Corralling guests wasn't as difficult as he imagined it would be. He met Juicy J for a night of partying in a California studio back when he was on the Incredibly Dope Tour;[9] Kendrick Lamar was a fellow *XXL* Freshman whom he talked to "all the time," and he connected with Cam'ron in New York, after taking a trip to Harlem one night at three A.M. to visit the Big L mural on the corner of 140th Street and Lenox Avenue (which subsequently led to a series of tracks they hoped to release as a *Step Brothers*-themed project).[10]

Working with Cam'ron, he told HipHopDX.com, had a profound effect on him. In their first session together, the beat for *Macadelic's* "Ignorant" was playing; Cam'ron thought the beat was crazy, but Malcolm wasn't sure about it. "I don't know if people want to hear that from me," he told Cam, who quickly shot back at him: "Fuck that. Fuck that shit! If you want to rap on this beat, rap on this beat." The experience instilled in Malcolm the confidence to simply not care. "That helped me learn to say, 'Fuck everyone,'" he recalled. "It let me know I can do whatever I want to do."[11]

The long shot feature was Lil Wayne—a big fish but one he felt confident about reeling in. For some time, he had wanted to get Wayne on a song. But he was insistent that the track they do together have some substance to it.

"When I was thinking about the record I wanted to get him on, I didn't want to get him on some club record, some swagged out record with me talking shit—like, yeah motherfucker, I got money, I'm successful, then have Wayne come in," he recalled. "I wanted to make a song that could do something in the world."[12]

He likened what he was attempting to do to "All That," a heartfelt collaboration with Bun B (from the mixtape *I Love Life, Thank You*, released in the fall of 2011 on the occasion of reaching one million Twitter followers). Finally, one night in California, he began work on a song called "The Question."

When his friend Jimmy Murton heard it, he felt he had finally found the perfect song for Wayne.

Malcolm had become friendly with Karen Civil, who ran Wayne's website—and she encouraged him to try getting Wayne on the song. From there, he contacted Mack Maine, president of Wayne's Young Money Entertainment record label, who he had also become increasingly friendly with. Malcolm was shy about approaching Mack Maine for the Wayne collaboration; he assumed artists did it all the time. But Mack Maine told him to email the song.

"It's all love," Malcolm recalled Maine telling him. "I'm gonna play it for him."[13]

Still, Malcolm wasn't expecting him to do it. It was Lil Wayne, after all, and while Mac Miller had a bit of a buzz, there was nothing in it for Wayne.

But to Malcolm's surprise, an email soon came back to him: YMCMB, it read, Malcolm recalled. When he opened the email, it was the full recording session. The only problem—there was no finished version of the song attached, so Malcolm couldn't tell what the song sounded like. Instead, he had to take all the files, individually, and put them in Garageband, then mix the track down himself. He described hearing Lil Wayne's raw vocals as "surreal."[14]

"The Question" would be one of *Macadelic*'s standout cuts, posing existential queries, things people ask whether they are famous rappers traveling from state to state to perform for raucous crowds or simply sitting in an office cubicle somewhere far less exciting.

"Sometimes I wonder who the fuck I am, so I've been lookin' in the mirror and it still don't make no sense," he raps.

Another standout, "Thoughts from a Balcony," brings his discontent to the fore: "Said I'll make it big when everybody know me / Well, I made it big and everybody phony." Not only are the songs more introspective, but the beats are more contemporary: "Loud," "Lucky Ass Bitch," and "Ignorant," ditch boom bap entirely. These are songs to be thrown in the mix at any late-night jam.

Franchise recalled going out one night with Malcolm to a club called Whim, in Station Square. "It was our own version of a New York City or Miami club," he said. "Where you walk in and there's like three bars in the middle of the room, the bathrooms are off to the side, then these little private rooms along the walls; there's this little-ass door to the middle, you walk back and that's where the actual club is—the stage, dance floor, and VIP. Man, it was sick. They played the song, and these Black shorties was in VIP twerking. I just remember how fucking excited he was about that."

While the beat selection showed a maturation, so, too, did the lyrics—*Macadelic* is peppered with drug references, the whole project sounding as if it were made by someone on a bender. "I got codeine in my cup!" he raps on "Loud." Another track, "Vitamins," finds him on a psychedelic trip, high off LSD or mushrooms.

Macadelic was indeed a turn for Malcolm. As an artist who had made his name as bit of an optimist—he had a "thumbs up" gesture that he'd often make in music videos and pictures—the mixtape was a gamble; it was plainspoken and aggressive, and featured innumerable nods to drugs and alcohol. This was Malcolm alright, but he was more weathered now, ornery even.

He was completely self-aware about everything. In a 2012 interview with Hard Knock TV, he broke down his discography: *KIDS* was all about goals and dreams, what he hoped to accomplish; *Best Day Ever* captured his excitement now that he'd done some of what he'd set out to do; and finally, *Blue Slide Park* was inspired by his longing for home.

"But *Macadelic* is more—*that's over*."[15]

All the criticism he'd taken had clearly gotten to him—particularly what was said about *Blue Slide Park*. "I'm not gonna act like I'm a superhero and sh— doesn't bother me," he told MTV News. "Of course it bothers me . . ."[16]

But it wasn't only the serious critics that got to him. Some things he heard closer to home may have stuck with him as well. "My dad used to talk all this shit on my music," he said. "My music would be being so successful [*sic*], he'd be like, *yeah whatever, but what are you saying*. And I'd be like, *fuck*."[17]

Maybe *Macadelic* would win over his dad. Maybe it'd win over the critics. Maybe it'd win over fickle rap fans who never paid him any mind. But *Macadelic*'s reception was mixed.

"It was a complete U-turn from *Blue Slide Park*," said Artie. "All his fans were like—'What the fuck?'"

If *Macadelic* puzzled his most ardent supporters, it did manage to connect with certain crowds who had never paid him any mind.

"Me and Vinny Radio, coming from Braddock, we grew up listening to straight hood shit, Meek Mill and shit like that," Franchise recalled. "I'd be coming back to the hood after tour and my boys would be like, 'Man, I don't even rock with Mac Miller.' But I felt like Mac gripped the ni**as when he did *Macadelic*. Ni**as in the hood were like, 'Your boy is hard, bro!' Shorties in the hood was like, 'I fuck with your boy Mac Miller, that boy is tight.' I'm like—'Yeah, he's white and he's gotta do what he's gotta do, but I been telling y'all my boy gets busy.' More of *our* people were gravitating towards him. And he always wanted that fan base. *Blue Slide Park*, they wasn't really excited about that. But *Macadelic*, he had Wayne on there, Cam'ron, Juicy J, plus the beats he chose—he won 'em."

In the spring, Malcolm hit the road. And he saw how *Macadelic* completely split the audience. Pumping the brakes on the easygoing style he'd presented on *Blue Slide Park*, it created a shift in his trajectory.

The timing was poor, because this tour was different. Previously, he had been playing to crowds of about 2,500 people a night. The new shows would be much bigger, college arenas, with crowds that—if all went according to plan—were as large as ten to twelve thousand people per night. Or, at least that was the expectation.

But the tour underperformed. Malcolm struggled to sell enough tickets to fill the arenas, and for many dates he came on stage to see the venues only partially filled. "The venues were too big," said Artie. "Things were just different. That review from Pitchfork hurt him. I felt like a lot of momentum slowed with that."

As an actual document, the review itself didn't hold much weight. You couldn't dance to the review, or rap along to the review. If you were hanging out with your friends on a Friday night, you wouldn't turn to one of them and say "Hey, let's go out and see the Mac Miller Pitchfork review." The review was, for the most part, nothing. Just a bunch of words on a screen.

But it was a small piece of a growing backlash to not only Mac Miller, but white rappers more generally, for Malcolm's rise did not occur in a vacuum, and had, if anything, only been part of a larger trend. YelaWolf, RiFF RAFF, Action Bronson, Machine Gun Kelly, G-Eazy, Macklemore, Iggy Azalea, Hoodie Allen,

Ricky Hil (the son of fashion designer Tommy Hilfiger)—in a post–Asher Roth world, the rap game was flooded with white rappers. Whether independent or signed to majors, some were finding success.

Perhaps the white rapper who triggered so much of the backlash was Kreayshawn, a tattooed white girl in bangle jewelry whose song "Gucci Gucci" had gone viral that summer, landing her a one-million-dollar record contract with Columbia Records.[18] The hype was initially justified; the song was a smash that people seemed to love. But within weeks of it going viral, Kreayshawn was dogged by controversy after tweets of hers surfaced in which she had used the N-word. She acknowledged her wrongdoing; still, she attributed her looseness with the word to being raised in Oakland, CA, where she said people of all races used it.[19]

"I feel like that word is used in the low-income community more than anything," she said. "I can see if I was some rich crazy trick and I was just saying this because it's hip-hop. I was raised around this. People call me that."

She dialed back her usage of the N-word, but as her career took off, her affiliation with rapper V-Nasty—one third of the White Girl Mob (with Kreayshawn and DJ Little Debbie)—who said the N-word liberally, set off a firestorm of bad publicity, so just as quickly as things were starting, they appeared to be ending. "It has taken a huge toll on what I been trying to do and what I been trying to push," Kreayshawn wrote in a Tumblr post not long after the controversy began. "I hope soon people will see the difference between us[;] even though we are still close friends doesn't mean I use [the N-word] too or defend it in anyway [*sic*] . . .[20]

Malcolm was not Kreayshawn. As far as anyone knew, he had never said the N-word, and his reverence for hip-hop culture ran deep. But within the culture, there seemed to be an uncomfortable energy surrounding white rappers—even Malcolm himself was uncomfortable with it, feeling a pang of guilt over being supported primarily by white people simply because they could identify with him.[21]

He struggled on the Macadelic Tour, seeing white people staring back at him from the crowd. ". . . I was the first rap show ever in all these colleges," he said. "Six thousand kids, and I'm the first hip-hop show because I'm white-college-friendly. That was always a demon for me. It was hard to sit here and know that, because I was a white dude, I was able to sell easier and be more marketable. That wasn't tight to me. I wanted to go through the same shit that everyone else did."[22]

If it wasn't white guilt getting him down, it was the fact that the shows were underperforming, failing sell out the arenas. He was depressed.

"I wanna get off this tour," he told DJ Clockwork. "This tour sucks."

The tour's conditions didn't help either. A college tour meant no liquor, no weed, no women—at least backstage.

"We couldn't do anything," said Clockwork.

But that didn't stop Malcolm from partaking on the tour bus; he'd find ways to get loose however he could.

"*Macadelic* was probably the druggiest tour," said Clockwork. "He was fucking with the lean, heavy. He was getting fucked up every night."

In addition to lean, he was also doing cocaine, molly, and anything else that was put in front of him. Anything that could get him through from one night to the next. The shows were work, so he treated them that way, heading straight to his tour bus after each gig to seek solace in the onboard studio. There, he'd sequester himself, Styrofoam cup clutched in his palm, trying to smile through the bullshit.

"If he had problems, he rarely showed it," said Franchise.

To the public, Malcolm still seemed like one of the biggest independent success stories in the music business. The tour was not the blockbuster he'd thought it would be, but *Macadelic* was music he stood strongly behind, and he was raking in money—on *Forbes* 2012 "Cash Kings" list, he placed number nineteen, with estimated earnings of 6.5 million dollars.[23]

A big chunk of that money was coming from performance fees. In 2010, a show would net him a cool five hundred dollars, if he was lucky. Now, he was charging upward of fifty thousand dollars, even when the arenas were half-empty. It was the kind of money that was sure to raise eyebrows, particularly from people who felt they were owed a few bucks—like Lord Finesse.

". . . Lord Finesse is suing annoying frat rapper Mac Miller, Miller's label Rostrum Records, and mixtape hub DatPiff, over the unauthorized use of his 'Hip 2 Da Game,' which serves as the instrumental for Miller's breakout track 'Kool-Aid & Frozen Pizza,' read a July 2012 news story on Spin.com.[24]

Finesse's argument was that "Kool Aid and Frozen Pizza" had kicked off Malcolm's career, and it wouldn't have been possible without his beat. It was a tough point to refute. At the time of the lawsuit, the video for "Kool Aid and Frozen Pizza" had collected nearly twenty-five million YouTube views, and *KIDS* had been streamed/downloaded nearly a million times. It wasn't the only thing that set Malcolm's career ablaze, but it certainly provided a spark.

"Look at this kid," an editor at *Complex* magazine said at the time. "He's like, a little white kid. But he's rapping on real hip-hop shit. This is crazy."

"I hated on every white rapper when they came out, including Asher Roth," said Peter Rosenberg. "Then I listened, and he's rapping on the Lord Finesse instrumental. Immediately, I'm like, 'Oh, well, that's pretty cool.' Like, 'It's hard for me to hate on this, this is pretty good.'"

Clearly, others felt the same. The song had worked wonders for Malcolm, and he was cashing in. "A lot of money was made on my song," Finesse said in a statement.[25]

But Finesse and Malcolm had initially spoken when the song first came out. They even made plans to work together.

"This was a completely positive conversation like, 'Yeah, I fuck with you,'" Will Kalson recalled. "Mac had been planning on doing '*92 Til Infinity* with Jazzy Jeff. He wanted to get Lord Finesse on there."

It was early in his career, though; *KIDS* had just come out. Eventually, Malcolm scrapped '*92 Til Infinity* in favor of *Best Day Ever*, which may have been the root cause of the issue. He had told Finesse one thing, then done another.

"I think Finesse felt slighted because they never actually worked together," Kalson said. "And he knew that Mac was performing the song every night."

Eventually, Finesse tried contacting Rostrum. The label wasn't selling the song, but Malcolm was indeed performing it, and those performances were, in fact, earning him money, none of which Finesse was receiving. Had he been given credit and compensation, he'd have likely felt differently. But according to Finesse, when he finally did connect with Rostrum—they told him to look at it as if Malcolm had done him a favor.

"I made every attempt to resolve this," Finesse said. "But when I reached out to these people their attitude was I should be grateful Mac was using my music to sell out concerts because it keeps me relevant."[26]

Malcolm held firm. Legally, he felt Finesse had no claim because the Oscar Peterson sample used on "Hip 2 Da Game" had never actually been cleared. But besides that, it wasn't like he'd copied the song word for word.

In a series of tweets posted when the lawsuit became public, Malcolm said he had only made the song to pay homage. "All I wanted to do is shed light on a generation that inspired me," he said. "I did nothing wrong."[27]

Still, the lawsuit was daunting. Finesse wanted ten million dollars in damages, a staggering sum. "Whatever is meant to happen, will happen," Malcolm said. "But I just know I don't have 10 million dollars."[28]

What was at stake was more than money, though. Rappers rapped over preexisting instrumentals every day; very rarely, if ever, did they get sued. Finesse, however, argued that there was a limit to what could be done with a preexisting instrumental. From his point of view, Malcolm hadn't done anything unique to the beat; he had simply rapped over it and presented it as his own.

"I love mixtapes but this is different," he said. "Mac didn't take a piece of music and create something new. He didn't transform it into something other than what it was. He just dropped the needle on my record and changed the title."[29]

Where the line between homage and outright theft was drawn would likely be decided in court, but until then the press had a field day. Here was another black eye for Malcolm, a white rapper already battling the perception he was a culture vulture.

"This isn't 50 Cent or Lil Wayne going off over hits that most of the audience surely knows," Brandon Soderberg wrote for Spin.com, "this is a young rapper playing on the ignorance of his very young fans. . . . [D]ude could've crammed in a shout-out or nod to the producer. That's just kind of how hip-hop works."[30]

Malcolm was unnerved. A full-blown crisis was unfolding.

"I was in Dubai and he called me in a panic like—'Yo man, can you talk to Finesse?'" DJ Premier recalled. "He's like, 'What should I do?' He was really worried. I told him Finesse is family and he's good people. It'll get handled. Get some lawyers. Let the lawyers deal with it and understand Finesse's point . . . revenue is being brought in for a song where you completely used his song and changed the name of it. But just let your legal people handle it."[31]

In the end, the lawsuit left Malcolm disappointed. He had always idolized artists and producers from the nineties; in his own way, perhaps misguided though it was, he felt that by repurposing their work, rapping on their instrumentals as such, he was making old-school hip-hop relevant to a younger audience, just as artists from the nineties argued that by sampling musicians from generations before them—and getting slapped with lawsuits too—they had done the same.

"I'm not out to do anything but show love to someone like a Lord Finesse," he said on the *Sway in the Morning* show. "That's been my thing. To put kids on to what he did, his generation, why he's important to hip-hop and just music in general . . . it just shows you gotta be careful; it's a new day and age, you don't know what can sneak up on you. This is something I did when I had no following. I did it strictly out of my love for hip-hop. And it came back to open up lawsuits."[32]

That it dovetailed with what was happening on the Macadelic Tour only added insult to injury. With each strike against him, his armor began wearing thin.

"*KIDS* to *Macadelic*, he was still happy Mac," said Will Kalson. "*Blue Slide Park* brought down his spirits a bit, but he was still a very happy person. After *Macadelic* . . ."

Fans picked up on the shift and began voicing their concern. On Twitter, Malcolm began receiving tweets asking what happened to the innocent kid he used to be. *When was I ever like this little-ass innocent kid?* he recalled thinking. He would retweet the comments, seemingly humoring the line of inquiry.[33]

His disposition wasn't the only thing fans noticed changing.

"People started seeing him pick up in weight," said Franchise. "He had a Macadelic Tour video come out. There were mad comments like, 'Fat Miller.'"

The issue: too much lean. Lean was syrup; it was all sugar, which made you gain weight. People began commenting about that as well, calling him a drug addict. Those tweets, too, he retweeted.[34]

He was either trolling, or the comments seemed to really affect him. To what degree he dwelled on them isn't certain, but he was at the very least aware of what people were saying about him. And he may have tried walking back what his fans were projecting on to him when, that summer, he tweeted:

"I am not even a real person to most of you. I am nothing but a name that is attached to something you love. Most of you will never meet me."[35]

Nevertheless, Rostrum was concerned. Wiz Khalifa and Mac Miller were about to begin a tour together, finally. Dubbed the Under the Influence Tour, it would also feature Chiddy Bang and a young rapper out of Compton who called himself Kendrick Lamar. Crowds would be as large as twenty thousand people. This was major step up, and Malcolm had to be in top form.

And so began a series of conference calls between Rostrum, Mac's parents, and the label's investors. The subject: Malcolm's lean usage.

The label proposed taking him off the tour; alternately, they wondered if it was a better move to keep him on tour and bring aboard a life coach.

But it was hard to stop a train halfway down the track. And besides, nobody seemed able to get through to him anyway.

"Everything was moving too fast," said Artie. "We were a community of people raising him, trying our best. And it was everyone's problem. But dude [was] running around, famous, from city to city, making a ton of money. He was charismatic and functional and he was always on time. He was professional and polite and happy. It's hard to pin someone like that down."

THIRTEEN

In the spring of 2012, amid a flurry of tour dates, and his rapidly expanding interest in pharmaceuticals, Malcolm traveled to Los Angeles to shoot an episode of the MTV show *Punk'd*.

He found the city so welcoming that by the summer he had decided to stay, renting a mansion in Studio City that set him back twelve grand a month.

The mansion, located at 4156 Sunswept Drive, was regal; it sat behind a security gate and was set back against a hilltop, splashed in white, with six bedrooms, seven bathrooms, a marble staircase, a backyard with a pool and hot tub, and more than six thousand square feet in which to lay up comfortably.

"It's *Scarface*," he said.[1]

Like Tony Montana, Malcolm was all ambition. It was par for the course; the music industry then was shifting from a business of selling albums into a business of attention.

For an independent artist in the Internet age, the key to success was activity. Activity meant attention. Attention meant buzz.

Between collaborations, mixtape cuts, and official remixes, his work ran the gamut. In 2012, he had songs with hip-hop heavyweights like Raekwon the Chef, Fabolous, De La Soul, and Talib Kweli, newcomers Meek Mill, French

Montana, Big Sean; Rostrum Records artists Wiz Khalifa and Boaz; and blog rap favorites Curren$y and the Cool Kids. He was so hot that even Justin Bieber asked him to get on a remix.

"The Bieber song," he explained, "the thing about features and doing different stuff is you have to be down to do whatever. And that doesn't exclude pop music. Personally, I see it as a different genre, a different group of people to impress."[2]

But in this flurry of activity, one project seemed to take precedence over the others. It was a collaborative EP produced entirely by Pharrell Williams, called *Pink Slime*.

The recording sessions for it started way back in 2011, in Miami, around the time *Blue Slide Park* was released, and yielded ten songs. Malcolm had worked with a handful of notable producers—Just Blaze, DJ Premier, Jazzy Jeff—but Pharrell was different.

"I'm such a Pharrell fan, in my head I'm just like, I don't know if Mac understands how crazy this is," said DJ Clockwork. "I'm sure he knew, but me, I'm looking at it completely different. Bruh, this is the greatest hip-hop producer in the world."

It was true, Pharrell's work with partner Chad Hugo had notched him innumerable hits with Jay-Z, Beyoncé, Justin Timberlake, Clipse, and others. And with his rock-rap band N.E.R.D, he'd proven to be an inspiration to kids who grew up with hip-hop but saw themselves slightly left of center.

Pharrell sat at the cultural nexus of many different movements, from skateboarding to music to art. He was a brand unto himself. And his beats were crazy. Perhaps he could do for Malcolm what he had done for so many others.

"It's always been a dream of mine to work with him," Malcolm said. "He wants me to shine. He wants people to leave this and be like, 'Yo, Mac Miller is the shit.'"[3]

And Pharrell really believed that, telling MTV that Malcolm was "what the game [has] needed."[4] With his independent success, Pharrell saw Malcolm as part of the new generation wresting power from the corporations.

"I was just looking at his movement and what he's doing online," Pharrell said. "I watched what he did on his own and thought that was interesting. I just felt like I had to do something with him. Mac's like a concert, festival centric kid. And we got them records, man. . . . It's that hype sh*t."[5]

A pair of songs—"Onaroll" and "Glow"—eventually did see release. They were strong showings, finding Malcolm in a loose mood, addressing the elephants in the room, namely his newfound millionaire status, his weight gain, and even the Lord Finesse lawsuit.

Anticipation was high for *Pink Slime*. Clockwork quickly incorporated "Onaroll" into Malcolm's shows and plans for the EP continued apace. But somewhere along the way things went awry.

"Pharrell wanted him to be like this rocker-rapper, on some Limp Bizkit shit," Clockwork said. "That's verbatim from Mac's mouth: 'He wanted me to be on some Limp Bizkit shit. That halted the process—because they weren't creatively seeing eye to eye. Mac wanted to do it this way and Pharrell wanted to do it this way."

Tracks they worked on would eventually pass from Malcolm to other artists—Travis Scott got one called "Flying High," and Azealia Banks got one that became "ATM Jam."

Malcolm, however, didn't seem too beat-up about it. In interviews, he continued to talk up the project, hoping it would one day be finished.[6] But he was also confident that, in the wake of *Blue Slide Park*'s bad reviews, he needed to have more faith in the vision he originally had for himself.

"I don't think anyone would have taken him seriously if he came out as this really edgy, hardcore lyricist," said Artie. "They put *Blue Slide Park* together to make him more kid-friendly, and there was nothing wrong with it. Benjy did the right thing. Mac approved of it too. [But] he always rapped about darker stuff. He was always that kind of artist from *Macadelic*."

That was the direction he seemed to be leaning in now, and it caused some friction between him and the label. "Rostrum, they wanted him to be like a pop star," said Clockwork. "Nitpicking at it—'Why don't you do this? Why don't you do that? Why don't you start sounding more like this person? We want you to make records like this . . .' and he was like, 'Bro, what? I'm not making no shit like that. I'm not going to make pop records, that's not who I am.'"

He asserted his independence in other ways too. That summer, on the Under the Influence Tour, an incident on the first night in Atlanta brought into focus how much distance had grown between him and the label.

"He was powerful and young and he was a lot different than he was the year before. He'd listen to me, but he was just more standoffish. He didn't smile as much, he was edgier, and I was just like, 'OK, maybe he's growing as an artist and it is what it is,'" said Artie. "So, he had an interview with CNN and I wanted him to look really nice. But I couldn't find him."

His mother was backstage at the show, and—according to Artie—she had found Malcolm with lean. So she pulled Artie aside, let him know, and then he darted off, only to locate Mac hiding behind his security guard.

"This security guy was mouthing off at me, telling me to leave him alone," he recalled. "I was like, 'Yo, dude, come here.' And he wouldn't come near me. He was pulling a power move on me. So, I gave it a second and I walked around the fenced-in area and I was like, 'Yo, you've got an interview, c'mon.' I just remember like, he was pretty messed up."

Here it was that the guy who practically discovered Malcolm, who had helped get his music on influential websites when few people were paying attention to him, who had worked for him for free until Rostrum signed him, was being treated like just some random label employee. Then again, it wasn't called the Under the Influence Tour for no reason. From the artists to the fans, everyone seemed to be high on something.

"Though the exact number of barfing, swooning kids wasn't quantified, this reviewer hadn't witnessed vomiting like this since *Bridesmaids*," wrote A.D. Amorosi after the tour's stop in Philly.[7]

But what was going on in the crowd paled in comparison to what was happening behind the scenes. Malcolm had a real problem. He was fully addicted to lean.

One producer who worked closely with Malcolm recalled trying to get in the studio with him in the fall of 2012. Malcolm begged off, though, telling the producer he had to head back east for something. The producer suspected, though he could not confirm, that he was on his way to rehab.

●●●

While it isn't clear if Malcolm ever did, in fact, enter rehab at that time, his music may provide some clues to his thinking. In a song uploaded to his SoundCloud account in October of 2012—"These Days (Dope Awprah)"—he says: "What the fuck happened to that nice kid / That you knew when he released that mixtape called *KIDS* . . . I think I need to see a doctor."

Not only were his label and parents concerned—his friends, too, felt he had an issue. They'd voice their concerns, though never too forcefully, hoping he'd take the hints.

"I don't think we ever had an intervention, nothing like that," said Clockwork. "We never had a sit-down with him. It's just one of those things where it's like—what are you going to tell him? That's his life, he is a superstar, what can I tell him that's gonna change his mind. This is my thought process at the time. So, I kept my nose out of his business, which probably wasn't cool."

But Malcolm didn't need an intervention to know he had a problem. He told *Complex* that he was "fucked up all the time," and that his friends had begun looking at him differently—something he took notice of.

"I was lost," he said.[8]

To get healthy, he first tried kicking his habit cold turkey. That didn't work, because he would only end up binging. Finally, though, without ever acknowledging how exactly he had done it, he managed to put lean to the side.

Perhaps it wasn't a matter of wanting to, but rather needing to, for there was a pressing concern—the comments he had been receiving about gaining weight really did have merit. Lean had caused him to pack thirty pounds onto his tiny frame.

"I was like, 'Damn, I'm fucking fat as hell,'" he said.[9]

Cutting the weight fast was essential, because he was about to be on national television. Practically since his career began, MTV had been supporting Malcolm. It seemed as if his every move was covered by MTV News; he'd taken home the Woodie of the Year Award at the 2012 mtvU Woodie Awards; he had also appeared at the network's flagship Video Music Awards, and made cameos on shows like *Guy Code* and *Hip-Hop Squares*.

Malcolm had only been in Los Angeles a short period of time, but execs at MTV felt he was living a young man's fantasy. He was newly famous, living in a big-ass house with his crazy friends in the City of Angels—the perfect setting for a reality television show, a format that, twenty years earlier, MTV practically invented.

Malcolm didn't have a ton of interest in making reality TV. It might pigeonhole him as, well, a reality TV star. Next thing he knew, he'd be on *Dancing with the Stars*. Heck, Vanilla Ice had his own reality show. "I don't wanna be 'the guy from the TV show,'" he recalled thinking. "I'm an artist and I wanna make music."[10]

But he had been dropping behind-the-scenes videos on YouTube for years. The videos featured his friends, and his friends were kind of interesting. Q was his straight-edged manager; Clockwork his music junkie DJ; Peanut, a late addition to his circle, his fashion-obsessed merch designer; Jimmy was a creative of some sort; finally, there was Big Dave, a hulking and humorous former NFL lineman, who worked as Malcolm's security. If he could incorporate his friends, maybe then a show would make sense.

"I'm shaking off the frat rapper thing; I don't want to jump into reality star next," he said. "But at the end of the day, I thought it would be a good thing for people to see who me and my friends are, because everyone has these preconceived notions."[11]

Still, YouTube videos shot by artists or their record labels were low-risk. Online, if nobody watched, no big deal. A network putting money into an actual production, hiring a crew to shoot, edit, and sell advertising against it—that was serious stuff. And it was a gamble.

"You had Quentin, Peanut, Jimmy, Big Dave," said executive producer Darin Byrne. "I thought no one would care about this group that nobody knew. Like, who is this person?"[12]

But Malcolm insisted. "He wanted all their names in the credits like a supporting cast," said Byrne. "He wanted to try to shine a light on all of them."

At the center was Malcolm, the planet around which everything orbited. The template for the show was *Rob and Big*. That show, based on the adventures of Rob Dyrdek and his friend Big, had been a breakout hit for MTV. The network felt Malcolm could be like Dyrdek, and his friends would be his Big.

Billed as a "docu-follow," the show wasn't so much about drama, more about letting viewers peek in on Malcolm's daily life.

"He was a homebody, he loved the house," said Byrne. "And I think he just loved giving back to his friends; having that kind of place where his friends could hang and create. He wasn't really a club guy, at all. I don't know what happened when we left, but I know he wasn't like, *let's go out and get messed up in L.A.* That wasn't him. He'd rather stay home and chill, make a beat, play video games, and have a party at his house."

While it wasn't scripted, episodes were loosely choreographed around the things happening in Malcolm's life. He was due to be crowned the Man of Next Year by *Complex* magazine, so that became an episode. He had alter-egos—Larry Fisherman and Larry Lovestein—so those became episodes. Pittsburgh was such a big part of his life, so heading home became an episode.

From these basic elements, producers sought to make television magic. And they did—like in the pilot episode.

"Bieber has one," Q tells Malcolm. "He drives it to Chick-fil-A all the time."

He's speaking of the Fisker Karma, an early Tesla competitor that *Complex* magazine was gifting Malcolm, a reward for having been voted, in an Internet poll, the "Man of Next Year." Malcolm had won the poll with fifty-nine percent of the vote, beating out ScHoolboy Q, Miguel, and other artists that *Complex* felt were on the verge of exploding.

Not everyone at *Complex* was excited about Malcolm's inclusion on the list. Some of the staff outright rejected him. But one writer, Insanul Ahmed, had written about him before. Each time he featured Malcolm on the site, he noticed an uptick in the site's traffic. The metrics proved to him that, despite *Complex*'s lack of enthusiasm, Malcolm was indeed popular. *Complex* didn't get it, but it was there.

"Man, this guy Mac Miller's really popular," Ahmed recalled the staff saying when they saw the votes. "What we wanted to get was fan engagement, we wanted to get people to the site. Mac winning by that large margin and getting his fan base to show up worked out for us. I don't think people were super excited for Mac himself, they were just like, 'Hey, at least the [website] traffic is there.'"[13]

Malcolm knew none of this, he just knew that he had won, and because of that, he was receiving a car. It would make for good television if MTV captured it all on camera, and so they began shooting. But then, in a plot twist straight out of *Curb Your Enthusiasm*, after Malcolm got the car, the hundred-thousand-dollar vehicle broke down.

Ahmed had been riding with Malcolm in the backseat—he was profiling him for having won the contest—and remembered the confusion that ensued as the car died on the 101 in LA.

"The car was smooth. It was a quiet ride. And when it stopped, I was like, 'Yo, are we stuck?' and he was like, 'Yo, man, the car . . . the car just stopped.' I said, 'What do you mean it stopped?' He says, 'Yeah we're stuck.' I'm like, 'Wait, what?!' Now, Fisker had gotten a lot of bad press because there was this whole thing during Hurricane Sandy, a bunch of the cars got wet and then caught on fire and like, exploded . . . at one point, Mac was like, 'Yo, man, maybe I just gotta turn the car back on.' But me and Q were like, 'Dude, do you smell that?' It smelled kind of smokey. Mac's like, 'I'm switching the car back on.' I said, 'Mac, I shouldn't tell you this, but Marc Ecko told me the cars do blow up, Marc Ecko said there's fires, don't turn it back on,' and he was like, 'Wait, the cars blow up?'"

The whole affair had turned into a calamity. And it gave Ahmed pause. In his career, he had interviewed numerous rappers and celebrities. Most assignments went smoothly. But not this one. And while his rapport with Malcolm may have been friendly, he wasn't sure what his reaction would be to being gifted something that didn't work. Not only did it not work, it now seemed to be a legit hazard. If he was someone of a different temperament, the car wouldn't be the only thing that blew up.

"He was having so much fun for a guy who just got a brand-new car that broke down," Ahmed said. "We got out of the car, we're waiting for the tow truck to pick us up—and he started freestyling about it. He said, "Imagine if you had given that car to Pusha T or Kid Cudi, and imagine it broke down. Man, they'd have been so fucking pissed. They'd have probably been yelling at you and shit.' But Mac, it just washed off of him; he didn't even care. The car was getting towed away and he was posing in front of it, making jokes."

For all Ahmed knew, this was just another day in his crazy life, and yeah, MTV was capturing it all for the show—not a bad thing!

The Fisker made for good comedy. It also made for, in a very roundabout way, Malcolm's highest-profile beef.

Until then, Malcolm and Donald Trump were only loosely acquainted. Malcolm had the song named after him, and Trump liked that. Trump wasn't sitting around listening to rap music, but by slapping his name on anything that could be built or sold—from steaks to buildings to suits—he had turned narcissism into an extreme sport. He reveled in anything that seemed to make his name more valuable.

Malcolm wasn't exactly a Trump fan. He didn't know much about him. "There was a phase that kind of happened where I liked making songs named after people," he said. "Like, I did one called 'Bruce Wayne.' The idea of the song—it's not like it's a song about Donald Trump. But the aura of the song is, kind of."[14]

"This is a time where people were making a lot of name songs," producer SAP said. "[Future's] 'Tony Montana,' all of that."[15]

And Malcolm just knew of Trump the way most people knew of him, as a rich guy symbolically linked to American excess, the crass commercialism and alpha male posturing that was the lifeblood of many a great hip-hop song. Trump himself had been name-dropped by countless artists, from the Beastie Boys and Prince to Rick Ross and Lil Wayne.

"Donald Trump" was a hit. But in the years that had passed since the song's release, a different Donald Trump had emerged.

No longer a playful and fun guy, Trump had spent the better part of a year arguing that Barack Obama hadn't been born in the United States and was thus ineligible to be president. "Show us your birth certificate," he demanded. It was the early days of the birtherism movement. He was toying with running for president himself.

All the while, he was endearing himself to an angry and aggrieved faction of the right-wing political establishment. These were the furthest things from his mind when Malcolm made the song.

"I think [Trump's] a dick," he told Marc Ecko when he was given the Fisker Karma. "When he started running for president I was like, 'Oh, fuck—this is horrible, I have a fucking song with this dude's name and now he's being such a douchebag.'"[16]

To add insult to injury, Trump felt he was responsible for the song's success. And that bothered Malcolm. He could have named it after Bill Gates; except, well, he didn't. And Trump was . . . Trump. He was a lightning rod for controversy, and *Complex* smelled drama.

"We had a policy at *Complex* when we would promote an article on Twitter. If it was something negative, we would never @ the artist," said Ahmed. "But when we were doing a tweet for that video, I was like, 'We have to @ Donald Trump because that guy's gonna respond, he's got thin skin.' And Donald Trump responded like fifteen minutes later."

Trump was livid, and on January 31, 2013, he wrote in a series of tweets: "Little @macmiller, you illegally used my name for your song 'Donald Trump' which now has over 75 million hits! Little @macmiller, I want the money not the plaque you gave me! Little @macmiller, I'm now going to teach you a big boy lesson about lawsuits and finance. You ungrateful dog!"[17]

It made for great headlines. But it stressed Malcolm out. He had just settled his lawsuit with Lord Finesse. Now this. "I was with him that day when he saw the tweets," said Statik Selektah. "He was like, 'Dude, this guy's fuckin' coming at me, he was just telling me he loves me.'"

And yet for all his tough talk, Trump never appeared to do anything. There are no public records of a lawsuit.

"He was just trolling," said the song's producer, SAP. "Just being a dickhead."

Malcolm soon took it all in stride. "I realized, who does Donald Trump beef with?" he said. "Me and Obama. So like, hey."[18]

Regardless, with his name in the news, it helped generate interest in the reality show, and when *Mac Miller and the Most Dope Family* premiered in late February, it proved a modest hit—around four hundred thousand people tuned in. It was a big number for MTV2, a small network lacking the distribution of the flagship channel.

Over six episodes, the show sought to introduce Mac's world. From parties at the mansion to fishing trips (where everyone got sick), to his mother's birthday, the show was frequently funny and lighthearted, and most of all, it allowed Malcolm to introduce different sides of himself—like, Larry Lovestein, a jazzman alter ego.

Malcolm would introduce other alter egos later in his career, but Lovestein proved a healthy diversion; complete with a self-produced EP titled *You*, by Larry Lovestein & The Velvet Revival—a fictional band with its own Twitter account and only one member, himself. The alter ego let him make another type of music that was near and dear to him—jazz—but do so without the expectations of it being released by Mac Miller (though anyone made aware of its existence would only know about it because it was made by Mac Miller).

And the show gave him space to work that part of his creativity out on camera. "I've known [Larry Lovestein] basically since I was born and I got to help him be on an MTV show," he said. "So I'm excited for the episode to come out where the world meets someone I've known my whole life."[19]

As for what was happening behind the scenes, the show steered clear of anything too raw for television, though in episode four, "PA Nights," he travels back to Pittsburgh for his mom's birthday dinner and does make an offhand joke about cocaine.

"Mac was the ultimate salesman. If he's in the room with anyone, he'll make you like him and like his music, too," said Insanul Ahmed. "I think [he] saw the show as an opportunity—*Let me showcase my personality and let me charm the audience; I just need people to see me be the harmless goofball that I really am*. The show just positioned Mac as being this fun-loving celebrity guy with a crew of rambunctious yahoos, or whatever, who are his friends . . . most of it is generally pretty harmless."

So, the cocaine? He was just joking—or at least that's how it appeared. If a stray Styrofoam cup was spotted on set, not much was thought was given. Malcolm was never late. He was always professional. And the production was smooth sailing.

Hiccups were few; at most, they were creative. "Breaking the fourth wall was something that he wanted to do a lot," said Byrne. "*House of Cards* was all the rage at the time; Kevin Spacey, at the end of every episode, does that little fourth wall break."

Malcolm wanted to do this often.

"He thought that would be more authentic in some way," Byrne said. "And we were trying to explain to him: in reality shows, you gotta get lost in the reality of it all. You have to have the viewers believe they are a fly on the wall, and you can't do that if you keep breaking the fucking fourth wall."

He felt the cameras added a lot of unnecessary pressure. When they were on, it was like he had to perform, even though he wasn't exactly performing.

"I'm kind of weird with cameras," he said. "Kinda paranoid. It feels like everyone's eyes are on you. Performing is a show. But the cameras are like behind-the-scenes stuff. My private life."[20]

On certain things, Malcolm would push back. The fourth wall, for instance. He knew what reality shows were. If he was going to do a show, he wanted to do it his way. The show was soft-scripted, no words put into his mouth, but there were things that, with each episode, had to be accomplished. It took some convincing to get him to sign on to that.

Nevertheless, it was an effort. He wanted to do anything but make a basic-ass reality show.

"This is cheesy," he said of some of things he was asked to do. "I don't want to be the Kardashians."

FOURTEEN

Hollywood is home to the entourage. More so than in New York, where space is at a premium, it is also about sprawl. It's an otherwise gritty place that looks more fabulous on television than it really is, but the rich and famous can, and often do, live in comically large houses with more space than is necessary, and thus, those spaces get filled with family, friends, and whomever else is temporarily deemed essential.

And in one of those houses—a mansion, in fact—is where Malcolm lived. More *MTV Cribs* than Airbnb, he was unlike so many of the famous people in town, for he kept a loose policy with the door. All you needed was to know him, or know someone who knew him, and you could find your way inside.

"If you were too young to get into a club, you could go to Mac's house," said a pal from nearby Sherman Oaks. "There, you'd see rappers, B-list actors, and a bunch of girls. It was the cool, hip spot to be at."

Malcolm purposely designed it this way. Kendrick Lamar. Tyler, the Creator, and Odd Future. YG. Nipsey Hu$$le. Heck, most of the record business, period, had decamped to the West Coast. And that was the precise reason he had moved there.

"[T]he most important people in hip-hop, right now, are out here," he said.[1]

And the house was good for a hang.

"Most of the time we [were] just there chilling, laughing," said the Internet's Matt Martians. "And, then somebody will go record . . . We go over there in the morning and we don't even make music most of the time."[2]

He went out of his way to make sure everyone felt comfortable. On hand he kept a big bag of weed; other substances were easily obtained—such was the makeup of the crowd who hung out there.

A key feature of the house was the studio, a windowless room that reeked of menthol cigarettes, with red walls and red lighting. Malcolm dubbed it "The Sanctuary."[3] "It looked like an opium den," Malcolm said.[4] In the studio he held court, working on a slew of projects. Chief among them was a new album.

Inside the studio, he had taken to putting on movies while he worked (of note: *Beetlejuice* and PBS doc *Birds of the Gods*). Documentaries about aquatic life, especially, were inspiring; underwater images served as a perfect companion for the hallucinatory states he found himself in while recording.

"I'm just really serious about movies, I take them very seriously," he said. "Not to do the cliche rapper, 'My life is like a movie,' but I just enjoy that concept . . . I always get pissed about movies, that they're not real. I always want them to be real."[5]

He even found that one doc, *Turtle: The Incredible Journey*, about a female loggerhead turtle's odyssey from a beach in Florida, around the globe and back home again—a trip that only one in ten thousand turtles are said to survive—synced up scene for scene with the new album he was working on. He had been hipped to it by his DJ, Clockwork, who had watched it while tripping on mushrooms.

"At first I just kind of brushed it off," Malcolm said. "But me and my boy Jimmy finally decided to watch it and [the album] just synced up perfectly. It was kind of creepy. Jimmy almost cried like four times."[6]

Whereas *Blue Slide Park* had been celebratory and fun, the new record continued the path he'd embarked on with *Macadelic*, more inward-focused and ornery.

Malcolm had changed. He knew it. And so did everyone around him. Two years before, it was all fun and games. He was traveling the world, a new city every night. But the constant grind had taken its toll. Fame, too, had worn him down.

"I had this idea of success in my mind and I think I reached a place and I was like, *Ah, this is awesome*; then all of a sudden something just shifted, where I just didn't," he said. "I mean, I was on the road for a long time. A long time. And I'm not trying to sit here and cry about anything, I'm good now, but something happened; I don't know what it was. But I just decided I hated everybody. I was just around so many people all the time that I just started hating everybody. I just didn't like to be around people . . . because you spend so much time in front of cameras, you spend so much time where you kind of have to be 'on,' where you have to 'be Mac Miller.' And Mac Miller to the world was this fun-loving little white kid, *I'm so funny, haha*. I'm just like, *Stop, man*. I just wanna sit down and chill out."[7]

The road had weathered him. Critics had beaten him down. The Lord Finesse lawsuit had been settled ("I'm actually legally not allowed to say anything about what happened," he told *Complex*[8]), but it showed him that, at the end of the day, music was a business.

Good intentions had their limits. People saw what they saw. And heard what they heard. What they had heard was a kid. A frat rapper. Maybe he *was* a frat rapper; after all, shows at and around college campuses were his bread and butter, and college kids loved him. If you smoked weed and drank, then did it all again the next weekend—well, Mac Miller was your guy (even if he didn't want to be).

If that gave people the wrong impression, he made his peace with it. "I realized, it's whatever," he said. "The truth is irrelevant. So I'm cool. I don't care. I realize that they don't know me. So say whatever you want. I've learned to find the humor in everything, even in the hatred."[9]

But it took work to block out the noise, and it left him drained. Besides, *Best Day Ever*, when everything was new and exciting—that, to him, was the peak.

"I don't think it's gotten much better than that," he said. "It's like losing your virginity. The whole time you're like, 'This is fucking crazy.' Then after having sex a lot more you're kinda just in there."[10]

Which isn't to say he was no longer enthusiastic; he was still wide-eyed in certain ways, pushing himself creatively. But he was eager to move on. At times, he was simply bored. "For the past year and a half, when I [perform] 'Knock, Knock,' it's fun, but when I say the lyrics, I don't feel anything," he said. "You're just kind of reciting."[11]

So he found other ways to entertain himself.

"There's this scene in *The Sopranos* where Christopher goes to a heroin dealer and doesn't buy any heroin, he wants to use him as a hit man. As he's walking away one guy's like, 'Yeah, I think he kicked his habit' and the other guy's like, 'He didn't kick the habit, he's just resting,'" said Insanul Ahmed, who had written the *Complex* Man of the Year story, which advanced the narrative that Malcolm had taken to lean after the bad reviews of *Blue Slide Park* but was now sober. "I did believe what he was saying was true, that he had fought it and he had stopped. Jimmy was basically Mac's best friend. Jimmy was like, the Turtle [from *Entourage*] of the group, the friend who's just there to be a friend. He was talking a lot about Mac really going through it and also about seeing Mac stop—he said he felt like Mac really did kick it. So, I believed it."

But his story didn't really add up. Ahmed spent a night in the studio with Malcolm. Watching him work, it seemed nothing had changed. Maybe he had kicked lean. But he was still indulging. "Weed and alcohol are not the same as other drugs, but usually when people are in sobriety or are going through rehab and stuff, they kick everything, they even stop drinking coffee," said Ahmed.

Malcolm wasn't alone in the studio that night. MTV cameras were present, and Earl Sweatshirt had shown up unannounced cradling a six-pack of beer and a bottle of Knob Creek. The energy, at first, was tense. A year earlier, *Complex* had revealed Earl's previously unknown whereabouts at the Coral Reef Academy in Samoa, where he had been sent by his mother to keep him out of trouble. The mystery surrounding his absence from Odd Future, while the group was surging, made him one of the most buzzed-about artists in music, complete with a Free Earl campaign, and a fawning eight-thousand-word profile published in the *New Yorker*.[12]

Complex had blown the lid off all of that, and Earl had recently struck back in "Chum," rapping: "Craven and these *Complex* fuck ni**as done track me down / just to be the guys that did it, like, 'I like attention.'" Now a *Complex* rep and Earl were set to meet face-to-face. It could have made for an explosive run-in, but then, nothing happened. Any lingering negative energy was dispelled with quickly, and the order of the day commenced. That was when Ahmed noticed something strange.

"I smoked weed with Mac. And he was drinking a lot, too," he said. "They made this song, 'Guild,' which was on Earl's album *Doris*, and did the whole thing from scratch that night. Mac drank the entire bottle of Knob Creek. He was just taking shots [of] it. He's like, 'Come on, take a shot.' I said, 'I can't, man.' I was so jet-lagged. But he finished that whole bottle by himself in three or four hours. We're chain-smoking blunts. If you're really trying to be into sobriety, you kind of have to go cold turkey on everything."

"Guild," on which Mac raps, "Moms love me cause I'm so commercial / Fuck 'em raw 'cause I know they fertile," would wind up being one of Malcolm's more eye-opening collaborations; paired with Earl, who wasn't lacking for credibility or critical acclaim, it seemed as if one of the most talked-about artists was effectively offering this corny white rapper a cosign. Serious music critics, who had thus far written off Malcolm as a kind of sad joke—a rapper they were forced to cover, due to his undeniable success—might have to think differently about him moving forward. Like, was this frat rapper kid now for real?

"Ni**as aren't expecting to hear Mac Miller," Earl said. "I wanted ni**as to see the Mac Miller feature, be like . . . 'Fuck . . .' like, 'This ni**a . . . this ni**a stink, he blew it, he doin' shit with Mac Miller . . .' And then that song comes on and it's like, 'Oh! Hmm, yeah.'"[13]

Of the many faces that breezed through Malcolm's house, Earl became one of Malcolm's better friends. Odd Future had a reputation for generally hating everything; their name alone Odd Future Wolf Gang Kill Them All—stylized as OFWGKTA—seemed at odds with nearly everything Malcolm stood for. Their salve was: kill people, burn shit, fuck school! But they found common ground.

"We're definitely kind of pretty similar people," Malcolm said. "We're both very nice. We're trying to do good things, but also we try to be assholes at the same time."[14]

On the point of being an asshole, Earl did think Malcolm kind of sucked. At least initially. That didn't prevent the pair from becoming friends. "[Odd Future member] Taco took me over to his house, I had only heard a few things about him, maybe heard one Mac Miller verse and was like, 'Oh, that was pretty trash,'" he said. "Then I went over to that ni**a's house, we was on the same page, became friends, and then just naturally started doing music. So, it was like we started on a completely fresh slate."[15]

"Guild" was performed by Earl in March of 2013. His fan base, rabid as they were, seized upon it immediately. Among folks who had potentially never cared for Malcolm, there may have been a slight bend of the neck.

The same month, another collaboration unspooled itself. It came from what appeared to be a parallel universe, not the booze-fest that birthed "Guild," or any number of the loosies that seemed to weasel their way onto the Internet. This song was unlikely to merit discussion in the comment sections of rap blogs or be picked apart on hip-hop message boards.

It was called "The Way," and was sung by a young lady who had been a child star of sorts, acting in the Broadway play *13* at the age of only fifteen, then landing a supporting role as Cat Valentine in the Nickelodeon television series *Victorious*—which, after four seasons, had just aired its series finale. Like Malcolm, and many a teen pop star before her, she built a dedicated following with cover songs uploaded to YouTube, while maintaining a candid social media presence.

Her name was Ariana Grande. And she was, in her own way, huge. Ariana hailed from Boca Raton, Florida, and *Victorious* was a major show, watched by millions each week. On the show, her character, Cat Valentine, was a positive Pollyanna, a favorite among viewers.

Ariana made frequent appearances on *Victorious* cast albums, occasionally dueting with star Victoria Justice; privately, though, she was toiling away on her own music, hoping to one day become a solo artist. As early as 2010, she was working on what she hoped would be her debut album, and after being sent some of her YouTube videos, she was inked by Monte Lipman to Universal Republic in 2011.

On November 22, 2012, Ariana tweeted: "Watching the parade from the couch all warm and cozy in our apartment. What are you thankful for at the moment?"[16]

Malcolm responded: "the velvet revival."[17]

Ariana wrote back: "I'm excited to listen to it, happy thanksgiving ♥"[18]

Malcolm's next message to Ariana read: "happy thanksgiving to you too. the homie larry lovestein wants to do a duet."[19]

To which Ariana wrote: "tell Larry I'd love to!"[20]

And Malcolm replied: "i'll let him know. he's very shy. check your dms."[21]

While it's unclear if this was a promotional stunt—it was social media, after all—Malcolm made numerous connections via social media, often popping into the DMs of artists he liked or wanted to collaborate with. And while it is unlikely that he foresaw what would come from just a few innocent tweets, he shot his shot regardless and it seemed to have worked. Shortly afterward, he and Ariana began spending time together, both inside the studio and out.

Friends who were around him at the time remember that when it came to Ariana, Malcolm was doing things that, to them, seemed slightly out of character. Perhaps they were, or perhaps they simply didn't know him as well as they thought they did. Case in point, it was November 2012 when Ariana was starring as Snow White in a play called *A Snow White Christmas* at the Pasadena Playhouse. She invited Malcolm to come see the play; on the date in question, he turned to Clockwork, and asked if he wanted to come along.

"A play—you're going to a play?" Clockwork recalled, surprised. "And he was like, 'Yeah, this girl I'm talking to is in this play, Ariana Grande.'"

Clockwork had no idea who Ariana Grande was, she was completely off his radar, but he remembered the play being "super dope," and afterward, he recalled standing outside the theater with Malcolm, waiting for Ariana to emerge. By then, he had been touring with Malcolm for two years, and seemed to believe he was fairly famous and well known. But when he was outside waiting with Malcolm, he observed how the paparazzi were swarming the venue, and paying absolutely no mind at all to his friend.

"They're acting like they don't know who he is," Clockwork said. "Or, maybe they really don't know who he is. But we're just standing there."

Malcolm just stood there, seemingly anonymous, smoking a cigarette and waiting.

"All these stars come out, everybody in the play comes out, and then boom—Ariana comes out," Clockwork recalled. "It's like my eardrums are about to bust. Little girls are going crazy. Cameras are going off."

As soon as Ariana saw Malcolm, she ran over and gave him a hug. The cameras began bursting then—*snap, snap, snap.*

Ariana rushed to get Malcolm out of the way, seeming to not want him swept up in the kind of tabloid celebrity life she was living. Clockwork, though, could see how the experience might become unnerving. Malcolm was famous in a way, but this was fame at a different level. His pal, who was rarely flustered, seemed uncomfortable.

"You feel like you getting attacked or followed," Clockwork said. "You can't see nothing . . . it's all these lights. I could see how it gives people anxiety. I could see how Princess Diana died off that shit. [Paparazzi] don't really give a fuck about your personal space. It's an adrenaline rush."

Ariana herself was not fond of the paparazzi, or the way she was perceived. She was a singer who became famous first as an actress, a child star who, at age twenty, was becoming an adult. For all that she already was, she wanted to be so much more.

"I have been doing TV for a while," she said. "But I'm very uncomfortable with it. In the sense that I just want to entertain people and make music. And all this stuff—I'm like, not very comfortable walking red carpets or having my photo taken when I'm not aware that my photo is being taken. There's just certain things that I'm never going to get comfortable with. But it just comes with the territory."[22]

The first song Malcolm and Ariana released was a duet of "Baby It's Cold Outside," the evergreen holiday tune made famous by Dean Martin and covered by everyone from Jessica Simpson to Michael Bublé.

But "The Way" was their real first look together. Built around a sample of Brenda Russell's 1979 hit "A Little Bit of Love"—popularized to nineties kids by its usage in rapper Big Pun's "Still Not a Player" in 1998—the song was Ariana's first single from her debut album, *Yours Truly.* The video saw the pair hugging up on each other, with Ariana cooing, "I love the way you make me feel, I love it, I love it," and Malcolm wrapping his arms around her waist. At the end, they shared a passionate French kiss.

Ariana denied that there was anything more to the kiss than met the eye. "He's one of my best friends, I had to have him on ['The Way']," she said.

"[The kiss] was directed, it wasn't just in the moment. I felt like it was a good choice. It's a romantic song."[23]

She also wasn't that taken with the kiss anyway; asked during a Power 106 radio interview to rate him on a scale of one to ten, she gave him a one. "Just 'cause [of] the cigarettes," she joked.[24]

Malcolm, too, played down the kiss. "That's the homie," he told MTV News, noting that she already had a boyfriend. "I didn't even know [the kiss] was going to happen and then we were shooting and the director was like 'This should happen' and I'm like 'Alright.'" When he was next back in Pittsburgh everyone was going nuts, he recalled. "Like 'You kissed Ariana Grande.' I was like 'Yeah, you know how I do.'"[25]

It was true, Ariana did have a boyfriend, YouTuber Jai Brooks. But the pair had broken up under mysterious circumstances shortly after the video for "The Way" was released that March. When interviewed on the *Ebro in the Morning* show, Ariana was asked directly: Are you in relationship with Mac Miller?

"It's not, no—there's nothing to know yet," she said, embarrassed. "I'm really honest and open with my fans. So when there's something official, or exciting . . . I'm living my life, trying to figure everything out. It's hard to update everyone on everything as it happens. Because you don't know what's going to happen."[26]

Pressed on if she was in love, she flatly declared: "No."[27]

Commercially, "The Way" did well, peaking at number nine on the charts. It was a staple on pop radio throughout 2013, and Malcolm seemed pleased—especially because he considered her a real friend. He also felt she was legitimately talented, and appreciated that the hard work she put into being taken seriously as a musician was paying off.

"She has an incredible voice," he said. "And I always tell her when I'm listening to her music, I always like her slow ballad songs, those are my favorites. But she's great, and I think she's gonna be very big and successful, which is dope. Seeing a bunch of people kind of coming around to the idea that she's not just this Nickelodeon star and musician—like, she can really do this. I'm glad I was part of one of the first things."[28]

Like Ariana, Malcolm was still trying to win over the skeptics. To accomplish this, he was still tinkering with his new record, which he had slated for a June release. He was calling it *Watching Movies with the Sound Off* (*WMWTSO*).

Work on the record drove him nuts. LA was a sprawling metropolis, filled with people and places to go. Any night, he could hop in his car and have an adventure. But instead, he chose the studio, a small, confining space, and drugs, which caused him to look inward. He worked late. Hours stretched on indefinitely.

"You could be in there 72 hours and think it's the same day," the rapper Da$h, one of Malcolm's collaborators, told *Billboard*. "Come in during the day, and come out in the pitch black."[29]

"He is nonstop," said the Internet's Syd tha Kyd. "He can go for hours. Ideas never stop flying through him."[30]

"It's dark in there," Malcolm said. "There's no concept of time or where you are. Separating myself from everything allowed me to explore my own mind."[31]

But it was all worth it. All great art required a little suffering, didn't it?

While making his landmark album *Darkness on the Edge of Town*, Bruce Springsteen spent six weeks recording one snare drum, over and over and over again. His engineer, Jimmy Iovine, thought he was absolutely nuts. But Bruce was defiant. There was a sound in his head that he wanted to hear on the record, and no matter what he did, he just couldn't get it right.[32] Until he did.

Queen's magnum opus, "Bohemian Rhapsody," took three weeks to record, requiring vocalists Freddie Mercury, Brian May, and Roger Taylor to sing their parts ten to twelve hours a day, continuously. The Beach Boys' "Good Vibrations" was a six-month affair, with a cost, accounting for inflation, of nearly four hundred thousand dollars—and it was just a single!

More contemporaneously, Kanye West had spent upward of three million dollars to make his 2010 LP *My Beautiful Dark Twisted Fantasy*, with its Hawaii-based recording sessions featuring a rotating cast of characters that included Beyoncé, Jay-Z, Kid Cudi, Drake, DJ Premier, the RZA, and dozens of others. And Dr. Dre was still working on *Detox*!

There was no proof, of course, that endlessly tinkering with a record, or any creative project for that matter, made it better—some of the best albums of all time, in fact, had been made relatively quickly. 2Pac's *All Eyez on Me* was recorded in two weeks;[33] Jay-Z needed just as little time to record *The Blueprint*, arguably his best album.[34]

Historically, Malcolm worked fast. But in his home studio, he was less rushed, and like a mad scientist at work on a new experiment, he gave himself over to the process. "I wanted to go insane over it,"[35] he said. "I wanted it to be that way."

Listening back to the album, he thought it was some of his best work. He had tweaked it a lot. An early version ended with him killing a girl, then killing himself. "It got to the point where my dad called me," he said. "Like, are you OK, what's going on?"[36]

But what he had now, he felt, built on his previous work. "The goals I'm setting for myself are high, so I'm just trying to get better," he told DJ Semtex. "And at no point have I ever thought that I was good enough yet."

Rostrum Records would release the album. They were excited to get a new record from Malcolm. But ever since *Macadelic*, they had been concerned about the way he was living. "It was definitely scary," Benjy told *Rolling Stone*. "I had never been that close to somebody who had issues like that."[37]

The label wouldn't argue—in fact, they *couldn't* argue—so long as Malcolm's music met their expectations. Rostrum prided itself on being artist-friendly, but they weren't dumb. Malcolm had young fans. They knew it, and so did he. On "Doodling in the Key of C Sharp," a stray song released to his SoundCloud, he rapped: "I still got some dumbass fans who want *KIDS* back / And I forget that they twelve years old, I must accept that . . ."

His increasingly downbeat music did not appeal to these fans. And after *Blue Slide Park*, the expectation was that he would build on its success.

One day, Benjy arrived at Malcolm's house to hear his progress on *WMWTSO*. Malcolm auditioned it for him, and Benjy seemed, for the most part, unmoved. A generally stoic and stone-faced guy, he was sometimes difficult to read—but he wasn't shy about vocalizing his enthusiasm when he felt it. "Plane, Car, Boat," a collab with ScHoolboy Q, was one of the songs he was undecided on. Malcolm's pals felt the song was good, but not exactly "the shit." Benjy offered feedback. And Malcolm listened.

What Benjy really wanted Malcolm to do though was think hard about which songs he wanted to shoot videos for. These would be the singles—and they'd dictate the album's commercial prospects.

"Benjy did what was basically his job," said Insanul Ahmed, who was present. "Just kind of being the dad of the whole thing."[38]

But as soon as he left the studio, Malcolm turned to Q, annoyed. "How could he say that about this record; man, he just ruined our confidence; he didn't even care that we did x, y, and z on this song, and he didn't notice I changed the drums on that song."

"They just seemed really not happy with the way the interaction went," Ahmed said. "Being in the room with them, it seemed fine to me, [but] there was some kind of baggage there."

In an interview with DJBooth.com, Benjy acknowledged that, as far back as *Macadelic*, he and Malcolm had begun to disagree over the direction of his sound. He wasn't sure Malcolm was well-established enough to pivot so strongly.[39]

Maybe a better move would be to shoot for a radio hit? Rostrum wouldn't chase after one, would never push him to make a song specifically for the radio, but with "The Way" in rotation, it couldn't have hurt to have a catchy Mac Miller single as a follow-up.

Sources close to both parties at the time believe that Benjy, upon seeing how well *Blue Slide Park* had done commercially, may have been disappointed that Malcolm had turned so hard in the opposite direction, abandoning his happier, more accessible sound for something that was notably abstract.

"I could see, being the owner of a record label, you might not appreciate the music in the same way," one source said. "Benjy probably didn't hear it the same way Mac did. There was a shift in the sound that Benjy didn't understand. *Macadelic* started that shift, and as it went along, Benjy may not have been prepared for it to switch up *that* much."

According to his friends, Malcolm's trust in Rostrum was fading.

"I definitely think that some animosity started to build against Benjy and Rostrum," said Will Kalson. "He didn't value Benjy's opinion as much after *Blue Slide Park*. Because even though it did well, Mac really cared about what people thought about him. I think he felt like Benjy led him astray in terms of the sound of the project. And that was why he started to do things dramatically different and completely rebel against the whole Rostrum system."

Kalson recalled Malcolm reading YouTube comments and being stung by the negative ones. Bad reviews clearly got to him. And perhaps unfairly, he may have believed Rostrum was at least partly responsible.

"Benjy did have a very specific sound that he tried to produce from his artists and Mac did not want to be held to that sound anymore," Kalson said. Benjy, he felt, pushed Malcolm to be as creative as possible, but come album time, there was something he expected that Malcolm didn't seem inclined to give him anymore. "Benjy was very critical of his music. Same with Wiz. I remember being in the studio before *Kush & Orange Juice* came out—Benjy and Wiz had an argument about *Kush & Orange Juice*. And that ended up being the project that broke Wiz."

Like *Macadelic*, *Watching Movies with the Sound Off* was darker and edgier than the music Malcolm had become known for; filled with hubris, a blend of anger and exasperation, it was Malcolm with something to get off his chest. The album was arguably his last-ditch effort for acceptance in a genre that was all too quick to rid itself of bad actors.

His aim: turn his haters into fans. To do that, he'd have to turn to the tastemakers. And just as he'd done with the blogs and media in the early days, he went right back to work.

One of his biggest haters was *Fader*, a magazine/website with a reputation for being an arbiter of all things cutting edge, placing artists like the White Stripes, M.I.A., Kanye West, Damon Albarn, Major Lazer, and Lil B on its covers long before they were famous.

"I remember being at the *Fader* Fort at SXSW, and Wiz brought him out onstage. We were like, 'Who is this little dude with the backpack on, jumping around onstage?' I think he did a song or two. And we were just not that into it," said Andy Cohn, *Fader*'s former publisher. "He was not accepted by the staff. The music, they didn't get it. It didn't feel on brand for *Fader*. Felt a little bit gimmicky. It felt a little young. [*Fader*] always tried to be a little more mature. They didn't get it and I didn't either. I just didn't love the music. I didn't connect with it. I don't think anyone really did."

But like an item on a bucket list that he wanted to check off, the *Fader* cover was something that Malcolm coveted. They might not like him, but he wouldn't be deterred.

"He was like, 'OK, these guys don't fuck with my music right now, but I'm not gonna give up'—clearly *Fader* was important to him," said Cohn.

Back then, magazine covers still mattered; for a celebrity, they were precious real estate, with the faces on them peering out from magazine racks, landing in a mailbox, or at the very least picked up at an airport to pass the time. This wasn't the Internet, where a soup of new content was published each day, replenished with every refresh of the browser. A magazine cover meant you were important.

While *Watching Movies with the Sound Off* was being prepped for release, Artie Pitt—aware that *Fader* did not like Malcolm—still went ahead and pitched the magazine a cover story. The staff had traditionally been cold on Malcolm, but they had to admit that his newer music had gotten, in their opinion, markedly more interesting. So they considered him for the August–September 2013 issue. Still, they weren't completely sold, and initially said no. And that's when Malcolm went into overdrive.

"Mac was really adamant about getting on the phone," Cohn said. "I never had an artist want to talk to me directly about being on the cover of the magazine. It was like, the coolest conversation. He was just so smart and mature about everything."

Many artists felt they deserved covers—that didn't mean they actually did. But the fact that *Fader* hated Malcolm, and he held no grudges, made an impact. Some artists took everything personally. Malcolm, however, saw it as an opportunity to sell himself.

"Look at the other end of the spectrum—you have Machine Gun Kelly," Cohn said. "A kid who goes on Twitter, publishes [editor in chief] Matthew Schnipper's email address, telling all his fans to bombard his email address telling him he's a fuckin' dick and a piece of shit and to light *Fader* magazines on fire, only because we didn't put him on the cover. For a kid to be passed over, then come back and almost take it—take it like a real adult—at his age and what he had under his belt at that time, was really, really impressive."[40]

So Malcolm made his case. He told Cohn that he appreciated *Fader* not simply loving him because they felt they had to, that they weren't, unlike many media outlets in the chummy back-slapping music media business, "yes men." He wanted *Fader* to know he was a real musician, who gave his all to the creative process, not just some white rapper profiting off of hip-hop. "What he really wanted to impress upon me was that he was not the same artist he was two years ago and that he understood why it didn't necessarily connect right away," Cohn said. "He was very self-aware."

Fader editor-in-chief, Matthew Schnipper, eventually agreed to the cover story; to pen it, he turned to Andrew "Noz" Nosnitsky. Noz had been one of the first journalists to write about Odd Future, and as a critic was renowned for celebrating undiscovered talent while savagely laying into those he deemed unworthy.

Dissing Malcolm on Twitter had become one of Noz's favorite pastimes, and unlike the Pitchfork review, which had clearly unnerved him, Malcolm was good-natured about Noz's ribbing. Rather than sic his fan base on Noz, he would respond to him directly with playful Internet banter, the type not uncommon in the social media age.

"Noz used to shit on him relentlessly," said Insanul Ahmed. But one of Malcolm's charms seemed to be that, once you got in a room with him, it was hard not to be taken with his charms. He began leaning into this strategy around then.

"Right after the *Complex* piece I did on him, he did a lot of press with people who used to shit on him," Ahmed said. "Another music critic, David Drake, called this the Mac Miller charm offensive. He was such a jovial guy. People liked hanging out with him."

Invariably, the music critics he charmed would write positive stories, but Noz was not easily swayed. A professional skeptic, he thought little of Mac's overtures, and in his *Fader* piece argued that critics actually hadn't gotten his music wrong at all: it really wasn't very good, he argued, derivative of the nineties in only the worst ways. He felt that if Malcolm had been labeled a frat rapper, it was likely because, at least back then, he really was one.

"He claims to have stumbled onto the persona, but it's a believable one," Noz wrote. The piece alleged that Malcolm's desire to make everyone feel comfortable made him overcompensate by outwardly projecting the image of "carefree party dude," even if that wasn't necessarily who he was.[41]

His new music, however, had redeeming qualities. Noz's take on *Watching Movies with the Sound Off* was that it had no hits. And that was its appeal. Describing it as "deeply insular," he noted that it was the kind of album that, in the nineties, would have only exchanged hands via dubbed cassettes, friends passing it on to others, as if to say: Check this out.

This, Noz seemed to suggest, was more authentic to who Malcolm really was—or, at the very least, more becoming of the man he was turning out to be. No longer a kid making boom bap songs, this was someone living in LA, filling his house with some of the most creative hip-hop artists of the day, who seemed to relish the opportunity to turn his haters into fans. The challenge alone was worth the fight.

Even one of his biggest critics, Jordan Sargent, got a crack at it. He had dissed Malcolm in Pitchfork, his review sending Malcolm into an emotional tailspin, but Malcolm came face-to-face with him, hoping to turn his hate into love, and ultimately win his approval. Like Noz, Sargent would pen a profile—this one for *SPIN*.

"I wanna say it was their idea to have this meet-up between me and him," Sargent said. "I didn't really want to be a huge part of the story. There's a history of rappers and journalists getting into physical altercations—it definitely crossed my mind."

But when Sargent and Malcolm finally met, he was taken aback by how nice he and everyone around him seemed to be. "Mac was kind of bashful, kind of awkward," he said. "It was disarming. And when we chatted, we got along fairly well. It wasn't combative. It was just nervous tension. At the time, his beard was grown out, and he had tattoos . . . he just looked like a young kid."

Sargent went into writing the profile having been Malcolm's fiercest critic yet. "This is just corny music," he recalled thinking of *Blue Slide Park*. But when he began collaborating with Sweatshirt and ScHoolboy Q, Sargent was interested in how someone who he felt was unimpressive had become close with rappers who were, according to him, "the coolest rappers going."

He, too, was taken with *Watching Movies with the Sound Off.* "I think that's his best album—I genuinely enjoyed the music," Sargent said. "And I didn't want to write a redemptive narrative story about him at the time if I thought the music was still shit. But that album is pretty dope. His music got better. That became apparent when I started reporting the story—that he was definitely a [real] musician. I went and saw him live; he played piano onstage, he covered D'Angelo. And that started to come through his work directly after *Blue Slide Park.*"[42]

Still, there was the lingering question, at the time, of whether it was all a ruse. "Mac Miller Is Cool Now," read the headline accompanying Sargent's piece.

"He was still perceived at that time to be on the boundaries—like, 'Should we be taking this person seriously?'" Sargent said. "It was supposed to come off like 'This is what this person wants you to think.' People took it as more like a declaration; whereas, it was more like this is what this person wants you to believe. It was true to a certain extent, and that was my objective observation, hinting at it like, 'Here's the new narrative on this person.'"[43]

In the article, Malcolm predicted that the artists in his circle would soon be running things. "I really envision all of us at the Grammys kicking it: 'Ha ha, bitch, beat you,'" he said. "No one is looking at music right now the way we are. There are no boundaries, bro."[44]

Some critics felt the same.

Calling it a "quantum leap in artistry," Craig Jenkins awarded the album a 7.0 in Pitchfork, writing: "Mac Miller of *Watching Movies*, who feels comfortable trading verses with rap nerd favorites like Jay Electronica and Action Bronson, largely succeeds in distancing himself from the guy peddling kiddie-pool deep rhymes about drinking 40s in front of the police just two years prior."[45]

And at *XXL*, Sean Ryon was equally impressed. Dubbing it an "engrossing listen," he said: "Mac Miller's sophomore effort is a surprising and focused album from an artist fed up with his public perception. He does enough here to prove his point."[46]

But not all were sold. Your humble narrator reviewed the record for *Vibe.* I felt that while the album was solid—"The Star Room," "Objects in the Mirrors," "S.D.S.," and "Gees" were standouts—at times the record was abstract to the point of being almost inaccessible; infused with self-pity, it seemed to circle the drain on a subject that Malcolm was unable, or unwilling, to fully address.

The heaviness was symptomatic of Malcolm's mood at the time, and even if the album suffered from it, there was nothing he could do. "The more I make this sad music," he said, "the sadder I get."[47]

His endless tinkering aside, a lot of the music was made spur of the moment, without a ton of premeditation. Like "REMember," a track he wrote in memory of Reuben Mitriani, a childhood friend that had recently passed away. Much like "Poppy," he cut the song almost as soon as he returned from the funeral.

"The first thing I did when I get home is made that song," he told Billboard. "That's why I love that song. Because it is that emotion. It's not in retrospect. I didn't wait two months and then make a song. I made the song . . . while the shit that haunted me from the funeral was still [there]."[48]

"Objects in the Mirror," he said, was a commentary on addiction—something he was well acquainted with. Using a woman as a metaphor, he compared his lust for a partner to his desire for a certain kind of high. "Youforia" was metaphorical too. On the track, he sings: "I been waiting so long (Been waiting) / To have you by my side (Tell you, 'I love you')". The song is notably vague, and could mean anything, but Malcolm did have something specific in mind when he wrote it.

"I realized everything is about the vagina," he said. "That is the mecca of life—the vagina. I realized it. Think about it. It's the most powerful thing in the world."[49]

There were other references to powerful things—like fentanyl, a synthetic opioid fifty times more powerful than heroin, which was only known, back then, to the most serious of drug users. "Love me, love me, that fentanyl, it numb me / Beautiful, it get ugly, turn you into a junkie . . ." he raps on "Someone Like You."

And on multiple songs (notably "S.D.S." and "I'm Not Real"), he addresses Mac Miller as a concept in people's minds—a persona, not a person—that isn't an accurate representation of who he actually is. "I just don't believe I am an actual person," he explained in an annotation on the lyric website Genius. "I'm actually just an idea to everybody. We don't actually exist as people to anybody, we exist thru [sic] the ideas that we give to the world."[50]

In his own way, too, he took out whatever frustrations he might have had with Benjy. His verse on "Suplexes Inside of Complexes and Duplexes" was said to have been written directly about their disagreements. Labeling him a "suit vest," he pictured Benjy telling him: "What the fuck you got to be sad 'bout? Go 'head and rap now."

"I feel like that's one big diss track against fuckin' Benjy," said Ritz Reynolds. "I'm sure Mac loved him. But when he came around, there was that mood, it was kind of like—*the suit is here.*"

For its June 18 release date, *Watching Movies with the Sound Off* went head-to-head in a sales battle with Kanye West's *Yeezus*, J. Cole's *Born Sinner*, and a new album from Quasimoto, producer Madlib's side project where he raps as his alter ego Lord Quas in a high-pitched voice.

"Let us not forget about Quasimoto, also dropping on the eighteenth," he told DJ Semtex in an interview. "J. Cole, Statik Selektah, Mac Miller, Kanye West, Quasimoto."[51]

When the dust settled, Kanye was number one on the charts, Cole was number two, and Malcolm was number three. With 102,000 copies sold in week one, he was surprised by how well the album performed. Given the record's themes, he said sales weren't on his mind when he made it.[52]

Regardless, the war between the artist and the suit was over. And the artist, Mac Miller, had won.

FIFTEEN

Malcolm toured in support of *Watching Movies with the Sound Off*. He dubbed the thirty-eight-date run of shows the Space Migration tour. As supporting acts, he brought Chance the Rapper, the Internet, and Earl Sweatshirt. In addition, a slew of REMember Music artists—the Come-Up, Njomza, Dylan Reynolds, Hardo, Choo Jackson, and Primavera Vills, all of whom he was hoping to break.

Some dates he was joined by Action Bronson; others, Meek Mill. Being a rap tour, it was also not uncommon to find Tyler, the Creator; Childish Gambino; Vince Staples; and ScHoolboy Q rocking. If there were any doubts that Malcolm not only belonged in hip-hop, but was also a real musician, someone worthy of praise and serious discussion, this was the tour that finally silenced them.

The last time Malcolm toured, he was playing arenas, venues he struggled to fill. Concurrently, his recreational use of lean became a full-blown addiction, and things got a little messy. But on this tour, he seemed to have a more firm grasp on how to handle his vices, and things were good.

To account for what had occurred when he tried selling out arenas, Space Migration was scaled back—venues were smaller and dates were fewer. At the Hollywood Palladium, he played for 3,800 people. At The Hard Rock Live, in Orlando, Florida—3,000. The Ritz, in Raleigh, North Carolina—1,400. These weren't big places. But smaller rooms meant fans were pulled in tighter, and onstage he was closer to the crowd. Like his early tours, the vibe was festive, the shows felt as much like a party as they did a concert.

His supporting acts, too, helped. Just as he had once done by making Kendrick Lamar his opener, with Chance the Rapper and The Internet and Earl, he was giving people a real reason to come out. For that, he often relied on Q, who just as he had done in his *Jenesis* magazine days, kept his ear to the street. "He was always in the know with who's poppin', who's coming out, all that type shit," said Clockwork. "He would tell Mac—'Yo, these are the artists that are poppin', bro. You need to go on the road with them.' So, Q brought Chance the Rapper, Vince Staples . . . it was a fucking packed tour. Everybody was cool."

If the goal was to give fans a good experience, he also wanted to make it positive for the artists touring with him. For his part, he may have felt that he was exhibiting good will, providing them a platform to reach fans who might otherwise not check for them. As a supporting act himself, his experience early in his career wasn't always so positive.

"When Mac first came out, Mac and Wiz were getting booked together everywhere," said Clockwork, who recalled Malcolm opening for Wiz at Roseland, in New York, and described it as one of the worst shows he'd ever done. "We came out and nobody moved. Those muhfuckas booed! But he knew why it was happening. He knew he was getting booed because he wasn't Taylor Gang and they just didn't fuck with his shit. Taylor Gang muhfuckas don't give a fuck about nobody but Taylor Gang. And when Mac first came out, Taylor Gang fans was not fucking with Mac."

That was then, though, and this was now. *Watching Movies with the Sound Off* had been successful, and Malcolm's depressed mood, which seemed to have informed so much of the record, appeared to have improved. The show, itself, was rather interesting—"You are about to begin a journey into the cosmos," an Orson Welles–like voice boomed as the night began. Mac was playing instruments onstage during the show, pausing to strum along to "Best Day Ever" on acoustic guitar; it was a rap concert, but it was so much more. Things were fun again.

Having a band, the Internet, helped. Fronted by Syd tha Kyd (vocals), Matt Martians (keyboards/vocals) and Steve Lacy (guitar), they refreshed Malcolm's sound, making it lush and organic. He relished in the fact that they were kids his age, too, not touring business lifers, like some musicians were, bouncing from one tour to the next, taking whatever gig came their way.

"I didn't hire no thirty-year-old studio musicians that want to stand back there and play," he said. "These are me and my homies that are my age. To have young people that love hip-hop and love playing instruments, really making music live right there for you, is a beautiful thing."[1]

The band upped the ante, made it a show worth seeing. "People never seen Mac with a band before," said Clockwork. "He's singing live, he's playing the guitar, he's on the drums. Our stage performance was so good. I thought—he's got a band now, oh here we go. But it fit perfectly. Everything was so tight. The Internet was so cool. They made me feel like I was the maestro. It made me feel like I was a part of something. That tour was literally the funnest tour that I was ever a part of."

The audience was still mostly kids, teens and twentysomethings in tank tops, snapbacks, Vans, and Supreme. But whatever Malcolm was selling, they were buying. They knew all the words to *Watching Movies with the Sound Off*, even though it had just come out.

Two years earlier, A.D. Amorosi at the *Philadelphia Inquirer* watched his show and said: "Mac Miller is the Ramones of rap with a predilection for keeping it simple . . . the goods were the goods and Mac Miller didn't have them."[2] Now, reviews were overwhelmingly positive.

"Mac's performance consisted of no gaudy chains, no posse to accompany him on stage and none of the antics he portrays on his *Most Dope* TV show. It was all about the music," Chris Harris wrote for *Vibe*. "As the crowd filed out, it was apparent Mac had conducted an out-of-this-world experience."

After a tour stop in St. Louis, Missouri, Brendan Smith wrote: "His set was equal parts hyper hip-hop, rebellious punk energy and shoegazing indie rock . . . Miller's performance proved he was more than just a rapper."[3]

And in the *Hollywood Reporter*, Jenevieve Ting described the show as "focused, raw, unapologetic," noting that he had "come a long way since his K.I.D.S. mixtape."[4]

Malcolm was really grooving now, in the zone. The tour ended in August; by September, he was on *Good Morning America* performing "The Way" with Ariana Grande (the song had peaked at number nine on the *Billboard* Hot

100); in October he was to leave for a string of European dates—this time as a supporting act for Lil Wayne. These would be arenas again, in places like Ireland, France, Belgium, Germany, Sweden, Norway, and Denmark.

He took MTV to Europe and shot parts of the reality show's second and final season there. One episode finds him in Ireland, where, between promotional stops, he traces his Irish heritage. Another episode sees him traveling home again, this time to receive the key to the city of Pittsburgh. Back home, he learns his grandmother has been keeping a scrapbook of everything he had ever done, then he stops at Timebomb and his old haunt ID Labs before receiving the key from Mayor Luke Ravenstahl—a key that his brother, Miller, who by then was working as a graphic designer, was asked to design. The mayor declares September 13, 2013, "Mac Miller Day," and viewers watch as Mac is unsure what to say for his acceptance speech.

"I'm not giving an amazing speech," he tells his mother.

"Just think amazing," she says. "You're amazing."

When he finally gets onstage, he thanks his brother for designing the key. "You're the talented one in the family," he says. "I just pretend."

Then he presses on.

"When I was about fifteen years old, I told everyone I would be a rapper. I'm gonna make music. They looked at me like I was crazy. But I did it. Not to be cliché and cheesy, but I'm gonna be cliché and cheesy. They say never forget where you came from. But it's true and I do believe we come from the greatest city in the world. Study hard and rep Pittsburgh, baby."

Shooting of the second season was much smoother than the first, though it had been delayed for a handful of reasons. One reason was that he just didn't want to do it.

"He was tired of it," said Bill Niels. "I remember him feeling like it was fake."

Other members of the Most Dope family complained about the cameras, a sentiment that seemed to be shared by everyone at the time—including Malcolm. "They would literally just be going about their day," said Bill. "And the MTV crew would stop them and ask them to do something again. Oh, say that again and do that again. They were tired of that."

His health was also a concern. He had notably sobered up, at least somewhat, to shoot the first season. But privately, MTV producers expressed concern about Malcolm's well-being. They wanted to shoot the show, but felt it was important for him to be in the right head space before they began.

When they were assured that he was healthy, they began making slight tweaks and set out to begin. Chelsea Fodero had come on as Malcolm's day-to-day manager, and she played a large role in the second season, providing a much-needed feminine voice on what was, for all intents and purposes, a sausage fest. Malcolm's mom, too, who shot the photo used on the cover of *Watching Movies with the Sound Off*—against a red background, Malcolm sitting naked at a table, an angel hovering above as a red apple sits in front, tempting him—got more camera time.

"The relationship with his mother was real," said Darin Byrne. "His mother was just a nice, kindhearted woman, and she stayed out of his way, let him be his own man, and his own creator. His mother made an impression on me, just as far as how proud of her son she was."

His dad was also a presence, having appeared in an occasional episode, as was his brother Miller (who, like his mom, had helped with *Watching Movies with the Sound Off*, designing the cover). Finally, there was the acknowledgment of Malcolm's girlfriend, Nomi, which took some cajoling on the part of MTV.

"He was cool with basically everything except his relationship," said Byrne, who noted that Malcolm always had misgivings about scenes with other women in them. It seemed to be a point of stress, and something that he didn't want to bring unnecessary attention to. For example, in season one he traveled to Las Vegas for his birthday party. When girls got involved with the day's shoot, he begged off. "He didn't take part in it," Byrne recalled. "He ended up going back and creating beats that night."

But there was always a desire, at least on MTV's part, to get Nomi into the show. Making reality shows with musicians was tough though because they wanted to keep their private lives private. "We definitely talked about it, and he was very much like, '*I don't want her to be a part of it*,'" Byrne said. "And I don't think it was just coming from him, it might have also been coming from her. I sensed when it came to personal relationships or hookups, he didn't want that to be captured. But Nomi—definitely—he was in a relationship with her. That was happening."

The relationship was a poorly kept secret for years. Nomi would periodically travel with Malcolm, accompanying him on tours. She'd been vaguely referenced in numerous songs. And he was open about *Macadelic*, saying that it was inspired by their ups and downs.

"*Macadelic* was all about us," he said. "This love/drugs stuff, how love and drugs are the same thing—our relationship was fucking me up. It made me think of myself as a bad person."[5]

The relationship had been a rocky one, though his friends say he loved her more than anything. "He would have done anything for her," said Clockwork. "Not that he had to—I mean, this is Mac Miller. At this point, he could have had any girl that he wanted. But he was really in love with her. He was dedicated to her. He was selfless when it came to her. He would send her flowers and shit when he was on the road. He would switch up whenever she would come to the shows. She would just bring the light—it was a good aura."

But he wasn't always faithful. One pal put it bluntly: "He cheated on her all the time."

Despite the tumultuous nature of the relationship, they were committed to making it work. "They was still deeply in love and still tryna work shit out, whatever *it* is," said Clockwork.

Acknowledging that it was "not the most healthy at times,"[6] Nomi kept a blog, which she updated often. She had always been a writer, and Malcolm encouraged her to publish, even when she didn't want to.[7]

In her writings, early on, she seemed as if she were head over heels for Malcolm, proud of what he had become. She would post photos of his wins—like *Blue Slide Park* going number one—and pen the occasional post hinting at their life together.

But as people involved with celebrities often do, she struggled sharing him with the world.[8] There was always distance between them. Work kept him on the road, and the more his star rose, the more she felt her grip on him loosening.[9]

Her posts would progressively change, mirroring the relationship itself. Sometimes, her mind wandered, wondering if sitting alone at her home in Philly was what people thought the life of a rapper's girlfriend was actually like. She openly wondered, on some occasions, why he wasn't texting her back.[10]

In one post, written in October of 2012, she flat-out declared her love for him, saying she didn't care about all the issues in their relationship—namely, the fact that he was becoming so famous, while all around him, there were all these other women.[11]

By the winter, according to her writings, the relationship had gone cold; but then, by spring of 2013 it was back on, when she moved to Los Angeles for an internship. In LA, she had her own apartment, enjoyed her work, and was closer to Malcolm. Still, she felt unsettled.[12]

The seesaw nature of their romance hit the skids again that summer. She likened him to a twelve-year-old[13]; Malcolm, meanwhile, told *Fader* the two were finished, then doubled back: "It's still not 100% over." The relationship, as far as anyone could tell, was *complicated*.

When it was good, though, it was good. On the road, Malcolm would dote on her. "When he started getting a little money, they'd go shopping and come back with bags and bags," recalled Clockwork. "The whole tour bus would be filled with Louis Vuitton, Gucci, crazy shit. He'd be on bended knee like, 'Whatever you want.'"

She was careful, however, to not lean on Malcolm for too much help. The occasional splurge—fine. But anything more, like a career boost, she seemed determined to achieve on her own. Arthur Pitt recalled her being very independent. She focused intensely on her writing, which most people around Malcolm believed she displayed a real talent for.

"She was a smart girl," he said. "And I think she always tried to do her own thing."

But the demands of his career had him always putting on a show. Perhaps it was for her. Perhaps for other people. Perhaps, sometimes, even for himself. There was a character he now played, and it was hard to tell where the person he pretended to be ended and the person he really was began.

In an interview with the *Huffington Post* to promote *Watching Movies*, he said: "Am I speaking to you as Malcolm McCormick right now? Or am I speaking to you as Mac Miller? Who knows? I don't even know anymore."[14]

That is, unless he was with Nomi.

"When it came to her, he wasn't Mac Miller," said Clockwork. "He was Malcolm."

• • •

While his relationship was the source of much anxiety—he and Nomi were back on when he left for a European tour in the fall of 2013—there were other issues that gnawed at Malcolm.

In an interview with *Fader*, he acknowledged that he'd gone through a dark period; his relationship, he said, had gotten to him, and his relentless touring schedule took its toll.[15]

The question of what effect touring had on him is an interesting one, for touring was one of the chief ways that money was made—not just for him, but for his label.

He worked himself to the bone, and while he never publicly acknowledged any issues with Rostrum, he did have his grievances. In 2013, according to *Forbes*, Wiz Khalifa had earned fourteen million dollars, while Malcolm had brought in six. Based on the nature of their 360 deals, Rostrum was allegedly taking a cut of this money. So, they were successful.[16]

But it was still operating as a small company with limited staff. Its two stars were often in competition for attention, with the chief breadwinner, Wiz, often appearing to win out. There was never any real beef between Malcolm and Wiz, but there was simmering resentment.

"Wiz felt like Mac was only successful because he came first, that he paved that trail," a source close to the label said. "Meanwhile, Mac really wanted Wiz to acknowledge him."

In the middle was Rostrum, which was spread thin. Making matters worse, the label seemed determined to expand, investing resources that Malcolm may have believed were better served supporting him, in breaking new, largely unproven artists.

"There was a lot of tension," said Artie, noting that he knew there were real issues when Malcolm hired his own publicity team. "I was working my ass off. And I heard from people that he wanted to leave. He talked about it too. He'd say: *'What are you doing, motherfucker? Why aren't I getting more of a push?* And I'd say, *'Dude, I love you, you know. But . . . I don't cut the checks.'* "

Malcolm seemed to believe he deserved better. A source close to the label recalled one particular incident, when the label pushed back about a video budget, that really got to him.

With tensions quietly brewing, in late 2013 Malcolm and Benjy met for dinner. The contract Malcolm had signed was due to end, and there was the prospect of future business to discuss.

In an interview with the website DJ Booth, Benjy recalled that the feeling between them was mutual: with Rostrum acting as manager and record label, things weren't really working out. Benjy suggested Rostrum stay on as management, while Malcolm signed a record deal elsewhere.[17]

But Malcolm didn't seem enthused about that idea. He told him he loved him, said he was proud of the things they'd accomplished, but that he wanted to go in a different direction.[18]

Artie was in bed when he got the news. It was New Year's Eve and he woke up to a missed call. It was four A.M. in New York; one A.M. in Los Angeles.

'Sorry, I can't do this anymore, I met with Benjy, I'm really sorry,' Malcolm wrote him. "I care about you more than music."

Looking back, Artie remembered how polite Malcolm had been about leaving. Still, he was stunned. "I thought I was gonna work with him forever," he said. "I was just kind of floating. Like, what the fuck? This sucks. Shit. Essentially, we had been fired."

While Artie took to crying in his Bedford-Stuyvesant apartment, Malcolm exited 2013 having engineered one of the most remarkable turnarounds in music history. He had not only released *Watching Movies with the Sound Off* to acclaim, he had also dropped *Live from Space* as a live album with five new songs (including "Life," the track he'd left off *Watching Movies* that finds him killing his girl), a beat tape (*Run-On Sentences Vol. 1*), and produced an entire mixtape, *Stolen Youth*, which had arguably launched the career of Vince Staples.

Staples was a rapper from Long Beach, California, who—when he met Malcolm—had not been very keen on rapping at all. At the time, he was palling around with Earl Sweatshirt, who had just returned from Samoa; accompanying him to Malcolm's house one day, he introduced himself. "*I know who you are, why don't you make more music?*," he recalled Malcolm asking him.

He told Malcolm he didn't have any beats. Malcolm told him he was making beats now, and said to return in two weeks.[19]

Two weeks later, Staples returned. Malcolm had beats ready to go and recording on *Stolen Youth* commenced. The mixtape took two weeks to record, a few months to polish; shortly afterward, it was out, released on the Internet, and Vince Staples's career began. He was never shy about crediting Malcolm for helping him—"There is no Vince Staples music without Mac Miller . . ." he once tweeted[20]—and he told *Complex* in 2013 that Malcolm was "one of my best friends in music."[21]

Malcolm shared similar bonds with ScHoolboy Q and Ab-Soul, who, along with Jay Rock and Kendrick Lamar, comprised the TDE supergroup Black Hippy. They, too, would hang around Malcolm's house; their frequent chill sessions led to numerous collaborations, with Ab-Soul recording much of his third album, *These Days*, in the Sanctuary.

"He was one of us," TDE engineer Derek "MixedByAli" Ali, said, calling him an honorary TDE member. "You could crack jokes on him and he wouldn't give a fuck. He was just the homie. He was our friend. He would come by Kendrick sessions and talk shit. This was before anyone blew up. Mac blew up way before anyone else. He would come through, chill and smoke. When he had his big ass crib in Studio City, we would go and just sleep at his crib for weeks at a time. We were just broke. He was family. It's really hard to explain. He was the fifth Black Hippy. He was with it."[22]

Another pal, Snoop Dogg, who he'd met socially, led to his appearance in a film: *Scary Movie 5*, part of an all-star cast including Charlie Sheen, Lindsay Lohan, Mike Tyson, Jerry O'Connell, Usher, Katt Williams, Ashley Tisdale, Katrina Bowden, Sarah Hyland, and many others. But it was comedian Mike Epps who he had to thank for his inclusion.

Originally, Epps was to be featured in a scene with Snoop Dogg, but an argument with producer Harvey Weinstein—in which Epps called Harvey a "bitch-ass ni**a"—led to him storming off. Snoop was stuck; he needed someone for the role, so he started dialing up people he knew. The only problem was, nobody was answering his calls.

"I called all kind of ni**as and Mac Miller picked up," Snoop recalled in a conversation with Schoolboy Q. "I'm like, *Mac, I need you in this movie, cuh.*

He's like, *What you need, Unc?* That ni**a showed up, we blew dope, he learned his lines and, ni**a, it was some classic shit . . . my ni**a was there for me."

Noting that Snoop hadn't called him, Schoolboy joked that he wanted to "get the white boy on the case."

"I needed to get the white boy because he had flavor," Snoop said. "I fucked with him, man. On some real shit I used to fuck with him, cuz. That's what hip-hop is about to where it don't have no color to it. We at the point now where we don't even look at where a ni**a from, what color he is, none of that shit. It used to be a time where we had walls and brackets to where you can't fuck with him because he this, and he that. I'm so thankful that hip-hop has grown, to where ni**as can do shit . . . That was my ni**a. I called him White Chocolate."[23]

Friends like these clearly had benefits. The film aside, producing for others made him focus more intensely on making beats; the more beats he made, the better he got. He had produced some of the beats on *Watching Movies with the Sound Off*, but was now taking the reins completely, as seen on one of his most interesting projects—a mixtape called *Delusional Thomas*.

A dark brooding work, *Delusional Thomas* finds his vocals pitched up into chipmunk-like squawk, not unlike the Quasimoto record, *Yessir Whatever*, he had talked up months earlier. He told *VICE* that he loved Quasimoto, and felt that pitched-up voice was similar to what the evil voice inside him sounded like.[24]

Delusional Thomas is an awkward and at times bracing listen; the lyrics on it are pained and dense, each line crafted to achieve maximum shock, a peek at his fractured psyche.

As on much of his music from this period, he's open about his addictions. On "The Jesuits," for instance, he admits that beating one addiction only leads him to another; deep inside, all he seems to be doing is running from himself. "I'm tired . . ." he declares.

On "Larry," he seems done with his fame, his legion of supporters, the Mac Heads, who track his every move, trapping him in a prison of their expectations. He calls them a "hundred million mini-me's," and seems inclined to get rid of them, somehow. And on "Grandpa Used to Carry a Flask," he talks of suicide, says he kicks it with "God and Satan," while keeping "coke in the Parliaments."

Guests are limited: just Earl Sweatshirt, Da$h, and Mac's old pal Bill Niels, who assists on the aptly-titled "Bill," the product of a spontaneous recording session that unspooled one day when Bill was staying with Malcolm at the mansion.

Described by Earl as "just some random-ass ni**a," when it was Bill's turn to rap, he stepped to the microphone. And Earl was blown away by what he heard. "[Bill] bodied everyone," Earl said, to the point where he and Malcolm had to rewrite their verses.[25]

But that was the beauty of the Sanctuary. Someone completely random could be sitting there, then find themselves on a song with two of the biggest artists in hip-hop. The vibe was free-flowing and improvisational, completely spur-of-the-moment.

Clockwork said Malcolm was "completely fucked up" when he made *Delusional Thomas*. But making it was helpful. It was a way to exorcise demons.

"It's therapeutic," Malcolm said. "I'm not a violent person at all. But have I had violent, evil thoughts? Yeah, doesn't everybody? I think it's kind of therapeutic to just take yourself there. Take a trip. It's all about the ride. And you go, and you just fucking become this psychopathic murderer, demented person. And then you live in that for a little bit. It's a subject. I don't want to stray away from any subject."[26]

Precisely *because* the music was shocking is why he wanted to do it. "I just feel like everyone has that shit in them," he said. "It felt so good to go in and just fuckin' talk about the sadistic urges that everybody else has but doesn't want to say."[27]

As for the alter ego, it was a way to channel his emotions into someone that was him, while not wholly representative of the character Mac Miller. Mac Miller would not get by making such a raw and unfiltered record, filled with anger and despair. "Everything that's done as Mac Miller is factual and based on factual information," he said. "Delusional Thomas, he's a character I created—he's like [a] psychopathic murderer."[28]

It wasn't on brand, but he didn't care. He just had to get it out. And whoever got it, got it. "We're all complex and we're all made up of more than one dimension," he said. "And the thing about this place that art lives in is that people get these labels. You brand yourself and have to stick to one brand, which I fucking hate. Like, human beings are more complex than just one simple brand."[29]

Another project he made around then would wind up among his most celebrated.

"I was not on planet earth when I made *Faces*," he wrote in a tweet. "Nowhere close."

"*Faces* was the craziest moment," said Clockwork. "It's really where you could hear his cry for help. *Faces* was a really dark moment for everybody. Like on a roller coaster, when you go up—*Blue Slide Park*; *Best Day Ever*; *I Love Life, Thank You*; *Macadelic*, then *Faces*. *Faces* is the drop."

Work on *Faces* began around the time *Watching Movies with the Sound Off* was being created, and continued through the new year. So too, did a separate project called *Balloonerism*, which was completed in late March. For reasons that aren't quite clear, he eventually scrapped *Balloonerism* (the record has since been leaked online) in favor of *Faces,* releasing it on May 11, 2014—Mother's Day. Friends dubbed it his "coke album," because Malcolm was back into drugs in a major way.

"He was partying hard, enjoying all his hard work, everything he had done," said Will Kalson, who was living in the mansion despite battling his own addictions. "I felt like he was just kind of enjoying it. I didn't feel like he was struggling, necessarily. But he was definitely going too hard, staying up all night doing coke in the studio. There was drugs everywhere. The Sanctuary was a place that everyone who was buzzing was trying to go to. So, of course, people are coming over with lean, people are coming over with drugs. I remember RiFF RAFF snorting lines of coke off the counter; Ab-Soul, he's pouring up."

At times, shit got messy.

"Things were getting kinda crazy," said a producer Malcolm had asked to work with his childhood friend Dylan Reynolds. "He was in a heavy cocaine period. This is definitely one of the madder periods. It was nuts in the house. It was complicated. I remember being there, and his pops was there. I don't think he had really seen him. He was really concerned, like: 'I wanna see my son, he's downstairs sleeping and if anyone's going to see him, I'm gonna see him!' Clearly, there was some sort of intervention shit going on. He probably looked at me and my buddy as people who were hanging on. Just [two] of the

ambiguous people showing up at the house. Meanwhile, Mac has been downstairs for two days or some shit, sleeping because he probably was on a bender."

The drugs were getting the best of him, and even when he was lucid, he
wasn't the nicest guy to be around.

"Me and Dylan Reynolds were working one time, and he just busts
in the room and goes, 'Change this, change this, change this' . . . just being
obnoxious," the same producer said. "He was the king of the castle. It was his
house and he did what he wanted. To be honest, I have a little bit of a temper,
and I got mad at him. Like, 'You little fucker, I will fight you.' I put my [fists]
up. I think Nomi was sitting right there. I was serious; like, 'Motherfucker, I
will punch you in your face.' And I just walked out."

But the drugs were necessary, in a way. They enhanced his writing;
when he was too tired to work, they kept him going. "Seventy-five percent of
the fuel tank of drug consumption is for the purpose of keeping the machine
running," the producer recalled thinking at the time. "He just wanted to create
and create."

It was hard to argue with the results. Though it played like a suicide note
written and recorded to rap beats, *Faces* was shaping up to be one of his better
mixtapes, arguably the best thing he had ever done. Still, the worries remained.
Everyone around him was united on one front: *Don't let him overdose.*

"There's a few times I went to sleep not sure I was gonna wake up,"
he admitted.[30]

"I thought that he could die any day," said Clockwork. "I had never seen
anybody go that ham before. I've seen bruh do enough drugs to where the
average person would have overdosed. It was everything but crack and heroin,
a smorgasbord of shit. You've got a table, you've got all your studio equipment,
but to the left and right of you is like two Jameson bottles, ten Styrofoam cups,
random powders here, balled-up dollar bills, baggies of drugs to the left, a
little weed right here. I ain't never seen no shit like that before. It was a candy
store. I would date girls, see certain girls, fuck on certain girls, I'd wake up in
the middle of the night, they're not even in my room. They in the fuckin' Red
Room doing drugs with this muhfucka. In the morning he'd be like, 'Bro, who
is your homegirl? She was all in the fuckin' studio doing all my drugs' . . . But
there was a lot of great things that came out of the shit."

And it wasn't like everyone was worried. To the uninitiated, it may have seemed as if Malcolm were doing a lot of drugs. He may have even thought that he was doing too much. But some of his close friends were even more into drugs than he was and to them he was something of a lightweight.

"I was basically a fucking drug addict in a mansion—Mac's mansion—with a five-hundred-dollar hoodie on," said Bill Niels. "I was no more than a drug addict on the street, just disguised in nice clothes with a famous friend. But Mac, I did not ever observe him to have an addictive personality like me. I remember one time we were doing coke, and there was this big pile of coke still on the table, and he was like, 'All right, well, I'm gonna go upstairs now and go to sleep. To me, that made no sense; I had to do every bit of drugs that was there until it was gone. I was an addict in the grips of addiction. I just couldn't stop. I just had no willpower and I just had to do everything in front of me. It always boggled my mind that Mac could just put it down."

Most importantly, he kept it together. "A lot of people think he was this big druggie and he wasn't," said Franchise. "I feel like he had binges. He had moments in time where he might've been using a little more than before; then he'd slow down or stop, and he'd gradually go back into it. He never looked like a junkie. He was never nodding off or looking weird to me. I know junkies from Braddock, [Pennsylvania]. I've seen it my whole life. He didn't look like the motherfuckers I grew up around."

Nevertheless, Malcolm saw his drug use as a portal for tapping an unknown source within himself. *Faces* is heavy. Life and death are its two overarching themes. Life, for he felt he had really made it; death, because he'd found out the whole pursuit was pointless. "I've been to the mountaintop," Prince once said. "There's nothing there."[31] Malcolm, it seemed, felt the same way.

The beauty of *Faces* is that, like much of Malcolm's music, it's a delicate dance between dark and light. He is equally boastful ("Here We Go") as he is depressed, at once pleased with how far he's come ("Insomnia") as he is bothered by how empty everything he's worked for seems.

One of the mixtape's real standouts is "Diablo," a lyrical workout over a piano loop cribbed from Duke Ellington's "In a Sentimental Mood," where he puts on an epic display of rapping virtuosity. The video, filmed in front of an Echo Park pizzeria—and featuring his mom serving hot dogs and pickles from a food truck dubbed "Old Jewish"— (also the theme of a limited line of T-shirts he made with brand Diamond Supply)—he dedicated to his dog Ralphie, who, during the making of *Faces*, had gone missing. Malcolm believed he'd been dognapped.[32] The loss of the dog—who he later learned was eaten by a coyote[33]—saddened him, and may have inadvertently contributed to the mixtape's darkness.[34]

Numerous tracks on *Faces* find Malcolm prophesizing his own death. Dubbing himself a junkie, on "What Do You Do" he says "a drug habit like Philip Hoffman will probably put me in a coffin." His displeasure with life, his desire to simply exit from it, is perhaps best evidenced on "Happy Birthday," a song about a party happening for him right upstairs in his own house that he neglects to attend because of all the phony people who might be there, and how miserable that scene would make him feel.

And that was an actual thing that happened. "He made the song on his birthday, and there's a big-ass party going on upstairs," said Clockwork. "I was in the studio with him. I'm thinking it's about to be a happy song, and he's like—'Fuck birthdays. I hate my birthday. There's a party going on upstairs, I don't even want to go to it.' It was just the energy, the space he was in."

Like much of his music, the songs seemed to be almost biographical—a selfie as rap song, as opposed to a picture, capturing him in his element, for better or worse. "It's just being able to get out a lot of emotion at once, a lot of thoughts at once," he said. "However you can feel, you can make a song for that moment, and do it very cleverly."[35]

Some of the record's influences were obvious—Hunter S. Thompson, whose gonzo style of first-person journalism seemed to seep into Malcolm's approach to songwriting; Charles Bukowski, the underground poet with his drunken bravado, whose character appeared to have become one with Malcolm's; and then Timothy Leary, the shaman who foretold the pleasures of psychedelics. All these voices could be heard, literally, on the mixtape; audio clips were stitched between songs, pulling the nearly ninety-minute project into a cohesive body of work.

Finally, it's a pair of songs—companions, of a sort—that really drill down into what seemed to be going on when *Faces* was made. One is "Funeral," a pulsing march, a kind of soundtrack to his own send-off—"play this at my funeral," he suggests. And another is "Grand Finale," similarly obsessed with his own death, asking to be buried in his hometown, Pittsburgh's Allegheny County.

He produced the song himself, playing simple chords on a Nord synthesizer he had just gotten. That the chords were simple didn't bother him; after all, the history of popular music came down to only a handful of progressions.[36] "You speak with your hands and how you touch the keys," he said. "'The Grand Finale' was this idea of like—this is it."[37]

The intention, he said, was that the song would be the last he had ever made.[38] It wasn't, but it did signal the end of one thing. After all the studio sessions, TV episodes, parties, drugs, breakups, and makeups, he was moving out of the mansion—it was RIP to the Sanctuary.

"I kept on trying to say goodbye to the studio," he said of the song's creation. "In my mind, it is very iconic and very legendary; that room, the Red Room. If all goes according to plan, and we're all legends at the end of this, that room is a huge thing."

Leaving the room, leaving that house, came with its own set of problems. The life he was running away from, he would now have to face. Uncomfortable with fame, uncomfortable with himself, he wondered how he might adjust.

He feared that he would not survive in the real world. But in the studio, in the Sanctuary, all was right. Described as a dark, depressing place, he still loved it. "It's bad, but it's beautiful," he said. "I'm not in a beautiful place, and I can look back and say—I did it, I made it out alive."[39]

SIXTEEN

A year later, Malcolm was living in Brooklyn. The sprawling Studio City mansion had been swapped for a two-bedroom, two-bathroom tri-level penthouse at 50 Bridge Street, in Dumbo, with a balcony overlooking the Manhattan Bridge, and in the distance, sweeping views of Manhattan. He had come with Nomi in tow, driving a U-Haul from Pittsburgh, where he had spent much of the summer of 2015, to New York. He seemed determined to make his relationship work.

He still had a place in LA, a spot he shared with his brother, but New York was his home now, and his first time without anyone from the Most Dope crew around.

Will Kalson was back in Pittsburgh, in recovery. Peanut and TreeJ started a clothing line, then got to squabbling about its earnings before the former decamped to Miami and the latter went back to the 'Burgh. Big Dave had been replaced. Jimmy Murton was on a journey of self-discovery.[1] And with other friends, Bill Niels started a clothing line, too, Daily Bread, before his addiction issues landed him in prison.

For better or worse, everyone was moving on. But Malcolm was Mac Miller—and had things to attend to. Namely, a new album, *GO:OD AM*.

He did the bare minimum to promote *Faces*. Not that it would have mattered. The song with Rick Ross—"Insomniak"—had potential to break through. But when *Faces* came out, hip-hop was changing. That January,

Macklemore & Ryan Lewis's *The Heist* was up for Best Rap Album at the 2014 Grammys; also nominated were Drake (*Nothing Was the Same*), Kanye West (*Yeezus*), Jay-Z (*Magna Carta Holy Grail*), and Kendrick Lamar (*good kid, m.A.A.d city*).

After *Blue Slide Park*, it looked like Malcolm was set for pop stardom; he'd be that white dude vaguely connected to Black rap whose domain was a white world. But he rejected it, and other white rappers were only too happy to step into the lane he'd helped carve out for them.

Macklemore was from Seattle, Washington, and although much older than Malcolm, had a similar story; he, too, loved underground hip-hop, had respect for the culture, and was independently successful. *The Heist* was a major hit. Songs like "Can't Hold Us," "Thrift Shop," and "Same Love" (which he performed live on the Grammys, with thirty-three same-sex marriages taking place right in front of the audience) were everywhere.

Kendrick Lamar's *good kid, m.A.A.d. city*, however, was a different kind of album. A concept record, it soundtracked a day in the life of a young kid in Compton. "My whole story is about kids trying their best—the [Black] male or people in general trying to avoid the circumstances that's around them," Kendrick told me. "A kid growing up in a city, Compton or wherever you at, trying his best to escape the peer pressures of wherever you coming from. I think everybody can relate to it at the end of the day."[2]

Unlike *The Heist*, *GKMC* didn't have any radio hits. Pop radio did not play Kendrick Lamar. Nor did urban radio; but then, Kendrick Lamar made art. And Kendrick had captured the zeitgeist. But when the award was announced, and Macklemore won, hip-hop fans around the globe let out a collective groan. Even Macklemore.

"You got robbed," he wrote Kendrick in a text message after the show. "I wanted you to win. You should have. It's weird and sucks that I robbed you."[3]

Afterward, things were different. An injustice had been done. Macklemore knew it. Kendrick knew it. America knew it.

Malcolm wasn't Macklemore. He wasn't Iggy Azalea, Action Bronson, RiFF RAFF, G-Eazy, or any other white rapper.

But it didn't matter. White rappers appeared to be taking over. Eminem, OK; but that was years ago and he was legitimately great. This new crop, talented, sure. But still. It wasn't just one white rapper. It was multiple white rappers.

"Hip-hop is white now," hip-hop legend Scarface said at the time. "I feel like we losing it. I feel like the people that are in control of what Hip Hop does is so fucking White and so fucking Jewish and so they don't give a fuck about what the culture and the craft really is about . . . I fucking hate that shit. That shit pisses me off."[4]

Around that time, J. Cole dropped "Firing Squad," addressing the issue head-on: "History repeats itself and that's just how it goes . . . Look around, my ni**a, white people have snatched the sound."

Elaborating on his stance, Cole told Angie Martinez: "Hip-hop is like, completely white. It's fine; anybody could do whatever music they want, it's art. Jazz is a [Black] form of music in its origins. And not only is it a [Black] form of music, it was the hip-hop of its day. It was that much of a rebellious music. It hit me: This is the point in time where you see that switch in hip-hop. It's not Iggy Azalea's fault. It's not Eminem's fault. And I don't want to put Eminem in a category with anybody in terms of skill level. What I'm saying is, there comes a time when the system realizes that, I can sell this white person a lot easier. I fast forward 20, 30 years from now, and I see hip-hop being completely white."[5]

This was all happening against the backdrop of a transformative year. A year when Eric Garner was killed by police in Staten Island, Tamir Rice was killed by police in Cleveland, Jerame Reid was killed by police in Bridgeton, New Jersey, Rumain Brisbon was killed by police in Phoenix, Akai Gurley was killed by police in Brooklyn, Tanisha Anderson was killed by police in Cleveland, Dante Parker was killed by police in Victorville, California, Ezell Ford was killed by police in LA, and John Crawford III was killed by police in Beavercreek, Ohio. And those were just the killings that made national headlines.

But it was the police killing of Michael Brown—"Hands up, don't shoot"—and the Ferguson Uprising that really crystallized, in the most painful ways, issues that had been afflicting Black America for more than four hundred years. When it came to Black life mattering, a white rapper sitting in his mansion all in his feelings was the last thing anyone wanted to talk about. Malcolm was alive and well; he just wasn't . . . important. No white rappers were.

On the flip side, you had Donald Glover. Glover, too, had been written off by critics early in his career; a television actor who wanted to be a rapper, his music—nerdy and self-effacing—defied stereotypes. But despite not fitting the mold, he had become increasingly popular, and was now becoming more vocal about social issues. A completely non-threatening person, a famous one at that, he had still, because of the color of his skin, come face to face with police on two separate occasions that year. Had any white rappers been approached by the police? He didn't know. But still, it gave him pause, and in a poem entitled "Childish Gambino is a White Rapper," posted to his Twitter account just days after Michael Brown was killed, he intoned:[6] "i wanna be a white rapper/i wanna be so white im the biggest rapper of all time/i wanna be so white i can have a number one song with cursing and parents are fine with it."

•••

By the time Malcolm was prepping his third proper album, *GO:OD AM*, the world still felt like it was unraveling. Donald Trump was running for president and Black men, like Freddie Gray in Baltimore, were still being shot by police.

Malcolm implored people to not vote for Trump ("I fucking hate you, Donald Trump," he said on *The Nightly Show with Larry Wilmore*[7]). And he was publicly supportive of Black Lives Matter, at one point asking, via Twitter, what "white people who listen to rap" had done to support the movement.[8] While it was unclear what an accounting of his own efforts looked like, the sentiment was felt—what was happening in the world wasn't lost on him, and he was not so self-obsessed that he was blind to inequality and injustice. He was even becoming more self-aware, or at least more honest, about how he, himself, had benefited from his white privilege.

"I'm sure that a lot of my success is due to being white," he said in an interview with journalist Craig Jenkins. In the same breath, he told Jenkins it wasn't something he could be "mad at," that he just had to do the best he could, and work, as he has done, to earn respect, despite the privilege he'd been afforded. Was this some sort of white guilt? Perhaps. And maybe it was justified, given how much easier it seemed, in his generation, for a white rapper to become successful.[9]

Still, respect was there. Barring the crème de la crème—Nas, Jay-Z, Kanye West, Nicki Minaj, Drake—he had collaborated with a who's who of rap's most celebrated artists, from underground stalwarts like Royce da 5'9" and Sean Price to popular faves like Future and Rick Ross.[10] There were still people he wanted to work with, like André 3000, Missy Elliott, and CeeLo, but the bucket list was shrinking. The culture he had wanted so very badly to be accepted into, he was now truly a part of.

He had even inspired others. "Watching this kid—we have different upbringings, but it doesn't matter, he has a love and passion for music, for hip-hop, he doesn't belong, all this shit, and I'm looking at him like *Yo, this is me*," said the rapper Logic. "When 'Donald Trump' came out, it was a fuckin' wrap. I made ten 'Donald Trumps' tryna be like this guy . . . I'll never forget when *Blue Slide Park* came out, I was on tour, and we had a show in Pittsburgh, and I went to Blue Slide Park, and I went to Frick Park Market, and I bought his sandwich, and I went to go eat it at the park. I listened to that album, I loved it. A lot of people didn't really like it, or said he went more pop—I loved it."[11]

He had become so successful that Warner Bros. offered him a deal that was previously unimaginable—ten million dollars. For a kid out of Pittsburgh who had done it all on his own, that sure was something. But did he want it?

"He was like, 'Cam, I'm never going to get no regular deal,'" the rapper Cam'ron recalled Malcolm telling him years earlier. "If I do a deal, it's got to be for 30 million or better. They got to give me the Michael Jackson [deal].' That's what he used to tell me. And he's like, 'It don't make sense. I'm going on tour, getting 40, 50, 60 thousand a show, 60 dates, and I'm making 80 percent off my music now. Why would I sign to a label?' And I was like, this is a smart young man."[12]

But the record business had changed. Blogs and social media had ceded their influence to streaming companies; streaming companies were in bed with the labels—the majors owned a piece of Spotify—and Warner was offering a lot of money. "It was pretty hard to say no to," said Big Jerm.

And it was Warner. They had some juice.

"Prince was on Warner Bros.," said Ritz Reynolds. "It's fuckin' Warner Bros. Like, yeah, *hell yeah*. The next level, let's go. I don't think Mac ever had radio airplay or anything. 'Missed Calls' was on there a little bit . . . it didn't really pick up steam. Maybe a major label could have pushed it better? But people didn't care what fucking label he was on. People didn't buy the shit because of the label."

The label didn't want to mettle with Malcolm's independence either. They just wanted to enhance it. "I'd like to think I kept some of my independence," he told Larry King. "But I think it was just time. They're a very independent-thinking company. Everyone at the office wears T-shirts. I haven't seen many suits."[13]

As is customary in deals of such stature, Warner also gave him a deal for his label, REMember Music. The company was a pet project he started in 2013; he funded it out of his own pocket. The label was committed to working with Vinny Radio, Franchise, Choo Jackson, Hardo, Dylan Reynolds, and Primavera Vills, all of whom he had known personally and professionally dating back to the Easy Mac days.[14] With Warner behind REMember, he hoped to put some real energy into its roster of artists.

If things seemed to be on the upswing, he said he owed it all to producer Rick Rubin. They'd connected after Malcolm left Rostrum and began seeking a new label home; one label he met with, Republic Records, was in business with Rick, and sent Malcolm to his house. They quickly hit it off.

"[He] comes down the stairs," Malcolm recalled. "He sits down next to me and the first thing he said was: tell me everything."[15]

Malcolm was taken by Rick's mystical presence. This was a man from the Long Island suburbs who couldn't play an instrument or operate a mixing board, but had still made it big in hip-hop, starting Def Jam with Russell Simmons. He'd then segued into rock production, working with everyone from the Red Hot Chili Peppers to Johnny Cash, and possessed an innate talent for connecting with artists in ways that brought out their best work (including Kanye West's recently completed *Yeezus* LP).

"Jimmy and everyone is like, but what does Rick do?" Malcolm recalled. "And I was like, uh, I don't know."[16]

Their relationship advanced quickly, with Malcolm calling on him for help when he felt his substance abuse issues were spinning out of control. One night, on tour in Europe, he was "super wasted." So he called Rick.

Rick invited him to his house, and Malcolm took him up on the offer, moving—in the summer of 2014—to a Malibu ranch with a private beach just down the block from the producer's home. Every day that summer, he'd head to Rick's house for some self-care—primarily, transcendental meditation and ice baths.

"I didn't go to rehab," Malcolm said. "I went to Rick Rubin's house."[17]

Rick made a big impression on Malcolm. He didn't want or need anything—and he was all about helping Malcolm get better. "I just did a lot of stuff with him that was just about getting healthy," Malcolm said. "He just really has a positive state of mind. I think there's people in the industry that will take someone who's fucked up on drugs and will try to milk that person for everything they can. Then there's people that understand that you need good soil for something to grow."[18]

All of which led him to *GO:OD AM*, his first project on a major. He saw it as a career reset, akin to a debut.

The first single was called "100 Grandkids." It was coproduced by Sha Money XL, a music executive who had helped launch 50 Cent and G-Unit before landing an A&R gig at Def Jam. Sha was a big Mac Miller fan; so big, in fact, he tried getting his boss, L.A. Reid, to do a deal with Rostrum for Malcolm, which Reid wasn't interested in. And Sha used him in a case study he presented to Def Jam.

"2010, I had just started at Def Jam, and I had just signed Big Krit," Sha said. "Mac was a big part of my case study on the type of artist that you want, and this is how you can read where they're heading. At that time, he was the most viewed artist on YouTube. I had K.R.I.T. I'm looking at what Curren$y is doing, what Wiz Khalifa is doing, what Kendrick is doing, what J. Cole is doing. The interesting part about Mac Miller, even though he was with Rostrum, he never really got a cosign from Wiz Khalifa. There was never no album, mixtape . . . they never made it look like they were family."[19]

For Sha, this was everything. He remembered Eminem, how Dre got him going, and then how Eminem got 50 Cent going.

"It wasn't the cosign," said Sha. "Mac really did his thing on his own, built his following. And he had his sound down pat since the beginning. He was hip-hop. He had no stutter moments. He had no moments where he didn't know. Now, some people are made because their managers and everyone else is inducing the shit, doing all this stuff behind the scenes. This kid didn't need no inducement, he didn't need no cosigns, he didn't need any of that shit. It's not easy and it's not something money could do. It was the time, the music, and the accuracy of him being authentic to who he was, which was his art. He was dropping joints. He had visuals. He had a personality. He had a lot of things artists take a long time to get to, that's why he ended up with a reality show. It just was in him. And he did it in a way where mothafuckas loved him."

One day, Sha received a call from Christian and Kelly Clancy. The Clancys were a husband-and-wife duo whose boutique management firm, 4 Strikes, had become one of the most well-respected in the music industry. Their star clients were Tyler, the Creator and Odd Future. "When the group wants to make a TV show, they help get it made; when they want to release a book of photos, they help get it published; when brands reach out to Tyler, they help him create a full-fledged commercial production company," Kevin Lincoln wrote of the Clancys in BuzzFeed. "We surround them with the best people," Christian said. "If we don't know how to do it, we find someone who does."[20]

Music industry veterans, the Clancys cut their teeth at Interscope, back when Marshall Mathers was king and 50 Cent ran hip-hop. But they eventually soured on the corporate side of the business. Then came Odd Future. ". . . I want to be a part of something that makes me feel 16 again," Tyler recalled Chris Clancy telling him. "I hate the industry and you guys make me feel young again."[21]

Malcolm had begun leaning on the Clancys for advice. He liked that they wanted to do their job but when it came to creative matters stayed the hell out of the way. "I'm not an A&R guy, I'm not trying to be an A&R guy," Chris Clancy told the *Rap Radar* podcast. "I'll tell you if I like something, and typically I'm wrong."[22]

Briefly, Malcolm was also aided by Ron Laffitte, former manager to Lady Gaga, whose clients at the time included Pharrell and OneRepublic; and Rich Egan, a Nashville-based manager who, years earlier, cofounded Vagrant Records, home to artists like PJ Harvey, Edward Sharpe and the Magnetic Zeros, and Dashboard Confessional.

"He was in a standstill," said Clockwork. "He was gonna go with the Clancys or he was gonna go with [Rich]."

At first, Chris Clancy didn't even like Malcolm. "He was the white college rapper guy that would go and sell out the House of Blues everywhere," he said. "There was like four or five versions of that." But the more acquainted they became with him, the more they saw the vision. Before long, they had fallen head over heels for him.[23]

"I was like, holy shit—he's like Neil Young," Clancy said. "He's all these things. Sooo not what I thought. I marginalized him. Simply because I didn't look under the hood. Basically, [it was] ignorance. It was only because I didn't listen. He got that a lot."[24]

They had other things they could connect on, too, like addiction, which Chris had dealt with earlier in life. Certainly, Malcolm could throw a rock in LA and find someone who'd been in recovery, but he couldn't always find someone who had overcome addiction *and* who was a great manager. And Chris and Kelly Clancy were great managers.

So when Sha's phone rang that day, and Kelly said she was working with Mac, he snapped to attention.

"I let Kelly Clancy know I'm in Malibu, I just bought me a crib off the coast—I'm stuntin' hard, feeling like Tony Stark," Sha said. "I told her I'm in my production bag, heavy. Mac Miller, we started talking about him: 'Yo, tell him I'm ready. I got some shit for him.' Within the same fuckin' hour, she's telling me, 'Go to his house right now.'"

Within minutes he was in his Audi on his way to Malcolm's new spot in Brentwood, MPC Renaissance beat machine in tow.

"He was cool as a mothafucka, smoking his little cigarette, just greeting me with love, respect, salutations, and shit," Sha recalled. "It was real good energy. He had a real mixing board in there; it wasn't just a fucking computer. It looked like a real studio. He put money into the shit. There's instruments laying around. A lot of different equipment. It had a vibe. It felt creative. The music was loud. It sounded good."

In LA, sessions like these were a dime a dozen, though. Producers and songwriters ran wild beneath the palm trees, trying to place their work with anyone who would take it. Sha, however, wasn't thirsty; he was an older dude, in his forties, and was a millionaire many times over. He'd been in hundreds of sessions. But this one was different.

"As soon as he heard the beat, he was like, 'Yo, can you bounce that for me?" Sha said, referring to the process of handing over the multilayered tracks of a beat so it can be recorded to. "I bounced it and gave it to him and he put it in Pro Tools and started doing all this stuff in Pro Tools and I was like, 'Oh shit, you know Pro Tools.' I was blown away. Flipping the beat in Pro Tools, chopping it up; he's not playing. I was like, 'I like this!' 'Cause I've been in sessions where the other artist, he can't even make a song. He can't even record. I've been in sessions where no vocals happen. Like, literally, no song."

Malcolm began adding his own instrumentation right there in front of Sha. Later, Big Jerm would add his own touch. "Working with Em and Dre, we did that all the time," Sha said. "We all share, because we wanna make music that lasts forever."

When it was done, Malcolm wanted to shoot a video for it. Directed by Nick Walker, it's a clip in two parts; the first half finds Malcolm watching over a stage as children perform a play below, thinking about his legacy; for the second part, he's in front of a lowrider, talking about the present. With its carnival vibe, the track and the video had a particular influence.

"['100 Grandkids'] reminded me a little of Eminem," Sha said. "It wasn't like there was something wrong with it—but I did see the stage and stuff and I was like, 'Oh, this is like some Eminem shit.'"

For Malcolm, it was a great reintroduction. *Faces* was *Macadelic* on steroids. "It's a great project because it's so raw," he said. "But every single song is about coke, drugs."[25]

But "100 Grandkids" was lighter, more fun and reminiscent of who Malcolm was when he had first become popular. On a major label, it felt like a new chapter. He was energized, focused, and ready to go.

"What's a God without a little od—just a G," he rapped on the song.

"I'm just being a human being again," Malcolm said. "I'm finally having fun again. Fun—there's nothing wrong that. This is my life, I enjoy it, and it's OK that I enjoy it. It's OK that I'm young and rich. Let's have fun. You've got to look in the mirror and tell yourself to stop being a little bitch: 'OK, dude, you're twenty-three and this is your fucking life. Go out there and do it, stop hiding,' because that was me before."[26]

When it came time to promote *GO:OD AM*, he was eager to talk about drugs, about how they had affected him. So when *Fader* approached him about making a short documentary called *Stopped Making Excuses*, he was an open book. On tape, he let it be known that if the choice was between being seen as a corny white rapper or overdosing, he preferred the former.

"He was the nicest dude of all time," said Scott Perry, the doc's director of photography. "He'd just moved to Dumbo, so we shot it at his apartment in New York, we shot in Pittsburgh at the Steelers game, and he had a charity softball tournament, which didn't make it in the cut—but we shot two days in Pittsburgh. We went in September. It was a beautiful city."

In Pittsburgh, Perry got to see just how big of a hometown king Malcolm was. "When we were setting up in his apartment, he was playing *MLB 2K* or some baseball video game—and he's playing as the Pirates—a Pittsburgh sports fan through and through. His Pittsburgh fandom was deeply authentic. His Steelers fandom was well-known. Following him on social media over the years, he's always been standing on the sidelines. So now we're at the game. Terrible Towel is a tradition there; someone comes out at the beginning of the game and gets everyone going. It's like throwing out a first pitch. And Malcolm got to do it. He was very much like a celebrity among the players. I remember the Steelers coming over as they were going back to the locker room, dapping him up."

While the doc made a point to highlight the respect Malcolm had earned from the music community, and his love for the Steel City, its anchor was his battle with drugs—and how he was overcoming it. "If you look at the documentary, it's [as] pretty raw and candid as someone can physically be," said *Fader*'s Andy Cohn. "I think that that was a comfort zone for him . . . it's the gift and the curse of being an artist and having those creative genes, which we all know come with some suffering involved."

He explained that his move to LA was all about getting far from home; he had been captivated by the energy in California, and he said he "caught the vibe."[27]

But before long, LA was killing him. Or maybe that was the easy answer. "To have all that space is a pro and a con," he said. "But it's really just something within myself."

He described how he spiraled, how things turned "toxic." The genesis was being indoors all the time; the boredom, he said, got to him, and drugs were a way to keep himself entertained.

"I hate being sober," he said. "I wanted a drug to do."[28]

But rather quickly he began to overdo it, as seen in a key moment in the doc—a studio session with French Montana, where Malcolm is holding a two-liter filled with lean.[29]

"This is too much; though; this is the pure," French says, trying to dissuade him.

Malcolm insists. And French tells him he isn't hearing him.

"This is not even the one you think it is," French says. "This is the one that's really *it*."

Malcolm shoots back: "More than Actavis?"

He liked Actavis, the company that made lean (and reportedly stopped making it after Justin Bieber became addicted to it[30]). He began sipping it on the Blue Slide Park tour, buying pints for two hundred dollars off a guy TreeJ met in Cali, who shipped it to him wherever he went.

"This right here, you're gonna miss a couple of shows," French says.

But some good *had* come from it. He'd made parts of *GO:OD AM* high as a kite. Warner Bros. had given him ten million dollars, the album had debuted at number four on the *Billboard* charts, and reviews had been overwhelmingly strong. Even his old foe Pitchfork called it his "most refined and well put-together project."[31]

People were loving the record. And his openness about his battle with substance abuse endeared him to many who were struggling with the same issues. He had to have done something right. The dark days weren't all for naught. They were for the art. "One thing that Mac did really well, he touched people. He made people feel something," said FakeShoreDrive's Andrew Barber. "People really thought that they knew him."

That didn't mean he took his ability to connect with people through his music for granted. With the way he was living—using drugs and alcohol to unlock his creativity—he was walking a thin line, and he knew it.

"I'm still here luckily," he said. "But you know you dance around the edge enough, there's a chance that you might fall off."[32]

SEVENTEEN

On July 4, 2016, Malcolm was due to leave for a series of shows in Europe. His team was en route to meet him, waiting for flights at the airport, when they received an email: The tour was canceled.

For months, Malcolm's struggles had been getting the best of him. Previously, he'd cited exhaustion for canceling gigs; now, he was publicly claiming the same.

The truth, however, was that he was going to rehab, a decision made after a final breakup with Nomi.

"Nomi left me," he told Clockwork one day at his Brooklyn apartment early that summer.

To cope with the breakup, he was indulging in massive quantities of cocaine, so much cocaine that Clockwork began wondering if his friend, whom he'd always had so much confidence in keeping it together, might really not be able to.

"I could see in his face and his jaws that he was all like wired and fucked up," Clockwork said. "And I'm sitting right in front of him. It was just me and him, and I asked him, 'Dude, are you OK?' And he like looked up at me like, 'Yeah! What do you mean? Yeah.' I'm like, 'You sure?' And he was like, 'Yeah, bro, I'm cool.' I was like, 'Alright.' I knew, deep down, he wasn't, but I kinda left it alone. That relationship shit can fuck you up."

According to one friend, Nomi's frustration with Malcom's drug use seemed to play a major role in her decision to finally end things for good. And in response to a question on her website, Taylor Magazine, she said she dated "someone with some serious mental health and addiction issues for the better part of six years." Malcolm, she alleged, suffered from a "mental disease," and accommodating his illness took a lot out of her.[1]

The Clancys urged Malcolm to go to rehab. Shane Powers, a close friend of the Clancys, recalled on his podcast that Chris often went to war with himself over being responsible for someone who didn't seem intent on surviving. "I don't need this. I don't manage people that are into killing themselves," Clancy was alleged to have said.[2]

Malcolm, who would later say he wanted to keep it together for Chloe, the Clancys' nine-year-old daughter (calling her his "guiding light,"[3]) spent about three weeks in rehab. At the same time, his buddy Bill Niels was dealing with his own addiction struggles.

"I got out of jail, went to rehab three times," Bill said. "I was court-ordered to a three-quarter house. I got there and there was no beds for me; a day later, a bed opens, and it was because this other kid got high and got kicked out, and he turned out to be a kid that used to play lacrosse with Mac. Two days later, he and his girlfriend were both found dead together. They both shot up, fell out, and died. I got his bed, and some of his stuff was still laying around. There was another kid who had been dead for two days, upstairs, and nobody had found him. It was a pretty hard-core environment. And Mac didn't really know, or understand, what was going on with me. He didn't understand how bad it got."

Bill was depressed. Life was kicking the shit out of him. Then he got a message from Malcolm.

"I'm in rehab," he said. He told Bill he was in there with an ultra-famous soul singer who was known all over the world for his virtuoso piano skills. "But *shhh*!—don't tell anyone."

And Bill didn't. But they kept in touch. Malcolm got clean, and so did Bill.

"We were both serious about staying clean," Bill said. "We were both real humble, like 'God bless,' saying recovery phrases and shit."

Bill felt that Malcolm was moving past a period in his life when he may have done things that went against his better judgment.

"Whenever I saw him start to do drugs, I knew it was against his principles to do 'em," Bill said. "I thought he did it to give himself some edge. I pictured him going out to California and all these other artists have this 'cool' edge, and someone he really looked up to, maybe they did drugs. Like, I grew up with Nirvana and Kurt Cobain. Kurt Cobain was a drug addict, and I wanted to be like Kurt Cobain. I thought it was cool as fuck to OD. I have a picture of myself in the sixth grade where I'm in this rag clothing, holding up this sign that says ADDICT. That's where this derives from. That's why I started taking pills at such a young age—I thought it was cool."

And he observed the same tendencies in Malcolm.

"The first time I noticed this in [Mac] was when we were in New York City, and it was John Geiger and Darrelle Revis backstage. I'm standing next to Mac, and they were like, 'What are you sippin'?' Mac said—'It's basically heroin in a cup.' But he said it in really bragging way. I just remember looking at him like, 'What the fuck are you doing, dude? Darrelle Revis is an NFL player, he doesn't think that's cool . . .' I remember Mac's demeanor saying that. He thought it was cool. That's why a lot of us started doing drugs."

Maybe it was all behind him now. He said he was clean, and together they were counting their days. He also seemed genuinely happy for the first time in a long time.

"I went out to a rehearsal with him for his first show of the Divine Feminine Tour," Bill said. "That's when I realized how stuck he was with Ariana. We were driving, and Ariana called him; all of a sudden, he's like, 'Heeeeeyyyy, babe . . .' His whole demeanor changed. He's like, obsessed with her. And God, who wouldn't be? She's Ariana Grande. It was crazy to me that he was dating her."

In the years since "The Way," Ariana had tripled her fame. While Malcolm was making his coke album *Faces*, she was racing up the charts with *Dangerous Woman*. But she always had a thing for Malcolm. And when she saw him going through a tough time, she was eager to lend her support.

"When he had to go to rehab, Ariana was there for him," a friend said. "He was done with Nomi. Ariana was available. And that's how they got together."

"She was visiting him all the time," another friend echoed. "She was up there at the rehab a lot."

Things got hot and heavy quickly. By mid-July, they were spotted together at Disneyland, and in August they were officially an item, with paparazzi photos of the pair, kissing at Japanese restaurant Katsu-Ya in LA, landing on TMZ.

"We have loved and adored and respected each other since the beginning, since before we even met, just because we were fans of each other's talent," she told *Cosmopolitan*. "We weren't ready at all, though, to be together. It's just timing. . . . We both needed to experience some things, but the love has been there the whole time."[4]

The photos sent Malcolm's profile skyrocketing. He was a successful rapper—people knew who he was—but his wasn't a face that looked out at you from the tabloids at the supermarket checkout line. Within weeks, the relationship was everywhere, and neither of them was good at discussing it.

Pressed by Ellen DeGeneres about her status, Ariana curled up, embarrassed. "This is so crazy," she said. "I've never had the relationship talk on a show before."[5]

Malcolm, too, was deflective. He was promoting a new record, *The Divine Feminine*, a concept album about love. That he had a record coming out about love, and he seemed to be in love—well, it didn't take a genius to assume Ariana had inspired the LP. But she didn't.

As far as back as the previous summer, Malcolm was talking about what would become the new album. "I think next I really want to just deal with making more songs about love," he told *Complex*. "That's something I really want to dive into, is just really getting into the ins and outs and the complexities of that emotion. So that's my plan currently. I'm just kind of exploring that a little more."[6]

Now the record was done. And people were asking him about it.

"It's crazy to me that people think the whole album is about her," he said. "Timetable-wise, how quickly do you think I can make an album? It's not songs about other women, it's songs about my perspective on love. But by the way, we're grown. There are people in my life that have affected my perspective on what love is. Everyone learns from all experiences in life. These are all things that are real to me in my life. But people saying that the whole album is about her is wild to me because it would be, literally, impossible."[7]

Still, Ariana had been featured on one track—"My Favorite Part." The song found Malcolm not rapping but crooning, "Before things come together, they have to fall apart," a decision he made courtesy of some Jameson whiskey he'd been sipping the night he recorded it.[8]

The record's genesis began with Tyrone "MusicManTy" Johnson, who had sent Malcolm a batch of beats long before the song was made. Malcolm didn't like any of them; he wanted ideas that were more musical. So MusicManTy dug into his hard drive. He found something he had made nearly a decade earlier, inspired by Stevie Wonder.

Malcolm really liked that one. "Send the files," he said.

But Ty didn't know where the files were. So he had to re-create the beat from scratch—and the original version was all live music. "Nothing is looped," he said. "I played every instrument from the beginning all the way to the end. I started with the Rhodes [electric piano]—'OK, this is the verse, this is the hook. Back when I made it, I didn't know how to loop or to chop or anything like that."[9]

Note for note, sound for sound, it took a week of sleepless nights. The risk with replaying a beat that an artist has already recorded to is that they'll love the original version, and feel that the new one doesn't match it. So Ty worked his ass off on it, trying to get it right.

"It was tedious," he said. "Now, from a music standpoint, some artists might not be so musically inclined. But he was. Because the hi-hats, they have a neo-soul swing. I didn't know if I had redone them correctly, if they were in the right pocket. They sounded close, but I wasn't a hundred percent sure. So I send it to him—he hits me back immediately: *It sounds good, but the hi-hats ain't the same.* I thought, *Oh yeah, this guy is dedicated; he's definitely got an ear.* And I went back and fixed them."

Malcolm loved the song. And he loved what making it with Ariana brought to their relationship. "It's very dope," he said. "And I like how that worked out . . . she's my best friend in the world."[10]

Now, while *The Divine Feminine* had been in the works for a year, and had not been completely inspired by Ariana, some of it was, in fact, made with her around. Not just "My Favorite Part," but other songs too.

One of the artists Malcolm had always wanted to collaborate with was CeeLo. He admired CeeLo's artistic growth, how he had started as a rapper with Goodie Mob, then gone on to be a genre-defying solo artist before collaborating with Danger Mouse as Gnarls Barkley. Here was a guy who simply did not stand still.

"That's someone who I wanted to learn from," he said. "Because that's someone who's in Goodie Mob—and then continued to evolve, evolve, and evolve. Because for me, I'm trying to learn how to use my voice in as many different ways as possible. I'm here to completely say I am trying to get better. I'm not at a point where I'm gonna say, *This is what it's gonna be.* I'm still figuring it out. I'm trying to get better, trying to learn what I'm gonna do. So someone like that who has jumped around with different styles—*The Odd Couple*, that Gnarls Barkley album, is [a] phenomenal album to me, I listen to that album all the time."[11]

When CeeLo got the word Malcolm wanted to collaborate, he was immediately down. He had been a fan for years, occasionally trading direct messages with him on Twitter.

"We drove from Vegas, got there, went straight to the studio, and him and Ariana were there," CeeLo recalled. "The titling of the album, the emotional state and creative space that he was in—I'm sure it was a product of that very loving environment. You could tell that they were just crazy about each other. They were all over each other, in each other's faces, very kissy. Which was sweet, because they looked like opposites of each other. They were really well meshed together. And I travel with my woman, too, so it was basically like a double date. We're a loving couple as well, so you can just tell when it's new, when it's fresh, when it's exciting. They were kicking it."[12]

Their collab, "We," would be a standout on *The Divine Feminine*, an album presenting a more mature, refined Mac Miller. This wasn't the lyrical dynamo that had spent six years and hundreds of songs trying to prove he was one of the best rappers in the game; this was an artist firmly in command of his voice, saying not every thought that came into his head—only the words that were necessary.

Sometimes the words were slow to come. While working on "Skin," he went through a period of writer's block. For two weeks, he struggled to find anything worthwhile to say. Then, he suddenly hit upon a verse and a chorus, only to step out of the studio and learn that the singer Prince had died—the cause, a counterfeit Vicodin containing a lethal dose of fentanyl.

"I cried for forty-five minutes nonstop," he said. "I didn't realize how affected I would be [by] that. It was hard to see. People love a fucking headline and it was hard for me to sit there and see someone who was obviously very private be turned inside out after his death. All this shit they were saying, I was just like, give it a second before you come with the drug stories."[13]

Another song that got attention was the raunchy "God Is Fair, Sexy Nasty," featuring Kendrick Lamar. Coming from two rapping-ass rappers, you'd have expected a lyrical competition. Instead, it was the complete opposite.

"I'ma take my time, I'ma hit that slow . . . you the only thing for me in this fucked-up world," Malcolm sing-raps over Tae Beast's lush production.

Malcolm described the track as a real journey to put together, one which was brought to life one night at the studio when Kendrick was in town to perform on *Late Night with Jimmy Fallon*. Playing Kendrick his new music, the Compton rapper seemed impressed.

"This is what you're supposed to be doing," Malcolm recalled Kendrick telling him that night in the studio. Then Kendrick hopped in the booth and just started making things up until they liked the direction the song was headed; settled on a lyric, he encouraged Kendrick to lay it down and he did.[14]

The song's poignancy is aided by its outro, in which Malcolm's grandmother, Marcia Weiss, tells the story of how she fell in love with Malcom's grandfather—"Poppy."

The story moved Malcolm so much that he recalled crying to it when he heard it, bawling his eyes out at the beauty of how pure the love was between his grandparents; in fifty years of marriage his grandfather never went to sleep at night without telling his wife he loved her.[15] In an interview with *Vogue*, Malcolm said he'd been chasing that kind of love his whole life."[16]

His grandmother added a personal touch to a record that felt near and dear to Malcolm's heart, one of his most pure creative works, almost selfish in its ambitions. To bring it to life, he worked with pianist Robert Glasper, whom Malcolm spent a lot of time palling around with.

"He would come to my shows—he even sat in with a piano trio I was playing with once in Brooklyn. Then there'd just be times where he'd be in the studio hanging, wasn't doing shit, and he'd call me up. I'd go by, and we'd listen to music," Glasper said. "When I got there for this session, the keyboard was set up; and this is when I realized how musical he was, because he sat down at the keys and started playing ideas, I was like, 'Yo! You play keys?' He was talking to me like a musician, he knew the terminology. Obviously, he's not a piano player, so he didn't have a major technique, but he just knew."[17]

Malcolm told him a bit about the vibe he was looking for; he'd recorded a mock-piano part himself that he wanted Glasper to replay. Glasper knocked it out in one or two takes, which took all of ten minutes. They made three songs for *The Divine Feminine*; only one made the cut, but the sessions were numerous, free-flowing, improvisational, and most of all . . . fun.

They also occurred during a period, pre-sobriety, when Malcolm was still drawing his power from drugs—particularly cocaine. "That was his usual thing," Glasper said. "He was doing coke and then he'd have a delivery guy come and deliver more coke. The last [session] we were at, he was super high. Super-duper high. Out of his mind. But he still was creating, he still wanted to create. And a lot of people can create like that. They get high, then create."

For Glasper, a jazz disciple who had just completed work on the soundtrack to the Miles Davis's biopic *Miles Ahead*—centered around the period in the 1970s when the trumpeter was awash in alcohol and cocaine—it was all par for the course.[18]

"I let him do his thing," Glasper said. "It was just studio shit. You know, cats just do their shit. They just have to have their vices and the things they do and when you're creating—I'm never one to jump in the way when someone's creating and doing that shit because that's what they need to do to create. If it woulda seemed like he was going overboard, and it was too much, and I got scared or something, then I'd say, *Hey, bro, I think you've had enough*. But it didn't get there, he was just high."

Nor did he think it was his place to interject. "I would never go to somebody else's session and be like, *Yo, quit doing drugs*. You want people to feel comfortable around you [in the studio]. So you gotta let them know, *Hey, whatever your vice is, I'm not judging, it's OK, it's all good. Let's create, we're here. It's all good.* Once you start being that person that nitpicks at their own shit, they're not inviting you back anymore."

Glasper felt that whatever he was doing was in service of his art. "He was just hungry to create," he said.

However Malcolm fed that hunger, the work proved cathartic. Though another radical departure in a career that seemed to career from one extreme to the next, for Malcolm, *The Divine Feminine* was a revelation. He had a new relationship, a new album. For the first time in a long time, he seemed to be happy.

"I needed to take some time to figure out what was important in my life," he said in an interview with *The Breakfast Club*. "I went out and got the big crib, and all the extra things, through all the vices in my life—this is what I'm supposed to do, I'm supposed to have this whip, I'm supposed to have this big-ass crib, I'm supposed to have parties—but . . . that's not really me. I'm just a pretty relaxed, chill dude. I don't need all that extra stuff."[19]

Even love and drugs, he felt, were things he didn't need. They were cool, but not necessary.

"I've always been fascinated by the similarities between [love and drugs] . . . I really feel like the two things can affect a human being in a very similar way," he said. "To get to the state I'm in now, I had to remove all aspects. Both of those things from my life. I had to get completely good. Figure out what I actually wanted to do. The universe has really been working in my favor since I started focusing on who I actually am."[20]

He no longer wanted to be associated with the drugs he had once so lovingly rapped about.

"There's no more drugs. Last time I was up here," he said, pointing at the liquor bottles behind the radio personalities, "we poured up at nine in the morning. I don't do anything. I smoke cigarettes. I just got tired of creating from that place, that space, about that space. Because it's like all of this—just drugged out, depressing, talking about sadness and all of that stuff—for as much music as I make, when you do that all the time, it gets repetitive for you. It stops being interesting. One of my things is I want to not be *this guy* in music. Not be the drug guy. Not be the love guy. Not be the depressed guy. The hip-hop arts guy, the happy guy. But try to capture what it is to be a human being, which is all of those things. Nobody is one thing, and it starts to feel very branded; like, when you go and order this, you know what you're gonna get. And everyone is so much more dynamic than that."

He wanted people to take *The Divine Feminine* for what it was, a collection of songs reflecting his perspective on love. He wasn't an expert on it; the music was just what he felt.

"I don't know what world I fit in," he said. "I don't know what radio type, where you'd play me. I don't fit into [radio] categories. I had a vision. I'm not here with the story of who I am as a human being. I'm here with an album that's about something. About an aspect of my life . . . what I think about [love]. I'm not the love guy. I'm just a guy."

•••

Malcolm was sober for nine months. He did the entire Divine Feminine Tour—October through December—sober. A completely clean tour. No drugs. No alcohol. No nothing.

"When I put that record out, that was the first time I had a clear head in ten years," he said.[21]

For a guy who had been high for what felt like most of his adult life, it was a big change. He told a friend that, one year, he'd spent a hundred thousand dollars on cocaine alone.[22] But that was all behind him now.

"On tour, the rest of the crew's still smoking weed, drinking, doing pills, whatever," said Bill Niels. "And there's two buses. His tour manager, specifically arranged for everything drug-wise to stay off that front bus. I remember him asking my advice. 'Do you think this is a good idea?' And I'm like, 'Yeah, yeah, you should definitely have this bus clean.'"

Sobriety did not come easily. Right after he got out of rehab he took his new sober coach, Shane Powers, to Lollapalooza. Powers was a former contestant on *Survivor*, former nightclub promoter, and former addict who once relapsed so hard he almost snorted his father's ashes. The Clancys tasked him with keeping Malcolm on the straight and narrow.[23]

"He had that sober coach dude around—Big Shane. I think [Shane] had worked with Justin Bieber before," said Peter Rosenberg, who bumped into Mac at the festival. "I think the whole thing was a little bit uncomfortable. We had quick conversations. 'Yo, you good?' He definitely seemed to be taking it very seriously. And he still seemed like himself. But I just have such a distinct memory of this unsaid thing. He knew exactly what I meant when I was asking him. He'd simultaneously tell me it was good and also I could see that it was like, 'I'm trying.'"

Back in LA, he had rented a house at 11659 Valleycrest Road, in Studio City. It was a much different house than the mansion he'd had during his filming of the MTV show. More suburbs than *Scarface*, the three-bedroom, three-bathroom house sat at the end of a quiet block; it was awash in natural light and had wooden beams splayed across its vaulted ceilings, brick stonework, and cedar hardwood floors.

"There's no extras," he said of the house. "There's no extra shit. As my house comes together, walking through it, there's no extra space, there's no extra rooms that are there for zero reason. Like, everything has a purpose."[24]

Case in point, on his wall he kept a framed poster of a tweet Jay-Z had written one night in the summer of 2017, after the Brooklyn rapper had been inducted into the Songwriters Hall of Fame. The multipart tweet storm listed all the great rappers he'd been inspired by, and included: Rakim, Big Daddy Kane, KRS-One, Chuck D, Ice Cube, Jaz-O, Eminem, André 3000, Nas, The Notorious B.I.G., 2Pac, J. Cole, Kendrick Lamar, Chance the Rapper, Jay Electronica, Lauryn Hill, MC Lyte, Queen Latifah, Common, Kanye West, Reverend Run, Grandmaster Caz, LL Cool J, 2 Chainz, Cam'ron, T.I., Q-Tip, Black Thought, Pharoah Monch, Scarface, De La Soul, Ice-T, Kool G Rap, Melle Mel, Kurupt, the Lox, DMX, ScHoolboy Q, Ab-Soul, Lupe Fiasco, Mos Def, Foxy Brown, Rick Ross, Quavo, Future, Travis Scott, T Grizzley, Redman, Ghostface and Raekwon, Wu-Tang, The Genius, Busta Rhymes, Treach, Young Thug, Beyoncé, Lil Wayne, Juvenile, B.G., Nipsey Hu$$le, Lil Kim, Slaughterhouse (including Joe Budden), Wale, MC Eiht, Too Short, E-40, Mac Dre, 50 Cent, Big L, Showbiz & A.G., Nice & Smooth, Fat Joe, Big Pun, the Digable Planets (especially Ishmael "Butterfly" Butler), Beanie Sigel, Young Chris, Freeway and the rest of State Property, Young

Jeezy, Pusha T, Playboi Carti, A$AP Mob, Sean Price, Mobb Deep, Kid Cudi, Tyler, the Creator, Earl Sweatshirt, Snoop Dogg, Slick Rick, Pimp C, Bun B, Big Sean, and Sauce Money.

Then, in a final tweet, he wrote: "Too many . .[Fabolous] , [Black] people really magic . Mac Miller nice too though ."[25]

Considering where Malcolm had been just a few years earlier, slammed by critics and reviled by hip-hop heads who pegged him as little more than a "frat rapper," the acknowledgment from Jay-Z, arguably the greatest rapper of all time, was a sign that what he had always dreamed of—to be recognized among the legends—had come true. It wasn't a Grammy, but then, the Grammys never got hip-hop right anyway.

Still, it was just Twitter, and there was real life to attend to. At home, Malcolm liked to hang out on the patio, which offered relaxing views of the canyons and mountains in the distance.[26]

He didn't live alone. Months earlier, he had been in Pittsburgh, due to meet Big Jerm at ID Labs with Ariana.

"I had two dogs at the time," Jerm said. "I was walking the dogs. I'm in Highland Park, which is not a bad neighborhood. It's like eight thirty in the summer, so it isn't dark yet. And these three kids—I saw 'em cross the street—were so young, like fourteen or fifteen. I'm thinking they're going to try to sell me candy bars. But then one kid tells me to give him whatever I had. I had my phone on me; might not have even had my wallet. I was walking my dogs! So I was just said—'I don't have anything.' And then he pulled the gun out. I think I said, 'You don't wanna do that.' He took it as me being tough. I just meant, *Hey, you don't want to shoot someone in broad daylight.*"

But then the kid pulled the trigger. And Big Jerm was hit. "It went in my chest kind of right below my shoulder, through my lung, and out. It didn't hit anything else. I got lucky," he said. "So, I actually met Ariana in the hospital for the first time. I don't know that she had ever been to Pittsburgh before. I think she was like, 'This is crazy here.' She didn't even know what to say or think."

Malcolm was concerned. He would put more than ten grand toward Jerm's hospital bills. "Get better," Malcolm told him, "then come to LA, stay with me."

So Jerm did. Though they had a significant age difference, Jerm had known Malcolm since he was a teenager. He produced *The High Life*. Now they were roommates.

In LA, Jerm found a very different Malcolm. The new Malcolm had little of the raw energy of the old Malcolm.

He would mostly sit around the house, not working, not doing anything, really, except play video games like *Madden* and *NBA 2K*; when he wasn't doing that, he was watching television. Sometimes they'd play tennis together, grab sushi. But for someone who spent his life above the clouds, Malcolm seemed as if he was grounded.

"He wasn't very motivated to do much," Jerm said. "We weren't really working a whole lot. I was used to him recording 24/7, so that's what I mentally prepared for. But I felt like he was kind of depressed. That was partially why he wasn't super motivated; he didn't have that *thing* to motivate him. He definitely seemed depressed. I think . . . with the drug thing, he felt that aided him in a way. He almost seemed—I'm not gonna say lost, because I don't know—but it's like he just didn't have that same spark or whatever, right then."

Perhaps it was his old nemesis Donald Trump winning the presidency that sent him into a depression. Perhaps it was something else. But the malaise lasted well into 2017.

Then a glimpse of his old self appeared. A performance at Coachella, in Indio, California, that April seemed to ignite something in him. Headlined by Radiohead, Beyoncé, and Kendrick Lamar, the two-weekend event—the highlight of summer musical festival season—saw him perform for one of the largest and most impassioned crowds he had ever been in front of. Ariana came out for a kiss midperformance, and he said had it was his "favorite" show he had ever done.[27]

One day around then, back at home, he pulled up a piece of music on his computer. It was all electronic pianos and swelling strings.

"Hey, Jerm," he said, "record me."

Over the track, Malcolm sang: "I just need a way out of my head. I was drowning, but now I'm swimming."

"When he first did that song, it was just kind of random," Jerm said. "I think he had had that beat for a little while. I don't think it was very thought-out."

But the song—"Come Back to Earth"—had a particular sound. A vibe. It felt like the start of something.

Ariana's Dangerous Woman Tour ran from the winter of 2017 through the following fall; Malcolm traveled along for some of the dates, joining her when she performed "The Way." But in the spring, when she left for the European leg of the tour, he hung back. Her gigs in Stockholm, Oslo, and Amsterdam went off without a hitch; however, after a show in Dublin, she traveled to Manchester, where, on May 22, with more than fourteen thousand people rejoicing inside the Manchester Arena, pink balloons falling from its rafters, an explosion occurred in the back of the arena. People were scrambling. Blood was everywhere. It was pandemonium. A suicide bombing had taken place. In total, more than eight hundred were injured, and twenty-three people died. Ten people hadn't even made it to their twentieth birthdays, with the youngest victim all of eight years old.

Ariana was deeply traumatized by the incident. She hadn't become a musician to cause pain. She had become a musician to bring joy. And now, this. So distraught was she over the events in Manchester, she thought she might never perform again.

"Initially, I went right home," she said. "I went to Florida. And I was like—I can't, I'm not putting on those costumes again, I can't sing those songs again."[28]

Malcolm was there to support her. He canceled a slate of festival performances and flew to Boca Raton to be by her side. Within a few weeks she decided the best way to honor the victims was to continue performing. The disruption of joy, of life, was what the terrorists wanted. So she got back to it, and two weeks later, at the One Love Manchester concert—in front of fifty-five thousand people—she even brought Malcolm onstage, duetting with him on "The Way" and "Dang!," the Anderson .Paak–assisted first single from *The Divine Feminine*.

Not long after the events in Manchester, Malcolm seemed energized again. He was hard at work on a new album he was calling *Guidelines*. And he was still sober.

"Ariana was really a huge reason why he stayed sober," said Clockwork. "Being with her made him wanna stay sober. He was taking everything seriously; he was in love, he was making money, doing shows. After shows, he wouldn't even go to the greenroom. Sometimes he'd kick us out, and he'd just talk to her, right after the show. We all knew that was good for him. Like, 'Bruh happy, he's like a child in a candy store right now, this is lovely.' When he was with her, he was completely one hundred percent sober."

But there were still concerns. When he was not on the road performing, Malcolm was less attached to the couch than he had previously been. He was leaving the house more. He said he was going to the studio. But sometimes he'd be gone three or four days. And nobody would know where he was.

"There would be times when Ariana would text me," Big Jerm said. "She'd be blowing me up. She couldn't get in touch with him and it's like, 'Yeah, he's not with me either,' so . . . I mean, she could be dramatic. But when I say dramatic—she assumed the worst. She knew things from the drug stuff before. She was very protective of him, in a loving kind of way. She just wanted to make sure he was safe or whatever. "Tell him to call me," she'd say. I didn't wanna get in the middle of their stuff. But I understood where she was coming from."

His management, the Clancys, who seemed to have been effective in helping Malcolm remove toxic people from his circle, also began—according to sources close to him at the time—struggling to keep up with him.

What Jerm later realized was that Malcolm may have been using him, either intentionally or not, as a buffer—a means of creating space between himself and those who had gotten too close. It was an awkward position for him to be in, but in the end, Jerm felt it was positive. Not just for him. But for Malcolm.

"I felt like we were close," he said. "And I felt like a lot of the original—I don't wanna say 'entourage,' because they were really his friends—but those original people that were around, like Jimmy and Q and TreeJ, were all back in Pittsburgh at that point. Ariana was so busy, he would have been alone a lot if I wasn't there. So, that was good."

But then Jerm felt he, personally, wasn't being productive. Malcolm kept leaving. And he wasn't involving Jerm in the music he was working on. Jerm assumed it was because the direction Malcolm wanted to go in, musically, was not one that he was proficient at. Still, Jerm was more than just a producer; he was a recording engineer who had sat in with Malcolm on hundreds of sessions. The ID Labs studio and production team had been a constant throughout Malcolm's career, and he had once called Jerm the most soulful dude he knew. There had to be something for him to do. So, maybe he wouldn't make the beats, but he could offer his insight. There had to be a reason Malcolm kept leaving him home, trying to get away from him.

Why am I out here? Jerm soon began thinking. And before long, he told Malcolm he was looking to head home. Malcolm didn't understand why he wanted to leave. *Why, when the whole music industry was in LA, would you go back to Pittsburgh? But OK, fine. If that's what you want.* So in June of 2017, Jerm went back home.

With Jerm out of the picture, Malcolm went on with his life. He worked on his music and his relationship with Ariana continued apace. Frequent appearances on each other's social media channels presented the image of a perfectly happy couple.

And for the moment, that's exactly what they were.

EIGHTEEN

On May 17, 2018, Malcolm crashed his G-Wagon into a light pole, nearly killing himself and his passengers before dashing off into the night. The police showed up at his house and arrested him. His blood alcohol level was nearly twice the legal limit.[1]

"He was the most polite and nice intoxicated person we've ever seen," the police said.[2] Naturally.

The crash came at a fortuitous time. A week earlier, in an Instagram story, Ariana had announced that she and Malcolm were no longer together, writing:

"Hi! This is one of my best friends in the whole world and favorite people on the planet Malcolm McCormick. I respect and adore him endlessly and am grateful to have him in my life in any form, at all times regardless of how our relationship changes or what the universe holds for each of us!" She continued: "Unconditional love is not selfish. It is wanting the best for that person even if at the moment, it's not you."[3]

A source told *Us Weekly* that the pair had been broken up since April, back when Ariana crashed EDM DJ Kygo's Coachella set for a surprise performance.

"Ariana was holding Mac together for a long time," the source said. "And it wasn't a good relationship for her."[4]

The singer would later tell *Vogue* that she had spent years worrying about Malcolm. While on the Dangerous Woman tour, she would try keeping tabs on him from afar, always concerned he might be on a bender. Describing the relationship as an imperfect one, she said she was the "glue," but over time found herself becoming "less and less sticky." The two eventually drifted apart, though that didn't stop her from thinking the world of him.

"He was the best person ever, and he didn't deserve the demons he had," she said.[5]

But at the time, because of the public nature of the relationship, and the speed at which Ariana appeared to move on— Pete Davidson seemed to be lying in wait—the perception was that the breakup sent Malcolm spiraling. Even if the breakup, Ariana's new fling, and the crash weren't all connected, the coincidental timing was too big to ignore.

When, a few days after the crash, Ariana began receiving messages implicating her, she responded by declaring the relationship "toxic," and said: "I am not a babysitter or a mother and no woman should feel that they need to be."[6]

The truth of the situation was complicated. Fans were blaming Ariana, but she'd tried hard to get Malcolm to remain sober. On his podcast, Shane Powers recalled how supportive Ariana had been in the early days; he would field calls from her, he said, where she would ask how she could be help. He credited her with helping Mac become healthy, and called her a "stabilizing force."[7]

And while it may have appeared that the breakup sent Malcolm spiraling, public comments he made more than a year earlier suggest he had already walked back his life of abstinence.

"I've spent a good time very sober and now I'm just, like, living regularly," he told *W* Magazine at the time. "I don't believe in absolute anything. That was a learning experience . . . it was important to let everyone know that I wasn't doing f—ing crazy amounts of hard drugs."[8]

On his podcast, Shane Powers recalled a conversation—Malcolm had called him one night, while he was out at a bar. He was sober at the time and wanted to take a drink. Powers tried dissuading him. Having gone through recovery himself, Powers seemed to know that sobriety took a lot of work. It took years, he felt, to really manage it right. It didn't come overnight. And

Malcolm wasn't really serious. He didn't want to do the work. Maybe it was laziness. Maybe it was something else. Whatever it was, he wasn't committed.

Malcolm told Powers that he was on edge and he needed to relax.

Powers told him that's why people drink. But he didn't think Malcolm should have a drink. When he started his sobriety journey, he had set a goal for himself: one year sober before drinking again in what appeared to be a moderation-based approach to alcohol management. It hadn't yet been a year.

Powers advised him not to take the drink, but Malcolm insisted. So Malcolm ordered a whiskey. Then another. And another. Eventually, the call ended. The kid hadn't done the work, and now he was drinking again. Nothing good could come from this.

All that sobriety talk, that recovery stuff—the things he had been talking up when he dropped *The Divine Feminine*—Malcolm thought he could control it. But that was addiction in a nutshell: a little voice inside that said all you needed was *a little bit*; then you needed more, and more, until nothing was ever enough.

Powers wasn't sure if Malcolm was an addict. Compared with say, Anthony Keidis, for whom addiction once meant a near-constant need to use, Malcolm seemed more like someone who merely enjoyed having a good time. He partied hard, that's for sure. But he kept it together. As far as anyone knew, he had never overdosed. He was rarely out of control. He was Mac Miller. He was a fucking star.[9]

An addict? Hell no. He was a musician. A rapper. A singer. A producer. And so many other things. Substances were a part of his lifestyle. This was Hollywood. This was entertainment. This was America, where everyone was on something, whether coke or crack or heroin or pills or lean or molly. If not that, then at least marijuana, which was legal in many places now, or alcohol, which was legal everywhere. Everyone needed . . . *something*. Anything to make a life manageable that, even when it seemed so easy, could still be so hard.

For his part, Malcolm saw the crash as a positive. It was a wake-up call. "I made a stupid mistake," he said. "I'm a human being. Like, drove home drunk, but it was the best thing that coulda happened. Best thing that coulda happened. I needed that. I needed to run into that light pole and literally, like, have the whole thing stop."[10]

By "stop," he meant pull back, go dark. Afterward, he wiped his social media accounts, resisting the urge to let his fans know he was OK.

"People who have been with me through being a 19-year-old wide-eyed kid to being a self-destructive, depressed drug user to making love music to all these different stages, they see something like that and they worry, so your first reaction is, 'Let me tell them I'm cool,'" he said. "But you just realize you have time. There will be a time to address those things, but it's . . . everything's gonna be fine."[11]

He told people who checked on him the same. He was fine. Everything was fine. "I hit him up about that—'Yo, you good?'" Peter Rosenberg recalled. "And he said: 'Yeah, that was one crazy thing. I'm good. Don't worry about it.'"

But others weren't so convinced. Clockwork remembered the crash. And he remembered Malcolm's attitude about it; that he told him he felt "invincible" right before he pressed down on the gas pedal. These were red flags that, for the most part, went largely ignored.

"I was kind of creeped out," he said. "Because, 'Bro, you had a whole other two lives in the backseat. You coulda killed everybody.' In my head I'm thinking this. And when he told me [he felt invincible], it just opened up so many things in my mind like, 'OK, I don't know what's going on with bruh. That was the craziest response I've ever gotten out of anybody. That's some you-tryna-die type shit. It left a lot of unanswered questions for me. Cause if the wreck wasn't a big wake-up call, then I don't know what was. After that wreck, mothafuckas should have formed like Voltron and went over there. Everybody should have sat down, talked. Maybe I should have told people what he told me. That probably woulda made people rally up too, but . . . I don't know. Maybe I shoulda shared that information. Maybe some people already knew he felt that way. Who knows?"[12]

Besides, as the saying goes, the show must go on. And away from the crash and the hubbub surrounding it, Malcolm had a new record to make. Records didn't make themselves. To make the meal, he had to spend hours, days, weeks, months in the kitchen.

Months earlier, his mood had been described as low. He had been sober. But he had also been operating in a minor key. Now, Ariana was gone, soon to be temporarily engaged to her funnyman boyfriend, in love with, what media outlets began calling, his "big dick energy."[13] It was time to reengage with the world once again.

New songs were coming together. He bumped into J. Cole in a studio in LA. Cole gave him a beat. He cut a record to it, called it "Hurt Feelings." Another song, "Self-Care" written before the crash, seemed eerily prescient, rapping: "That Mercedes drove me crazy, I was speeding/ Somebody save me from myself, yeah . . ."

Then he was in Hawaii. Recording more. He also had some singer-songwriter material he was working on. The producer Jon Brion, known for his work with Fiona Apple, Kanye West, and on numerous soundtracks (in particular *Eternal Sunshine of the Spotless Mind*) had met Malcolm in passing one day while visiting another friend who was attempting to get sober.

Brion thought nothing of the meeting but later received a called from Warner Bros. exec Lenny Waronker, who told him Malcolm wanted to work with him. When Malcolm played him his new material, these raw, emotive songs, Brion implored him to continue.[14]

"I think he wasn't sure if this confessional, singing, non-beat-driven stuff that he'd been working on was good or not," Brion told the *New York Times*. "He was clearly trying to sort through his demons and was just being very, very honest, not trying to hide any of it."[15]

There was a loose concept for these records forming in Malcolm's head. There was a hook from *Faces*, "Ave Maria"—"It all just keeps spinning / Gotta keep swimming."

He liked that word, "swimming."

In Chile, where he had traveled for Lollapalooza that March, he worked more. Another song came—"Perfecto."

He had bassist Thundercat, one of his closest friends and a frequent collaborator, add his rippling grooves to "What's the Use?"* Then there was "Ladders"—up-tempo, funky, and alive. Others were more plaintive; "Wings"

---

* They'd bonded, years earlier, through their mutual love for LA jazz club the Baked Potato, where Malcolm had performed as Larry Lovestein and where Thundercat's father, a former jazz musician, once played. (assets.billboard.com/articles/columns/code/1566467/thundercat-qa-coping-with-loss-surprising-snoop-and-the-jazz-roots-of)

scans as a note by an angel making its ascendance. Hip-hop, R & B, funk, soul; this album would defy categorization. It had no genre.

"I'm at this point where it's just free-form, Jackson Pollock throwing shit against the wall," he said. "And that's just exciting to me, to not have any type of structure . . ."[16]

Malcolm had been working to be this creatively free his entire life. But a batch of songs remained unfinished. They were slightly different. Similar, but different. More singing, less rapping, less funky—*less dark*. These were songs for a potential companion album. *Swimming . . . in Circles*. That was the concept. Two albums, maybe three. But definitely two halves that formed a whole, displaying the dualities of Malcolm McCormick.

The drugs were back now. In Chile, he had people traveling with him, people that other people there did not know. Anytime Malcolm had strange people around, they knew—those were his drug dealers. The vibe was weird.

But the new music was good too. It built on *The Divine Feminine*, which was a good record, a strong record, though not exactly a hit record, despite debuting at number two on the charts.

Not that it mattered. Malcolm had worked hard to build his fan base, the Mac Heads. These kids were loyal. Wherever he went, they went right there with him.

To get his buzz going, he dropped a couple of singles—"Small Worlds" (featuring John Mayer on guitar), "Buttons," and "Programs." They were warmly embraced by his fans; it was seen as a welcome return and a sign of good things to come.

• • •

On August 1, Malcolm was performing. He was at the offices of NPR, sitting in front of a microphone, a gray shirt over his lean frame, brown dad hat atop his head.[17]

Backing him for his *Tiny Desk Concerts* performance were Justus West on guitar, Klynik on keys, Joe Cleveland on bass, Kendall Lewis on drums, Robin Fay Massie on violin, YaShauna Swan on second violin, Lelia Walker on viola, and Melanie Hsu on cello. To his immediate right was Thundercat, who he'd pleaded with to cut loose from a tour in Eastern Europe just to be there that day, and with whom he'd periodically trade witty banter.

"[Mac] really wanted it to be magical every time he would do something," Thundercat said. "He wanted to feel comfortable in front of everybody, to a degree—he wanted to introduce people to how it really works for him. And he didn't think I was going to show up . . . And I showed up. It was one of those moments, like, no way, *you're really* here."[18]

Swimming was out in days. Who knew what it would do in the marketplace. Who cared. The music business had changed considerably since the Rostrum days; no longer were big first week sales important. Now it was all about streams. Algorithms had encroached on DJs, playlists had supplanted radio, and Twitter, Instagram, and Reddit had laid waste to music critics.

"You have to kind of be the architect of what you're making and not think about what the current world is doing, or what the climate is right now, or what people are gravitating towards," Malcolm said. "I'm just trying to make music for people who have similar thoughts or feelings as me."[19]

In his own way, Malcolm was stuck in a previous era. He was still making albums, complete, singular, artistic statements; all anyone wanted was fast food, and here he came with a whole-ass meal.

Home for him was not on the charts, though he always charted well. No, his home was on the road, in front of the fans, where all those years ago he laid claim to his future. First in his Honda, then in Will Kalson's Volvo, then a Sprinter van, before graduating to the big leagues: a tour bus. It all happened so quickly, and yet, not really. It had been nine years since *The High Life*, a decade since the Ill Spoken.

Beedie—Brian Green—he remembered him. Back in March, at a Pittsburgh Starbucks, when Malcolm was home to accompany his friend Dylan Reynolds to the hospital for cancer treatment—he shaved his own head in solidarity—Malcolm saw Brian in line, jumped on his back.

"Surprise—it's me!—Little Malcolm. Here's my number, text me," Mac said. "For sure, for sure," Beedie said, but he never did.

All Malcolm really wanted was to hang out again. He was in Pittsburgh more these days, reconnecting with childhood friends, supporting the ones who had always been there for him; he seemed to be searching for parts of himself that he had lost along the way.

Bill Niels saw him in April. Malcolm played him *Swimming*, the early version, then they went to the movies. Him, Q, Malcolm; three old friends, former roommates, together again. Inside the theater, they watched *Rampage*, laughing among themselves. Afterward, they went for burgers. More laughter. More fun. It was like old times, except it was not. The kids they thought they were, they were no longer. They'd been a few places, seen a few things.

Bill had taken to rapping. He had always rapped but never with any real dedication; Malcolm encouraged him, but Bill had spent years dealing with drug addiction. He was clean now. Better. And rapping his ass off. "Send me a beat," Bill said. But Malcolm was busy. So Bill would check in every once in a while, send him positive messages. Then the breakup with Ariana came.

"Are you alright, what's going on with you?" Bill texted him.

"Read the news," Malcolm texted back.

"I don't give a fuck about the news," Bill responded. "I'm asking you if you're OK."

Malcolm was silent. And then: a meme. LeBron James crying. That was it. After breaking up with one of the most famous women in the world, that was all he had to say.

"I mean, all the joking that we do as friends together is a defense mechanism," Bill said. "I think he just wanted to keep a positive view of things. He just didn't wanna be negative. Ever. He was just a positive person. He always so forgiving and positive. Like, 'Oh, don't worry about that, everything's fine.' I think it was good that he was a positive person and he was keeping a positive attitude, but I think he was throwing things under the bus that he needed to deal with in a different way that he never did."

Bill still wanted that beat, though. The songs he had been writing were raw and emotive, exploring addiction and trauma, heavy themes that permeated his existence. One night in late August, he texted Malcolm again:

"I'm planning on putting out this EP and I have 5 songs, I really think that it would be completing the story just to have your touch on it. It was really hard recording and writing this stuff about myself, talking about all this rehab, lying, and doing heroin, it sucks, but I really felt it necessary to express that."

Malcolm got the message, read the message, was moved by the message.

"Miss you, man," Malcolm said. "I'ma sit at my computer right now. Give me a moment."

Then, all of a sudden, an MP3 arrived. It was little more than a kick and a snare, with a beautiful chord progression layered atop, courtesy of his Fender Rhodes. Bill sat there, just listening. The beat that would soon become "New Wings"—from Bill Waves's *For the Lost Children* EP, and the last song Malcolm would produce in his lifetime—was simple and direct. All that music Bill was making was music he thought nobody, not even his friends, were paying attention to. But Malcolm heard; he was paying attention even when it seemed that he wasn't.

"I love you, man," Malcolm wrote him. "Proud of you. Every day."

Malcolm had time that night to make a beat for Bill, because, well, time was all he had now. Dating Ariana, a mainstream celebrity, had turned him into a tabloid magnet, and the car accident hadn't helped. Every time he left the house now, paparazzi were on his ass. In turn, he had become a complete homebody.

"I just stay in the house," he told FakeShoreDrive's Andrew Barber one night in late June, after Barber stopped by with his artist Valee. "Anytime I go out, something bad happens. I go out, and people write about me. They just had me on TMZ."

"He was on a self-imposed exile," Barber recalled. "But he was in great spirits. Everyone was chilling, having a good time. He was giving a little perspective and game to Valee about how to maneuver in the industry, tips on how to survive, without being preachy. But that made me feel sad for a moment. Like OK, that sucks; you got all this money, fame; you were just dating Ariana Grande. Literally, you could go do anything in the world that you want right now, but you're staying isolated in the house."[20]

Being home had its perks, though. Just as before, back when he'd had the mansion in Studio City, artists stopped by; the vibe in the new house, despite the isolation, was—as always—creative. One night that June, the rapper/ singer Post Malone stopped in, leading to a jam session with him, Malcolm, Thundercat, and producer Frank Dukes (who Malcolm had worked with but never actually met).

"Mac was the first artist to get me, Mac was the first one that tweeted me," Post Malone said. "It's so weird, because I listened to him since the beginning. I was like, *This guy is fucking awesome, this guy is cool as shit.* And then to be able to meet him, and become friends was just like—I look up to you. Now we're sitting here playing beer pong. We were sitting there playing beer pong, and we were like let's make a fucking album, we were coming up with names."[21]

Recording for the proposed album never took place, but it seemed that only when he was creative—in the studio or on the stage—was Malcolm now free. Like the NPR *Tiny Desk Concerts* performance, where fresh off a coast-to-coast flight, he was seemingly unbothered by anything, back in his element, rapping about those years, so long ago.

"He told me that he was a little nervous," *Tiny Desk Concerts* producer Bobby Carter recalled. "This was the first time they would perform these songs live . . . He was the real deal."

The performance was haunting; microphone beneath his jaw, he appeared joyful yet still strangely somber, the lightness and darkness that had defined him for so long embodied in one seventeen-minute clip. Looking out at the camera, out at the world, out at you, his lyrics from "2009" seeming to echo like a coda.

"It ain't 2009 no more / Yeah, I know what's behind that door . . ."

"That was the year that all this really started for me," he said in an interview with Apple Music 1 radio host Zane Lowe to promote *Swimming*. Behind the door, he said, was a "crazy world."

And the crazy world came with so many crazy things, all of which he had experienced, and thankfully lived through. Creation, he said, was the impetus for everything; the compulsive need to create was the thing that made him open that door in the first place, and what led him down the paths, both good and bad, that his life had taken.

"The real addiction and the real self-destruction [have] always come from creating," he said. "Because that's just where I've put all my energy. And it's just, that has taken up so much space in my brain that in the past I hadn't left room for an actual life to be happening. It was just all making music, all the time . . . you run out of life to talk about."[22]

Then there was a series of small shows. They were just for the fans, at the Hotel Cafe, in LA. Three nights, August 3 to 5, with his new band, priming himself for the road.

"It ain't 2009 no more / Yeah, I know what's behind that door . . ."

The Hotel Cafe was tiny. It fit only two hundred people. That's why Adele, John Mayer, Ed Sheeran, and countless others liked it. That's why Mac Miller liked it.

And more than two hundred people showed up each night. Lines snaked around the block. They had to turn people away. The shows were great.

"He brought it every single night," said the Hotel Cafe's Gia Hughes. "The energy was super high. People were really, really excited. A lot of people might be more guarded or aloof, but he just seemed like he gave himself to people. He wanted his fans to feel seen and heard by him, and that is rare. Mac Miller—people felt connected to him. It came down to his energy and his disposition, how happy and kind he seemed to be. He was a light."[23]

"It ain't 2009 no more / Yeah, I know what's behind that door . . ."

In the crowd, new friends, old friends, everyone friends.

"We were staying at a hotel, and my wife befriended an older couple sitting poolside, having some drinks, listening to some music," CeeLo recalled. "And it turns out, it's Mac Miller's parents. He calls me—'Hey man, I heard you met my parents!' So we posse'd up, went over there together, to the show, with his parents. He also had Lil Xan there; Jason Sudeikis was there. He was one of those lightning rods that could have brought a room full of very interesting people together, which he did. His thing was not a phase or a joke or a facade, it was a very real thing. Mac Miller was one of those genuine articles."

He even saw someone he hadn't seen in years. That had been happening lately, like the time, around then, when he reconnected with Nomi Leasure in a Brooklyn bar, gulping down pale ales as she knocked back martinis. They hadn't seen each other in two years, not since they had lived in the Dumbo apartment. There was a lot to unpack, and so the night wore on until the bar was set to close, when she spoke of her new relationship, and he seemed to indicate he was looking to put his previous one behind him.[24]

But it was not Nomi at the Hotel Cafe that night, no. That night, as Malcolm walked off the stage, there he was—Benjy Grinberg. Despite any differences they might have had, neither had ever uttered a bad word about the other. They were just a couple of Jewish kids from Pittsburgh who loved hip-hop and made history together. They shared a hug. It was all love.

"It ain't 2009 no more / Yeah, I know what's behind that door . . ."

And backstage, his family—mother, father, brother—and other famous friends.

"I always detect this moment watching someone perform where I can tell they've finally got rid of the nerves," John Mayer, who played on *Swimming*, told Malcolm after one Hotel Cafe show. "And I remember the lyric—it was *shame on you*. You said *shame on you*, and I saw this glint in your eye—*now you're here*."[25]

Wasn't this what it was all for? All that torture? To have this moment, this respect—this life! A most dope one indeed. How far he'd come.

It was, after all, in 2009, when he sat on the porch at his parents' house, searching for names. A name for the crew, for the movement, that's what Malcolm needed. A bunch of names were on the table. But Q—his old friend Q—had one that everyone, especially Malcolm, liked.

"We should call it Most Dope," Q said. "Because everything we do is more dope than everything else, and we're just the most dope out of everybody else."[26]

Malcolm loved it. "Let's go get tattoos," he said. He wanted everyone to get something permanent on their bodies representing an idea that, in theory, didn't even really exist yet—he was that confident and that convincing.

And they went down that very same day to Sinners & Saints Tattoo Shop in Pittsburgh's East End, the whole crew, and made it official.

"This shit's gonna blow up," Malcolm told them.

Now he was here. Now he was here. Now he was here.

"It ain't 2009 no more / Yeah, I know what's behind that door . . ."

But something wasn't right.

"Have I done drugs? Yeah," he told *Rolling Stone* while promoting *Swimming*. "But am I a drug addict? No."[27]

In truth, he was at war once again with the demons he fought from within. As far back as July, he had been dabbling, putting in orders for large amounts of drugs—Oxycodone, Xanax, and cocaine.[28]

At one LA recording studio that summer, an influential songwriter recalled walking into the lounge only to find Mac Miller passed out on the floor. He was so drunk and high that he didn't even know where he was.

"This guy's a mess," the songwriter recalled thinking, while picking him up.

He had a sober coach, managers, and a family who loved him dearly. But there was only so much they could do. They had lives, too. Many of his close friends, The Most Dope Family, were gone. They were busy pursuing other things, caught up with their own personal struggles, or excised from Malcolm's circle for reasons that, to them, were never quite clear.

Malcolm once wrote on Twitter, years earlier, "The happiest little kids are the saddest little kids when they're alone."[29]

Now he was alone. Perhaps he always was. Ariana, with whom he'd shared such a passionate, loving, public relationship, would later tell *Vogue*: "I loved him," but still—"I didn't know him."

He had demons, that much she knew. He had spent much of his career fighting back those demons, trying to find himself in the music along the way.[30]

"I don't really know who Mac Miller, the artist, is . . ." he once confessed.[31]

What he was searching for at the time was a North Star, something to aim at, somewhere to go, and something to say. He was always searching. Through six albums, nine mixtapes, dozens of collaborations—in total, more than six hundred songs—he was always searching, his greatest addiction, his raison d'être, the creative act itself.

And it was all right there. He was all right there. You just had to listen.

"I lived a certain life for ten years and faced almost no real consequence at all," he said. "I had no version of the story that didn't end up with me being fine."[32]

"It ain't 2009 no more / Yeah, I know what's behind that door . . ."

Two days later, in the early morning hours of September 7, 2018, Malcolm McCormick opened that door for the last time.

Finally, he was home.

EPILOGUE

On the morning of September 7, 2018, Malcolm's personal assistant found him on his bed in a "praying position." He was unresponsive, turning blue, and had fluid leaking from his mouth.

His assistant called 911 and performed CPR.

Police who arrived at the scene noted, inside his home studio, a small bag containing a "white powdery substance," an iPad with "linear white powdery residue" on it—white lines, in other words—and an empty bottle of liquor. Inside Malcolm's bedroom was a bottle of prescription medication (prescribed to him), another empty bottle of liquor and in his right pocket a twenty-dollar bill with a white powder residue on it.

Three days earlier, according to a DEA report, he allegedly made two purchases of drugs—one from a madam named Mia Johannson, delivered to him by a sex worker whose services he paid for named Karla Amador; and another from a dealer named Cameron James Pettit.

The drugs—cocaine, Adderall, Norco, Xanax, and Oxycodone—were found inside a coat in his closet. Among them were six "blues," purchased from Pettit, that were thought to be Oxycodone, and later tested positive for a lethal dose of fentanyl. A magazine with blue powder residue was found inside an open safe, as were a "rolled piece of paper and a credit-style gift card."

Malcolm was pronounced dead at 11:51 A.M. He was believed to have crushed and snorted the counterfeit Oxycodone containing fentanyl, leading to his death. The Los Angeles County Coroner determined Malcolm had passed away accidentally due to mixed drug toxicity—fentanyl, cocaine, and ethanol were present in his system at the time.

His assistant noted that, beforehand, Malcolm's mood had been positive, he had no known health issues or illnesses, but he did struggle with sobriety—when he "slipped," he would consume drugs, specifically Xanax and assorted opiates, in "excess." His most recent "slip" had been days earlier, on September 4.

Although just one among hundreds of thousands of opioid-related deaths to have occurred since the start of the opioid crisis in 2010, and just another in a series of fentanyl-related incidents that had recently taken the lives of musicians Prince, Tom Petty, and Lil Peep, Malcolm's death—like theirs—was a horrific tragedy. Many who saw him in the weeks before his passing said he seemed to be in good spirits, and like *The Divine Feminine* before it, *Swimming* had been a creative leap, opening a new chapter in the book that he was writing for himself. He was set to begin a tour that October that would find him in venues he had never played before, like Madison Square Garden, where he once said it was his dream to perform.[1]

There was no inclination his death was planned, although in countless songs, and in numerous interviews, he made it clear he knew the risks of his lifestyle. Among his dozens of tattoos, including MOST DOPE spelled across his fingers, the Pittsburgh Pirates logo on his right hand, John Lennon's face, and the A Tribe Called Quest–inspired words BEATS, RHYMES AND LIFE, was an Outkast quote: "Only so much time left in this crazy world." Indeed.

Malcolm long admired tragic figures, artists who lived hard and died just the same. One of his least known but most brilliant songs is an instrumental called "M.H.B." Released in 2013, just ahead of *Watching Movies with the Sound Off*, it features clips of cult comedian Mitch Hedberg detailing his unlikely rise over a plaintive piano. Hedberg, who in 2005 also died of an accidental overdose,[2] was a major influence on Malcolm.

"If you spend your whole life preparing, then you're never going to do anything," he recalled Hedberg once saying. "Just jump in and do it. That's the best way to get better at something. Do it while you suck at it."[3]

Back when he was still Easy Mac, not yet Mac Miller, Malcolm had jumped right in. Now, all these years later, he was here. He was excited for his upcoming tour, tweeting his enthusiasm about it the day before. That night, after reportedly spending the evening out with friends watching the Philadelphia Eagles play the Atlanta Falcons, he returned home and found himself, in a way, back where he'd once started—livestreaming to his fans.

"I don't know if I'll ever do this again," he said ominously, as he turned the camera to his home studio to make beats on Instagram Live. Later, he took to Instagram Stories, placing the camera in front of his turntable as "So It Goes," the last song on *Swimming*, played out. At one o'clock in the morning, he wrote on Twitter about the song's ending:

"I told Jon Brion to play the ascension into heaven and he nailed it."

A few hours later, he exchanged direct messages on Twitter with a producer, Tee-WaTT, telling him he planned to record on a number of his beats. "I'ma go in on a shit load of these [*sic*]," he wrote.[4]

These were not the actions of someone who wanted to go.

News of his death hit with enormous impact. Tributes poured in from: Drake, J. Cole, Kendrick Lamar, G-Eazy, Chance the Rapper, Lil B, Earl Sweatshirt, Vince Staples, Wiz Khalifa, Shawn Mendes, Post Malone, Miguel, Snoop Dogg, Maroon 5, Elton John, Liam Gallagher, Halsey, and . . . Ariana Grande. In Pittsburgh, hundreds of people gathered for a vigil held in his honor at Blue Slide Park. And the following month, a commemorative concert called "Celebration of Life," at the Greek Theatre in Los Angeles, saw Travis Scott, John Mayer, Rae Sremmurd, SZA, Anderson .Paak, Vince Staples, Action Bronson, and Thundercat perform; by video, Pharrell Williams, Donald Glover, Pusha T, G-Eazy, and Tyler, the Creator, sent their love.

Despite his records never garnering much radio play, Malcolm remained a cultural and commercial juggernaut. In his life, he sat for hundreds of interviews, and answered thousands of questions. His music videos have been viewed hundreds of millions of times, and his six studio albums—including *Circles*, released posthumously—all charted in the top five on *Billboard*. He earned a 2019 Best Rap Album Grammy nomination for *Swimming*.

Perhaps most importantly, he always remained loyal to his fans. One supporter recalled the Mac Heads putting together a scrapbook: It featured their favorite lyrics, photos of their Mac Miller tattoos, letters, and other assorted ephemera. When he was presented with it, he was so overcome with emotion that he reached out to some of the contributors to thank them personally. He was not above responding to seemingly random fans directly on Twitter, giving his time to listen to their concerns while offering his advice and/or support. It is unknown how many lives he saved through the struggles he endured.

Though his later music saw him venture beyond his comfort zone, Malcolm will likely be remembered as a hip-hop legend. He leaves behind a treasure trove of unreleased music (perhaps it will one day be released), and the lingering question of where his creativity would have taken him had he lived.

Nevertheless, through the power of the Internet, where much of his journey began, fans new and old continue to discuss, debate, and dissect the massive amounts of himself that he left behind. They toast to his legacy, they turn up in honor, and they continue to celebrate Mac Miller and his most dope, most extraordinary life.

ACKNOWLEDGMENTS

This book would not exist with the love and support of my wife, who when things got dark was my life-affirming source of light, provided me space and time to work, and offered me priceless insight regarding its execution and content. This book would also not exist without my daughter, who was born when the project was in its infancy, was a bottomless well of inspiration, and kept me sane throughout.

I also want to thank my father—for everything, but especially for putting the music in my soul as a youth. And I want to thank my mother, for putting the fight in me, and whose passing when I was young taught me so much about loss. Finally, thank you to my extended family, every last one of you; now you get to read the thing I've been talking about all these years at Thanksgiving.

Most importantly, I'd like to thank Mac Miller, who despite his tragic death, undoubtedly lived an interesting life, one worth writing about. And I want to send a special note of gratitude to all the people who talked to me for this book, many of whom didn't know me from a hole in the wall but opened their doors not only to their homes but to their deepest memories and reflections during a time of tremendous grief. Thank you to Artie Pitt, for being a friend in real life and for pushing me to keep writing. Thank you to Clockwork, for the hours you sat getting drilled with questions. Will Kalson, for the trips down memory lane. Bill Niels, for a tough but honest conversation. TreeJ, because you hadn't talked to anyone in years, but you talked to me. Darelle Revis, for taking the time out of NFL retirement. Brian Green, for being a real one. Soy Sos, for giving it to me straight. Franchise, for picking up that call. Palermo Stone, for being the dot that connected so much of this story. Peanut, appreciate you. Big Jerm, for being there from day one, and really being open to talking about everything. Justin Strong, thank you for putting me back in the Shadow Lounge, despite never having been there. Sap, for having such a strong memory of what went into "Donald Trump." Statik Selektah, for the hours of game you gave me (and Malcolm). Peter Rosenberg, for years of friendship and good talk. Wendy Day, for the Eminem stories. Ruddy Rock, for being you. Seth Zaplin, for being a New York City nightlife legend. Phonte, for mothers. Sha Money XL, for all you've done for the culture. Rondell Conway and Vanessa Satten, for the years of work you put in documenting hip-hop for real. Jayson Rodriguez, for flipping me that crucial MTV *When I Was 17* transcript (Magic Johnson couldn't have thrown a better alley-oop). Bun B, for being so gracious with your time, and giving up so much game. CeeLo, for jumping on the phone with one of your biggest fans. Ritz Reynolds, for "Missed Calls" and taking such a deep dive into your memory banks. DJ Premier, for everything you've ever done, and being there for Malcolm when he needed you. Just Blaze, for nerding out with me. Andrew Barber, for perceiving something about Malcolm few probably would. Darin Byrne, for your sharp recollection of the MTV show. Insanul Ahmed, for the many hours you put in documenting Malcolm in his early years, and for your honesty in all matters. Andy Cohn, for picking up that call and making that cover happen. Scott Perry, for working with Malcolm on the *Fader* doc "Stopped Making Excuses." Jordan Sargent, for being open to talk. Logic, for being willing to admit when you were inspired by someone—something not all artists, let alone popular ones, are willing to do. MusicManTy, for making magic with Malcolm and Ariana. Robert Glasper, for bringing such a crucial part of *The Divine Feminine* to life and being open about your experiences with Malcolm. Gia Hughes, for working at those final shows at the Hotel Cafe, and your willingness to discuss them. All the professional journalists, amateur journalists, bloggers, radio broadcasters, DJs—anyone who ever documented anything about Malcolm, and tried to do so in an honest and accurate way—thank you so much. Without you all this book would not be possible.

Let me also extend my appreciation to Abrams, everyone from the HR department to accounting to tech support to the person who takes out the office trash—you have no idea how much you matter. Now, specifically, let me thank my editor, Samantha Weiner, for her patience and care. This book was a labor of love, and I am certain that my delays, my endless tinkering, and my inability to leave well enough alone drove you up the wall, but in the end I think it was all worth it. Shout out Jamison Stoltz, too, for your leadership. Thank you to my first agent on this book, William LoTurco, for your attention, care, and belief that there was a book in me to be written. And thank you to my second agent on this book, Robert Guinsler, for stepping in at a crucial moment, providing great compassion and a steadying presence. Also thank you to Annalea Manalili, copy editor Janet Rosenberg, and proofreaders Mark Amundsen and Joy Sanchez for really helping tighten things up. And designer Eli Mock for making the book look so beautiful. Michael Pratt, too, deserves a ton of credit—as my assistant, you did a bang-up job as a transcriptionist, researcher, and travel buddy. Good people are in short supply, and I am super grateful to call you a friend.

Now we come to the end. And as anyone who has ever done it knows, writing a book is triumph of will; but often, so too is finishing one. If you have come this far, I want to thank you. You have been on this journey with me from page one, and the hours we have spent together have meant the world to me. I hope they have meant the world to you, and that one day in the near future we get to do it all again.

NOTES

PROLOGUE

1. Patrica Garcia, "Mac Miller on Love, Ariana Grande, and the Last Thing That Made Him Cry," *Vogue*, September 27, 2016, www.vogue.com/article/mac-miller-the-divine-feminine-album.
2. Mary Wormcastle, interview by author, September 11, 2018.
3. Rembert Browne, "Mac Miller Finds the Way," *Grantland*, August 20, 2015, grantland.com/features/mac-miller-good-am-album/.
4. DJ Clockwork, interview by the author, August 1, 2019.
5. Bun B, interview by author, July 15, 2020.

ONE

1. David Nasaw, *Andrew Carnegie* (New York: Penguin Press, 2006), 113–14.
2. Ibid.
3. R. Jay Gangewere, "Henry Clay Frick: 'The Man' Was a Businessman," *Carnegie*, March/April 1997, carnegiemuseums.org/magazine-archive/1997/marapr/dept2.htm.

TWO

1. Aron A., "Mac Miller's Mom Shares Original Birth Announcement on Birthday," HNHH, August 21, 2019, www.hotnewhiphop.com/mac-millers-mom-shares-original-birth-announcement-on-birthday-news.69990.html.
2. "Mac Miller—Everything You Need to Know (Episode 36)," *Fader*, October 27, 2016, YouTube video, www.youtube.com/watch?v=j0KRaf8YJB4.

3. Insanul Ahmed, "My Son Is a Rapper: Meet Mac Miller's Mom, Karen Meyers," *Complex*, May 11, 2014, www.complex.com/music/2014/05/mac -miller-mom-karen-meyers-interview.

4. "Mark McCormick," McCormick Architects + Designers, n.d., mccormickarch .com/about/.

5. Donald Miller, "Spinning Off Mt. Lebanon Library's Success Story, *Pittsburgh Post-Gazette*, August 17, 1997, 90.

6. Ahmed, "My Son Is a Rapper."

7. Mac Miller, interview by aliattherave, May 31, 2011, YouTube video, www .youtube.com/watch?v=CCWn2AuDs_M.

8. Insanul Ahmed, "Mac Miller's 25 Favorite Albums," *Complex*, June 19, 2013, www.complex.com/music/2013/06/mac-millers-25-favorite-albums/.

9. Matthew Strauss, "Mac Miller on His Days as a Dickhead Weed Dealer," Pitchfork, September 16, 2016, pitchfork.com/thepitch/1293-mac-miller -on-his-days-as-a-dickhead-weed-dealer/.

10. John Norris, "Mac Miller Talks Ariana Grande, Donald Trump, Making the Soulful Celebration of Women & Love 'The Divine Feminine,'" Billboard.com, September 14, 2016, www.billboard.com/articles/columns/hip-hop/7510294/ mac-miller-ariana-grande-donald-trump-divine-feminine-interview.

11. Ahmed, "Mac Miller's 25 Favorite Albums."

12. "Mac Miller, the Albums That Changed My Life," posted by Bill My Zoot, Kanye to The, September 7, 2018, www.kanyetothe.com/threads/mac-miller -the-albums-that-changed-my-life.8084951/.

13. Rob Boffard, "Mac Miller Doesn't Perform 'Donald Trump' Anymore and Was Inspired by Bob Dylan on 'The Divine Feminine,'" Exclaim!, November 22, 2016, exclaim.ca/music/article/mac_miller_doesnt_perform_donald_trump _anymore_and_was_inspired_by_bob_dylan_on_the_divine_feminine.

14. Ibid.

15. Ahmed, "My Son Is a Rapper."

16. Tracy Certo, "Mac Miller remembered by four Pittsburghers who knew him well," NEXTpittsburgh, September 10, 2018, nextpittsburgh.com/features/ mac-miller-remembered-by-four-pittsburghers-who-knew-him-well/.

17. Adam Reinherz, "Mac Miller, global rap icon, remembered as genuine, appreciative friend," *Pittsburgh Jewish Chronicle*, September 21, 2018, jewishchronicle.timesofisrael.com/mac-miller-global-rap-icon-remembered -as-genuine-appreciative-friend/.

18. Justin Jacobs, "Mac Miller raps his way into the spotlight," *Pittsburgh Jewish Chronicle*, September 5, 2010, jewishchronicle.timesofisrael.com/mac-miller -raps-his-way-into-the-spotlight/.

19. Jen Long, "'One day kids are gonna learn my songs': Best Fit meets Mac Miller," The Line of Best Fit, June 20, 2012, www.thelineofbestfit.com/ features/interviews/mac-miller-99283.

20. "About Us," St. Bede School, n.d., www.saintbedeschool.com/apps/pages/ index.jsp?uREC_ID=1929448&type=d&pREC_ID=2063816.

21. Alex Oh and Jacob Paul, "Mac Miller's Blue Slide Park Vigil," *Tartan*, September 16, 2018, thetartan.org/2018/9/17/news/mac-miller.

22. Alyssa Adoni, "Young Mac Miller Freestyle on a School Bus," May 8, 2019, YouTube video, www.youtube.com/watch?v=6CxNuhIx2dM&ab_channel =AlyssaAdoni.

23. Adam Reinherz, "Mac Miller, global rap icon, remembered as genuine, appreciative friend," *Pittsburgh Jewish Chronicle*, September 21, 2018, jewishchronicle.timesofisrael.com/mac-miller-global-rap-icon-remembered -as-genuine-appreciative-friend/.

24. "Passover with Mac Miller," *Forbes*, December 21, 2011, YouTube video, www .youtube.com/watch?v=RRqcS5sm6D4&ab_channel=Forbes.

25. Jacobs, "Mac Miller raps his way."

THREE

1. Will Kalson, interview by author, June 1, 2019.

2. Insanul Ahmed, "25 Things You Didn't Know About Mac Miller," *Complex*, January 29, 2013, www.complex.com/music/2013/01/25-things-you-didnt -know-about-mac-miller/guitar.

3. "Mac Miller, the Albums That Changed My Life," posted by Bill My Zoot, Kanye to The, September 7, 2018, www.kanyetothe.com/threads/mac-miller -the-albums-that-changed-my-life.8084951/.

4. Ibid.

5. James Rudolph, "Childhood memories of Malcolm McCormick," *Cal Times*, September 21, 2018, www.caltimes.org/4734/showcase/my-memories-of -malcolm-mccormick/.

6. Ahmed, "25 Things You Didn't Know."

7. Mac Miller, interview by *The Come Up Show*, March 17, 2011, YouTube video, www.youtube.com/watch?v=oyMWRedER04&ab_channel heComeUpShow.

FOUR

1. Brian "Beedie" Green, interview by the author, June 2, 2019.

2. Bill Niels, interview by the author, August 13, 2019.

3. TreeJ, interview by the author, August 11, 2019.

4. Mac Miller, interview by Jayson Rodriguez, *When I Was 17*, MTV, September 4, 2012.

5. Ibid.

6. Ibid.

7. Mac Miller, interview by Sway's Universe, "Mac Miller & the Sway in the Morning Mystery Sack: Story of Lost Virginity & Favorite Genre of Porn," Sway's Universe, May 3, 2013, YouTube video, www.youtube.com/watch?v=_UM _qYoUeSo&t=84s&ab_channel=SWAY%27SUNIVERSE.

8. Miller, interview by Rodriguez.

9. Ibid.

10. Ibid.

11. Ibid.

FIVE

1. Brian "Beedie" Green, interview by the author, June 2, 2019.
2. "But My Mackin' Ain't Easy," mixtape tracks posted by Keyn0te, January 20, 2011, DatPiff, www.datpiff.com/Mac-Miller-But-My-Mackin-Aint-Easy -mixtape.190925.html.
3. Owners of Frick Park Market, interview by the author, September 11, 2018.
4. Ibid.
5. Soy Sos, interview by the author, June 4, 2019.

SIX

1. Will Schube, "The Crash and Resurrection of Benjy Grinberg, the Chief of Rap's Last Great Independent Label," *Tablet*, March 16, 2020, www.tablet mag.com/sections/arts-letters/articles/benjy-grinberg-rostrum-records.
2. Arthur Pitt, interview by the author, June 19, 2019.
3. Terry Gross, "The Lyrics and Legacy of Stephen Foster," NPR, April 16, 2010, www.npr.org/templates/story/story.php?storyId=126035325#:~:text =Known%20as%20the%20%22father%20of,%22My%20Old%20 Kentucky%20Home.%22.
4. "Pittsburgh Music History: 1865 to 1929," Pittsburgh Music History, n.d., sites.google.com/site/pittsburghmusichistory/chronology/1865-to-1930.
5. "Pittsburgh—The Crossroads of Jazz," Pittsburgh Music History, n.d., sites .google.com/site/pittsburghmusichistory/pittsburgh-music-story/jazz.
6. "Pittsburgh Music History: Doo-Wop & Vocal Groups," Pittsburgh Music History, n.d., sites.google.com/site/pittsburghmusichistory/pittsburgh -music-story/doo-wop.
7. Eric Arnum, "Clubs Around Country Get Wired for Webcasts," MTV, July 26, 1999, www.mtv.com/news/516248/clubs-around-country-get-wired-for -webcasts/.
8. Neil Strauss, "A New Industry Threat: CD's Made from Webcasts," *New York Times*, December 12, 2001, www.nytimes.com/2001/12/12/arts/the-pop -life-a-new-industry-threat-cd-s-made-from-webcasts.html.
9. Lola Ogunnaike, "And They Said He Couldn't Run a Major Record Label," *New York Times*, March 2, 2003, www.nytimes.com/2003/03/02/arts/ music-and-they-said-he-couldn-t-run-a-major-record-label.html.
10. Ed Masley, "A rapper on the rise," *Pittsburgh Post-Gazette*, July 24, 2005, www.post-gazette.com/uncategorized/2005/07/24/A-rapper-on-the-rise/ stories/200507240188.
11. Benjy Grinberg, interview by Latif Tayour, *It's Show Business with Latif Tayour*, January 14, 2020, podcasts.apple.com/us/podcast/15-benjy-grinberg -of-rostrum-records/id1481980802?i=1000462446775.
12. Ashley Westerman, "50 Years Later, The Archies' 'Sugar, Sugar' Is Still 'Really Sweet,'" NPR, September 20, 2019, www.npr.org/2019/09/20/761616330/50 -years-later-the-archies-sugar-sugar-is-still-really-sweet.
13. "Nitty," profile page on iMusic.am, n.d., imusic.am/ar/zJ7MsR.

14. Josie Roberts, "The hip-hop pulse," Trib Total Media, June 28, 2005, archive
.triblive.com/news/the-hip-hop-pulse/.

15. Keith Nelson Jr., "Tour Tales: DJ Bonics saw Wiz Khalifa bring Pittsburgh
to Africa and has memories from '2009 Tour,'" Revolt.TV, March 26, 2019,
www.revolt.tv/2019/3/26/20825280/tour-tales-dj-bonics-saw-wiz-khalifa
-bring-pittsburgh-to-africa-and-has-memories-from-2009-tour.

16. Michael Machosky, "ID Labs in Lawrenceville keeps Pittsburgh on the
hip-hop map," Trib Total Media, July 31, 2011, archive.triblive.com/news/
id-labs-in-lawrenceville-keeps-pittsburgh-on-the-hip-hop-map.

17. Masley, "A rapper on the rise."

18. Aaron Jentzen, "Prince of the City," *Pittsburgh City Paper*, October 5,
2006, www.pghcitypaper.com/pittsburgh/prince-of-the-city/Content
?oid=1334078.

19. Roberts, "The hip-hop pulse."

20. Kimbel Bouwman, "Interview with Benjy Grinberg, president of Rostrum
Records and A&R; and manager for Wiz Khalifa, Mac Miller," HitQuarters,
October 17, 2011, web.archive.org/web/20121115012505/http://www.hit
quarters.com/index.php3?page=intrview/opar/intrview_BGrinberg.html.

21. Masley, "A rapper on the rise."

22. Pitt, interview by author.

23. Masley, "A rapper on the rise."

SEVEN

1. Ali Shaheed Muhammad and Frannie Kelley "Microphone Check—Mac
Miller: 'It's OK to Feel Yourself,'" NPR, September 29, 2015, www.npr.org/
sections/microphonecheck/2015/09/29/444212099/mac-miller-its-ok-to
-feel-yourself.

2. "Mac Miller Finally Comes Outside, Launches New Material & Reminds
Us He's Funny as F*@k!," *Ebro in the Morning*, HOT 97, August 7, 2015,
YouTube video, www.youtube.com/watch?v=fxNvmVDiwD8&ab_channel
=HOT97.

3. Soy Sos, interview by author, June 4, 2019.

4. Ross Scarano, "Mac Miller's 15 Favorite Movies," *Complex*, January 31, 2013,
www.complex.com/pop-culture/2013/01/mac-millers-15-favorite-movies/
royal-tenenbaums.

5. Jim Straub and Bret Liebendorfer, "Braddock, Pennsylvania Out of the Fur-
nace and into the Fire," *Monthly Review*, December 1, 2008, monthlyreview
.org/2008/12/01/braddock-pennsylvania-out-of-the-furnace-and-into-the
-fire/.

6. Franchise, interview by the author, July 16, 2019.

7. Palermo Stone, interview by the author, July 11 and 22, 2019.

8. "Chatting with Ls: Mac Miller," *2Lsonacloud* (blog), June 17, 2009, miss6one5
.blogspot.com/2009/06/chatting-with-ls-mac-miller.html.

9. "Nas & Jay-Z Talks About Big L + Unseen But Seen Footage," posted by

BigKeemzHD, May 8, 2014, YouTube video, www.youtube.com/watch?v=uv4LnKdFLHc.

10. Daniel Sozomenu, "'Flamboyant:' How Rap Legends Remember Big L 20 Years After His Death," *Vibe*, March 28, 2019, www.vibe.com/features/editorial/flamboyant-how-rap-legends-remember-big-l-20-years-after-his-death-635681/.

11. Ibid.

12. "Nas & Jay-Z Talks About Big L," YouTube video.

13. Adam Fleischer, "Big L Would Have Been 40 Today: Here's How He Impacted Jay Z, Mac Miller and More," MTV, May 30, 2014, www.mtv.com/news/1835250/big-l-40th-birthday-legacy-jay-z-mac-miller/.

14. Mac Miller, "When I Was 15 . . . (vol 1?)," May 19, 2009, YouTube video, www.youtube.com/watch?v=JhwoQwJdrp0.

15. Mac Miller, interview by Jayson Rodriguez, *When I Was 17*, MTV, September 4, 2012.

16. Mac Miller, interview by Waskool, Freshen up a Bit, December 24, 2009, web.archive.org/web/20110122065152/http://waskool.blogspot.com/2009/12/mac-miller-interview-with-waskool.html.

17. Miller, interview by Rodriguez.

18. Ibid.

19. Mac Miller, interview by aliattherave, May 31, 2011, YouTube video, www.youtube.com/watch?v=CCWn2AuDs_M.

20. Ibid.

21. Miller, interview by Waskool.

22. Mac Miller, interview by itsbongoboy, September 13, 2010, YouTube video, www.youtube.com/watch?v=Ypuf-hUeYyc&ab_channel=itsbongoboy.

23. Amanda Waltz, "Remembering Malcolm McCormick," *Pittsburgh City Paper*, September 19, 2018, www.pghcitypaper.com/pittsburgh/remembering-malcolm-mccormick/Content?oid=10757539.

24. Ross Scarano, "Mac Miller's Guide to Pittsburgh," *Complex*, February 1, 2013, www.complex.com/pop-culture/2013/02/mac-millers-guide-to-pittsburgh/taylor-allderdice-high-school.

25. "Footnotes: Mac Miller," *Fader*, August 15, 2013, www.thefader.com/2013/08/15/footnotes-mac-miller.

26. Scarano, "Guide to Pittsburgh."

27. Miller, interview by Rodriguez.

28. In September of 2019, the artist Kyle Holbrook completed a mural of Malcolm himself. It stands at 204 Paulson Avenue, in the East Liberty neighborhood.

29. "Pittsburgh PA," on MLK Mural, n.d., www.mlkmural.com/mlk-mural-pittsburgh.

30. "Mac Miller Mural—Kyle Holbrook, MLK Mural Project," September 7, 2019, Artworld, YouTube video, www.youtube.com/watch?v=s5o1W-7pBZk.

31. Miller, interview by Rodriguez.

32. rtmadminnpc, "Working to guide youth to greatness," *New Pittsburgh Courier*,

October 12, 2011, newpittsburghcourier.com/2011/10/12/working-to-guide-youth-to-greatness/.

33. Shawn Cooke, "On the heels of Wiz Khalifa and Mac Miller, Pittsburgh hip hop faces a cloudy future," *Pittsburgh City Paper*, December 16, 2015, www.pghcitypaper.com/pittsburgh/on-the-heels-of-wiz-khalifa-and-mac-miller-pittsburgh-hip-hop-faces-a-cloudy-future/Content?oid=1874195.

34. Ibid.

35. Ibid.

36. Joyce Gannon, "Pittsburgh near bottom in U.S. diversity ranking." *Pittsburgh Post-Gazette*, May 14, 2015, www.post-gazette.com/business/career-workplace/2015/05/14/Pittsburgh-near-bottom-in-diversity-ranking/stories/201505140165.

EIGHT

1. Ross Scarano, "Mac Miller's Guide to Pittsburgh," *Complex*, February 1, 2013, www.complex.com/pop-culture/2013/02/mac-millers-guide-to-pittsburgh/taylor-allderdice-high-school.

2. Rory D. Webb, "Macadelic and the State of Mac Miller," *Pittsburgh City Paper*, March 26, 2012, www.pghcitypaper.com/Blogh/archives/2012/03/26/macadelic-and-the-state-of-mac-miller.

3. Aaron Jentzen, "Prince of the City," *Pittsburgh City Paper*, October 5, 2006, www.pghcitypaper.com/pittsburgh/prince-of-the-city/Content?oid=1334078.

4. "McKeesport is 4th most dangerous city in America, according to study," Pittsburgh's Action News 4, March 12, 2019, www.wtae.com/article/mckeesport-is-4th-most-dangerous-city-in-america-according-to-study/26797844#.

5. Mac Miller, interview by itsbongoboy, September 13, 2010, YouTube video, www.youtube.com/watch?v=Ypuf-hUeYyc&ab_channel=itsbongoboy.

6. Geoff Edgers, "They took Grandmaster Caz's rhymes without giving him credit. Now, he's getting revenge," *Washington Post*, September 29, 2016, www.washingtonpost.com/entertainment/music/they-took-grandmaster-cazs-rhymes-without-giving-him-credit-now-hes-getting-revenge/2016/09/29/f519c35a-7f3e-11e6-8d0c-fb6c00c90481_story.html.

7. MrDaveyD, "Hip Hop History: The Behind the Scenes Story of Sugar Hill Gang," Davey D's Hip Hop Corner, October 4, 2013, hiphopandpolitics.com/2013/10/04/hip-hop-history-behind-scenes-story-sugar-hill-gang/.

8. David Menconi, "The riff that lifted rap," *News & Observer*, July 14, 2011, web.archive.org/web/20110714175053/http://www.newsobserver.com/2010/03/14/385149/the-riff-that-lifted-rap.html.

9. Ben Westhoff, "Filming Straight Outta Compton Got a Lot More Real Than Anyone Intended," *LA Weekly*, August 11, 2015, www.laweekly.com/filming-straight-outta-compton-got-a-lot-more-real-than-anyone-intended/.

10. "Screw Rick Ross," Smoking Gun, July 21, 2008, www.thesmokinggun.com/documents/crime/screw-rick-ross.

11. Ben Sisario, "Akon's Rap Sheet Is Revealed," *New York Times*, April 17, 2008, www.nytimes.com/2008/04/17/arts/17arts-AKONSRAPSHEE_BRF.html.

12. Dave Lifton, "Read Chuck D's and LL Cool J's Complete Beastie Boys Rock and Roll Hall of Fame Induction Speeches," Diffuser.fm, April 16, 2012, diffuser.fm/read-chuck-ds-and-ll-cool-js-complete-beastie-boys-rock-and -roll-hall-of-fame-induction-speeches/.

13. Ibid.

14. Vanilla Ice, interview by Dimitri Ehrlich, *Interview*, July 14, 2011, www .interviewmagazine.com/culture/vanilla-ice.

15. James Bernard, "Why the World Is After Vanilla Ice," *New York Times*, February 3, 1991, www.nytimes.com/1991/02/03/arts/why-the-world-is -after-vanilla-ice.html.

16. Robert Hillburn, "The word on Vanilla Ice: Despite chilly reception from critics, this white rapper is today's hot property," *Baltimore Sun*, March 28, 1991, www.baltimoresun.com/news/bs-xpm-1991-03-28-1991087175-story .html.

17. Michael J. Mooney, "For us, Rob Van Winkle will always be Vanilla Ice." *Miami New Times*, November 26, 2009, www.miaminewtimes.com/music/ for-us-rob-van-winkle-will-always-be-vanilla-ice-6366096.

18. Hillburn, "Word on Vanilla Ice."

19. Ken Parish Perkins, "Vanilla Ice shrugs off conflicting stories about his background," *Salt Lake Tribune*, November 23, 1990, 82.

20. Ibid.

21. Bernard, "Why the World Is After Vanilla Ice."

22. "Vanilla Ice says 'Sorry'—Arsenio Hall interviews Vanilla Ice about MC Hammer," posted by ecks4fun, April 30, 2010, YouTube video, www.youtube .com/watch?v=yscu0SDTFYI&ab_channel=ecks4fun.

23. Wendy Day, interview by the author, November 18, 2016.

24. "Dr. Dre Tell How He Discovered Eminem In 'The Defiant Ones,'" posted by Bubba Alpine, July 13, 2017, YouTube video, www.youtube.com/ watch?v=wgztAU7p-WM&ab_channel=BubbaAlpine.

25. Eminem, interview by Mike Tyson, "Eminem | Hotboxin' with Mike Tyson," Mike Tyson, March 19, 2020, YouTube video, www.youtube.com/watch?v =vvSySR8RdzY.

26. Eddie Fu, "Eminem Recalls Being Evicted the Day Before the Rap Olympics Loss That Helped Him Get Signed," Genius, March 23, 2020, genius.com/a/ eminem-recalls-being-evicted-the-day-before-the-rap-olympics-loss-that -helped-him-get-signed.

27. Anthony Bozza, "Eminem Blows Up," *Rolling Stone*, April 29, 1999, www .rollingstone.com/music/music-news/eminem-blows-up-91979/.

28. Ibid.

29. "Dr. Dre Tell How He Discovered Eminem," YouTube video.

30. Bozza, "Eminem Blows Up."

31. "Dr. Dre Tell How He Discovered Eminem," YouTube video.

32. Ibid.

33. Richard Harrington, "'Murder,' Cashing in on Violence," *Washington Post*,

November 2, 1994, www.washingtonpost.com/archive/lifestyle/1994/11/02/
murder-cashing-in-on-violence/6cc116b8-e10c-4c5f-a8ac-852e27283718/.

34. "Dr. Dre Tell How He Discovered Eminem," YouTube video.

35. "Time Alone: Mac Miller," Mass Appeal, September 29, 2016, YouTube video, www.youtube.com/watch?v=JSWeciyoxgs.

36. Fiona Sturges, "In the rap battle, Sparxxx may fly," *Independent*, November 16, 2001, www.independent.co.uk/arts-entertainment/music/features/rap-battle-sparxxx-may-fly-5362884.html.

37. Matthew Trammell, "What Is the Place for White Rappers Today?" *Fader*, October 6, 2015, www.thefader.com/2015/10/06/white-rappers-mac-miller-vince-staples-interview.

38. Jesse Serwer, "DJ Screw: from cough syrup to full-blown fever," *Guardian*, November 11, 2010, www.theguardian.com/music/2010/nov/11/dj-screw-drake-fever-ray.

39. Michael Hall, "The Slow Life and Fast Death of DJ Screw," *Texas Monthly*, April 2001, www.texasmonthly.com/articles/the-slow-life-and-fast-death-of-dj-screw/.

40. "Bun B on Pimp C's Reaction When DJ Screw Died from Drinking Lean (Part 3)," VladTV, October 30, 2018, YouTube video, www.youtube.com/watch?v=_HcKVGQ1Yuc&ab_channel=djvlad.

41. Jessica Koslow, "CAM'RON & JIMMY JONES LAUNCH SIZZURP," HipHopDX, March 20, 2004, hiphopdx.com/news/id.2460/title.camron-jimmy-jones-launch-sizzurp#.

42. Jayson Rodriguez, "PIMP C DIED FROM ACCIDENTAL COUGH-MEDICINE OVERDOSE, SLEEP CONDITION: AUTOPSY," MTV, February 4, 2008, www.mtv.com/news/1580916/pimp-c-died-from-accidental-cough-medicine-overdose-sleep-condition-autopsy/.

43. Mac Miller, interview by Jayson Rodriguez, *When I Was 17*, MTV, September 4, 2012.

44. "Flashback: Mac Miller on Being a White Rapper and if it Helped His Career," VladTV, September 16, 2016, YouTube video, www.youtube.com/watch?v=XBz5SK33kDE&ab_channel=djvlad.

45. Mac Miller, interview by Leah Benoit, "MSU & U Episode 23: Entertainment—Mac Miller Interview," MSU&U Telecasters, November 22, 2011, YouTube video, www.youtube.com/watch?v=a3Qmr98Sw6I&ab_channel SU%26UTelecasters.

46. Mackenzie Brown, "Student, manager finds niche in hip-hop world," *Globe*, June 29, 2016, ppuglobe.com/2016/06/student-manager-finds-niche-in-hip-hop-world/.

47. Priya Pansuria, "Youngest in Charge: Quentin Cuff." AudioKorner.com, July 1, 2012, audiokorner.com/2012/07/youngest-in-charge-quentin-cuff/.

48. Brown, "Student, Manager finds niche."

49. "Mac Miller on the Origins of His Name," MTV News, September 7, 2018, YouTube video, www.youtube.com/watch?v=EqKP-sA6bCk&ab_channel TVNews.

50. Pansuria, "Youngest in Charge."

51. Kate Magoc and Rory D. Webb, "Shadow Lounge prepares to close after over a decade in a changing neighborhood," *Pittsburgh City Paper*, March 27, 2013, www.pghcitypaper.com/pittsburgh/shadow-lounge-prepares-to-close -after-over-a-decade-in-a-changing-neighborhood/Content?oid=1632528.

52. Scott Mervis, "Shadow Lounge Memories: The artists reflect," *Pittsburgh Post-Gazette*, March 28, 2013, www.post-gazette.com/ae/music/2013/03/28/ Shadow-Lounge-Memories-The-artists-reflect/stories/201303280211.

53. Deborah M. Todd, "Freestyle contest puts All-Star rappers on their toes," *Pittsburgh Post-Gazette*, June 29, 2009, www.post-gazette.com/life/ lifestyle/2009/06/29/Freestyle-contest-puts-All-Star-rappers-on-their-toes/ stories/200906290158.

54. Rory D. Webb, "Macadelic and the State of Mac Miller," *Pittsburgh Post-Gazette*, March 26, 2012, www.pghcitypaper.com/Blogh/archives/2012/03/26/ macadelic-and-the-state-of-mac-miller.

55. Justin Strong, interview by the author, June 17, 2019.

56. Mac Miller, interview by Naomi Zeichner, *Fader*, June 5, 2013, www.thefader .com/2013/06/05/interview-mac-miller.

57. Nomi Leasure, *Peek* (blog), March 2012, peek-mag.tumblr.com/post/ 19562365653/my-life-is-fascinating-and-no-not-just-because.

58. Josie Roberts, "The hip-hop pulse," Trib Total Media, June 28, 2005, archive. triblive.com/news/the-hip-hop-pulse/.

59. Big Jerm, interview by the author, October 4, 2019.

60. Michael Machosky, "ID Labs in Lawrenceville keeps Pittsburgh on the hip-hop map," Trib Total Media, July 31, 2011, archive.triblive.com/news/ id-labs-in-lawrenceville-keeps-pittsburgh-on-the-hip-hop-map.

NINE

1. Scott Mervis, "Warner Bros. signs local rapper Wiz," *Pittsburgh Post-Gazette*, July 17, 2007, www.post-gazette.com/ae/music/2007/07/17/Warner-Bros -signs-local-rapper-Wiz/stories/200707170234.

2. Cody McDevitt, "Music Review: WAMO hip-hop show best when lyrics are clear," *Pittsburgh Post-Gazette*, July 22, 2007, www.post-gazette.com/ae/ music/2007/07/22/Music-Review-WAMO-hip-hop-show-best-when-lyrics -are-clear/stories/200707220193.

3. Matt Diehl, "Wiz Khalifa," *Interview*, May 23, 2011, www.interviewmagazine .com/music/wiz-khalifa.

4. Wiz Khalifa, interview by Eric and Jeff Rosenthal (ItsTheReal), *A Waste of Time*, January 23, 2018, podcast, soundcloud.com/awasteof time/167-wiz-khalifa.

5. Ibid.

6. Ibid.

7. Benjy Grinberg, interview by Latif Tayour, *It's Show Business with Latif Tayour*, January 14, 2020, podcast, podcasts.apple.com/us/podcast/15-benjy -grinberg-of-rostrum-records/id1481980802?i=1000462446775.

8. Benjy Grinberg, interview by Latif Tayour, *It's Show Business with Latif Tayour*, January 14, 2020, https://podcasts.apple.com/us/podcast/15-benjy -grinberg-of-rostrum-records/id1481980802?i=1000462446775.

9. "2011's Top 40 Best Bets," *Billboard* 123, no. 3 (January 29, 2011): 11–27, ezproxy.nypl.org/login?url=https://www-proquest-com.i.ezproxy.nypl .org/trade-journals/2011s-top-40-best-bets/docview/851272691/ se-2?accountid=35635.

10. Ruddy Rock, interview by author, 2021.

11. Kimbel Bouwman, "Interview with Benjy Grinberg, president of Rostrum Records and A&R; and manager for Wiz Khalifa, Mac Miller," HitQuarters, October 17, 2011, web.archive.org/web/20121115012505/http://www.hitquarters .com/index.php3?page=intrview/opar/intrview_BGrinberg.html.

12. Rock, interview with author.

13. Ray Waddell, "On the Road," *Billboard* 123.1 (2011): 18, ProQuest (web), January 19, 2021.

14. Skyzoo (@skyzoo), "In 2009 a kid from PGH hit me on MySpace, said he was a fan/fellow MC & wanted to collab. We connected and made 'Pen Game'. Years later everytime we hung out he'd say 'I was the only 17 yr old with a Skyzoo verse! They can't fuck with me!' His name was Mac Miller. RIP my G," Twitter, September 7, 2018, 5:23 P.M., twitter.com/skyzoo/ status/1038175935407828992.

15. Mac Miller, "Friday Night Drunk Talk," *ListenToMac* (blog), October 16, 2009, listentomac.blogspot.com/2009/10/friday-night-drunk -talk.html

16. ——, "I Love College?," *ListenToMac* (blog), October 17, 2009, listentomac .blogspot.com/2009/10/i-love-college.html.

17. ——, "The Beauty of Travel," *ListenToMac* (blog), October 19, 2009. listentomac.blogspot.com/2009/10/beauty-of-travel.html.

18. ——, "Stay Focused," *ListenToMac* (blog), October 20, 2009, listentomac .blogspot.com/2009/10/stay-focused.html.

19. ——, "Gone for the Weekend . . . ," *ListenToMac* (blog), October 25, 2009, listentomac.blogspot.com/2009/10/gone-for-weekend.html

20. ——, "Memories Don't Live like People Do . . . ," *ListenToMac* (blog), October 18, 2009, listentomac.blogspot.com/2009/10/memories-dont-live -like-people-do.html?m=1.

21. Deborah M. Todd, "Like Wiz Khalifa, rapper Mac Miller is another talent from Allderdice," *Pittsburgh Post-Gazette*, August 12, 2010, www.post -gazette.com/ae/music/2010/08/12/Like-Wiz-Khalifa-rapper-Mac-Miller -is-another-talent-from-Allderdice/stories/201008120489.

22. Insanul Ahmed, "25 Things You Didn't Know About Mac Miller," *Complex*, January 29, 2013, www.complex.com/music/2013/01/25-things-you-didnt -know-about-mac-miller/guitar.

23. Mac Miller, interview by Mr. Peter Parker, "Mac Miller Soundset 2011," The Mr. Peter Parker Show, June 8, 2011, YouTube video, www .youtube.com/watch?v=Sdks7KWapbk&.

24. Ben Boskovich, "Mac Miller: Hip Hop's Rising Valedictorian," *WHIRL Magazine*, July 26, 2012, whirlmagazine.com/mac-on-top/.
25. "Footnotes: Mac Miller," *Fader*, August 15, 2013, www.thefader.com/2013/08/15/footnotes-mac-miller.
26. Brenton Blanchet, "Mac Miller's Victory Lap: Collaborators, Friends Remember 'Best Day Ever' 10 Years Later," Grammy.com, March 31, 2021, www.grammy.com/grammys/news/mac-millers-victory-lap-producer-rapper-friends-remember-best-day-ever-10-years-later-anniversary.
27. Bouwman, "Interview with Benjy Grinberg."
28. Steven Roberts, "Wiz Khalifa's Kush and Orange Juice Hits Big on the Internet," MTV, April 14, 2010, www.mtv.com/news/1637073/wiz-khalifas-kush-and-orange-juice-hits-big-on-the-internet/.
29. Darrelle Revis, interview by author, August 6, 2019.
30. Greg Fleming, interview by author, March 12, 2020.

TEN

1. Rita Kempley, "KIDS." *Washington Post*, August 25, 1995, www.washingtonpost.com/wp-srv/style/longterm/movies/videos/kidsnrkempley_c029f5.htm.
2. Review of *Kids*, *Time Out New York*, n.d., www.timeout.com/movies/kids.
3. Kenneth Turan, "'Kids': Grossing Out the Old Squares," *Los Angeles Times*, July 28, 1995, www.latimes.com/archives/la-xpm-1995-07-28-ca-28836-story.html.
4. Mac Miller, interview by *YRB*, "YRB Mac Miller interview & freestyle," August 30, 2010, YouTube video, www.youtube.com/watch?v=aAmjZ_p_PwQ&ab_channel=MacMiller.
5. Michael Cohen, "Art Commotion—Larry Clark Interview," Harmony-Korine.com, 1996, www.harmony-korine.com/paper/int/lc/commotion.html.
6. Mac Miller, interview by itsbongoboy, September 13, 2010, YouTube video, www.youtube.com/watch?v=Ypuf-hUeYyc&ab_channel=itsbongoboy.
7. Chris Martins, "Mac Miller Is High on Life (and Maybe, Probably, a Girl)," *Complex*, September 14, 2016, www.complex.com/music/2016/09/mac-miller-divine-feminine-interview-torrid-romance.
8. Miller, interview by itsbongoboy.
9. Miller, interview by *YRB*.
10. Just Blaze, interview by author, February 19, 2020.
11. Donna Claire-Chesman, "Rostrum's Benjy Grinberg Remembers Mac Miller," DJBooth, December 5, 2018, djbooth.net/features/2018-12-05-benjy-grinberg-remembers-mac-miller.
12. Mac Miller, interview by Leah Benoit, "MSU & U Episode 23: Entertainment—Mac Miller Interview," MSU&U Telecasters, November 22, 2011, YouTube video, www.youtube.com/watch?v=a3Qmr98Sw6I&ab_channel SU%26UTelecasters.

13. "Wiz Khalifa Is MTV News' 'Hottest Breakthrough MC of 2010!'" MTV, July 25, 2010, www.mtv.com/news/1644383/wiz-khalifa-is-mtv-news -hottest-breakthrough-mc-of-2010/.

14. Rostrum Records, "PRESS RELEASE: ROSTRUM RECORDS SIGNS MAC MILLER, PREPS 'K.I.D.S.,'" July 21, 2010.

15. Mobb Deep, "Quiet Storm," Genius, March 14, 1999, genius.com/Mobb -deep-quiet-storm-lyrics.

16. Nate Santos, "Hey Young World," *Source*, February/March 2012: 60.

17. James Sullivan, "The kid's all right," *Boston Globe*, December 2, 2011: G22.

18. "Mac Miller Teared Up Recording Poppy | Inside the Lyrics," *Fuse*, June 4, 2012, YouTube video, www.youtube.com/watch?v=7mVfAGG_3K8&ab _channel=Fuse.

19. Statik Selektah, interview by author, May 15, 2019.

20. "Mac Miller Releases K.I.D.S. on Ustream," posted by Pitpanther01, January 19, 2011, YouTube video, www.youtube.com/watch?v=jayallvQrSQ&ab _channel=Pitpanther01.

21. Chris Richards, "A Mac Miller fan responds," *Washington Post*, December 6, 2011, www.washingtonpost.com/blogs/click-track/post/a-mac-miller-fan -responds/2011/12/06/gIQAOLSxZO_blog.html.

22. Mac Miller, interview by HardKnockTV, "Mac Miller Talks Macadelic, Criticism, Cam'ron, ASAP Rocky + More," HardKnockTV, April 11, 2012, YouTube video, www.youtube.com/watch?v=Gemttzg6As8&ab_channel =hardknocktv.

23. Jonathan Tobias, "DXnext: Mac Miller, HipHopDX, November 4, 2010, web.archive.org/web/20150403024724/http://www.hiphopdx.com/index/ dxnext/id.185/title.dxnext-mac-miller.

24. Nathan Tempey, "Sway Lounge Is Closing by the End of the Month," Gothamist, December 13, 2015, gothamist.com/arts-entertainment/sway -lounge-is-closing-by-the-end-of-the-month.

25. "R.I.P. Harold Hunter 1974–2006," Splay, n.d., www.splay.com/harold/ recent_thoughts.html.

26. Seth Zaplin, interview by author, August 19, 2019.

27. "Sean Price + Buckshot + Sabzi of Blue Scholars + Team Facelift + Kick Drums and more," *Time Out New York*, March 15, 2012, www.timeout.com/ newyork/music/sean-price-buckshot-sabzi-of-blue-scholars-team-facelift -kick-drums-and-more.

28. Ruddy Rock, interview by author, January 11, 2021.

29. Rock, interview by author.

30. Arthur Pitt, interview by author, June 19, 2019.

31. Christie Craft, "Mac Miller Kills Sway + Releases New Mixtape," *Lifestyles of the Bitch & Shamele$$* (blog), August 18, 2010, bitchandshameless .wordpress.com/category/roxy-cottontail/.

32. Zaplin, interview by author.

33. Ibid.

ELEVEN

1. "The 100 Best Mistapes of 2010 (49–21), *XXL*, December 31, 2010, www .xxlmag.com/the-100-best-mixtapes-of-2010–49–1/.
2. Mac Miller, interview by aliattherave, May 31, 2011, YouTube video, www .youtube.com/watch?v=CCWn2AuDs_M.
3. Bill Niels initially flew in too but left after realizing he had nothing to do.
4. Mac Miller and Most Dope, interview by *JENESIS Magazine*, November 8, 2011, YouTube video, www.youtube.com/watch?v=dPcu3 LIsN6g&t=122s&ab_channel=JENESISMagazine.
5. Ibid.
6. DJ Clockwork, interview by author, August 1, 2019.
7. Rondell Conway, interview with author, July 12, 2019.
8. Peter Rosenberg, interview by author, February 28, 2020.
9. "03/11/11 07:42PM," Mac Miller TV, www.ustream.tv/recorded/13263914.
10. Ibid.
11. Mac Miller, "Fun Is 4 Everyone: Volume 3," April 10, 2011, YouTube video, www.youtube.com/watch?v=a7-rdgVA0m4&ab_channel.
12. Just Blaze, interview by author, February 19, 2020.
13. 9th Wonder, interview by David Astramskas, October 10, 2011, Ballislife, ballislife.com/9th-wonder-interview-talks-jay-z-defends-mac-miller/.
14. Brian "Z" Zisook, "Mac Miller Cleared Sufjan Stevens Sample on 'Donald Trump' for Free," June 15, 2017, updated February 12, 2018, DJBooth, djbooth.net/features/2017–06–15-mac-miller-donald-trump-free.
15. Lauren Carter, "Mac Miller Talks Twitter Exchange with Donald Trump," *XXL*, July 14, 2011, www.xxlmag.com/donald-trump-gives-mac-miller -props-for-donald-song-via-twitter/.
16. "Mac Miller Talks Twitter Exchange with Donald Trump," *XXL*, July 14, 2011, www.xxlmag.com/donald-trump-gives-mac-miller-props-for-donald-song- via-twitter/?utm_source smclip&utm_medium=referral.
17. Steven Horowitz, "Donald Trump Brands Mac Miller 'the Next Eminem,'" HipHopDX, August 18, 2011, hiphopdx.com/news/id.16501/title.donald -trump-brands-mac-miller-the-next-eminem#signup.
18. Mac Miller, interview by Im Brandon Arroyo, "Flashback | Blue Slide Park, Starting Out, Cleveland, Pittsburgh," The Arroyo Show, June 6, 2020, YouTube video, www.youtube.com/watch?v=Qzr23Mjrf-Y&ab_channel heArroyoShow.
19. Mac Milller, interview by *Billboard*, "'Blue Slide Park'Track-by-Track," *Billboard*, November 7, 2011, YouTube video, www.youtube.com/ watch?v 50Rn8S2Q2w&ab_channel=Billboard.
20. Michael Machosky, "ID Labs in Lawrenceville Keeps Pittsburgh on the Hip=Hop Map," Trib Total Media, July 31, 2011, archive.triblive.com/news/ id-labs-in-lawrenceville-keeps-pittsburgh-on-the-hip-hop-map/.
21. Mac Miller, interview by Leah Benoit, "MSU & U Episode 23: Entertainment—Mac Miller Interview," MSU&U Telecasters, November 22,

2011, YouTube video, www.youtube.com/watch?v=a3Qmr98Sw6I&ab_channel SU%26UTelecasters.

22. Ibid.

23. Ibid.

24. u/Always_Touch_Myself, "Any comments on Mac Miller's Album Leaked—Blue Slide Park?" Reddit, n.d., www.reddit.com/r/hiphopheads/comments/m4ys7/any_comments_on_mac_millers_album_leaked_blue/.

TWELVE

1. J. Freedom du Lac, "Giving Indie Acts a Plug, or Pulling It Pitchfork Web Site Rises as Rock Arbiter," *Washington Post*, April 30, 2006, www.washingtonpost.com/archive/lifestyle/style/2006/04/30/giving-indie-acts-a-plug-or-pulling-it-span-classbankheadpitchfork-web-site-rises-as-rock-arbiterspan/916639c1-aee4-4ceb-90a5-09c384af9b72/.

2. DJ Premier, interview by author, February 4, 2020.

3. A play on Heiroglyphics classic jam "'93 Til Infinity."

4. Ritz Reynolds, interview by author, July 16, 2020.

5. Zack O'Malley Greenburg, "Mac Miller: Indie Music's Savior?," *Forbes*, December 19, 2011, www.forbes.com/sites/zackomalleygreenburg/2011/12/19/mac-miller-indie-music-savior-30-under-30/?sh=23d5b29011f9.

6. Ibid.

7. Jordan Sargent, "Mac Miller Is Cool Now," *Spin*, July 18, 2013, www.spin.com/2013/07/mac-miller-watching-movies-tour-interview/.

8. Talib Kweli, "88-Key on His Relationship with Mac Miller," Facebook, May 20, 2021, www.facebook.com/watch/?v=478774239871854.

9. Michael Saponara, "Juicy J Talks Crafting 'Neighbor' With Travis Scott, Working On A$AP Rocky's Upcoming Project," *Billboard*, September 26, 2018, www.billboard.com/articles/columns/hip-hop/8476970/juicy-j-interview/.

10. Sryon, "Mac Miller Reveals Possible Project with Cam'ron," HipHopDX, February 14, 2012, hiphopdx.com/news/id.18680/title.mac-miller-reveals-possible-project-with-camron#.

11. Andres Tardio, "Mac Miller Says 'Tde Will Be a Big Part' of Next Album, Talks Bond with Schoolboy Q, Ab-Soul & Cam'ron," HipHopDX, September 10, 2012, hiphopdx.com/news/id.21079/title.mac-miller-says-tde-will-be-a-big-part-of-next-album-talks-bond-with-schoolboy-q-ab-soul-camron.

12. Mac Miller, interview by *XXL*, "Mac Miller Talks Working with Lil Wayne on Macadelic," *XXL*, December 30, 2014, YouTube video, www.youtube.com/watch?v=AhA-BYnXD0U&ab_channel=XXL.

13. Ibid.

14. Ibid.

15. Mac Miller, interview by HardKnockTV, "Mac Miller Talks Macadelic, Criticism, Cam'ron, ASAP Rocky + More," HardKnockTV, April 11, 2012,

YouTube video, www.youtube.com/watch?v=Gemttzg6As8&ab_channel =hardknocktv.

16. Rob Markman, "Mac Miller Speaks His Mind on Macadelic." *MTV*, March 19, 2012, www.mtv.com/news/1681340/mac-miller-macadelic/.

17. Ibid.

18. Tamara Palmer, "Rapper Kreayshawn Inks Deal with Columbia Records." MTV, June 8, 2011, www.mtv.com/news/2495595/rapper-kreayshawn-inks -deal-with-sony-records/.

19. "White Rapper Kreayshawn Defends Using N-Word," NewsOne, June 9, 2011, newsone.com/1298105/kreayshawn-defends-nword-gucci-videeo -white-rapper/.

20. Kreayshawn, *Kreayshawn* (blog), July 25, 2011, kreayshawn.tumblr .com/post/8046550036/blah-blah-blah-yeah-im-that-white-rapper-chick 2011.

21. Matthew Trammell, "What Is the Place for White Rappers Today?," *Fader*, October 6, 2015, www.thefader.com/2015/10/06/white-rappers-mac-miller -vince-staples-interview. 2015).

22. Ibid.

23. Zack O'Malley Greenburg, "Cash Kings 2012: Hip-Hop's Top Earn-ers," *Forbes*, September 5, 2012, www.forbes.com/sites/zackomal leygreenburg/2012/09/05/cash-kings-2012-hip-hops-top-earners/ ?sh=220e868e5101.

24. Brandon Soderberg, "Worst Beef Ever: Mac Miller vs. Lord Finesse," *Spin*, July 13, 2012, www.spin.com/2012/07/worst-beef-ever-mac-miller-vs-lord -finesse/.

25. Steven Horowitz, "Lord Finesse Issues Statement Regarding Mac Miller Lawsuit," HipHopDX, July 12, 2012, hiphopdx.com/news/id.20398/title .lord-finesse-issues-statement-regarding-mac-miller-lawsuit.

26. Ibid.

27. Alex Gale, "Mac Miller Hit With $10 Million Lawsuit by Lord Finesse," BET, July 11, 2012, www.bet.com/news/music/2012/07/11/mac-miller-hit-with -10-million-lawsuit-by-lord-finesse.html.

28. Mac Miller, interview by Sway's Universe, "Mac Miller Speaks on $10 Mil-lion Dollar Lawsuit with Lord Finesse," Sway's Universe, August 29, 2012, YouTube video, www.youtube.com/watch?v=bHrinYZHsKM&ab_channel =SWAY%27SUNIVERSE.

29. Horowitz, "Lord Finesse Issues Statement."

30. Brandon Soderberg, "Worst Beef Ever: Mac Miller vs. Lord Finesse," *SPIN*, July 13, 2012, spin.com/2012/07/worst-beef-ever-mac-miller-vs-lord -finesse/.

31. Premier, interview by author.

32. Miller, interview by Sway's Universe, "$10 Million Dollar Lawsuit."

33. Mac Miller, interview by HardKnockTV, "Mac Miller Talks Lil Wayne, Rumors, Drugs, Kendrick Lamar + More," HardKnockTV, April 13, 2012, YouTube video, www.youtube.com/watch?v=4bIaATqlCe0&t=391s&ab _channel=hardknocktv.

34. Ibid.
35. u/GlitterRitz, "As Requested, 150 Deleted Mac Miller Tweets," Reddit, n.d., www.reddit.com/r/MacMiller/comments/a2t5i9/as_requested_150 _deleted_mac_miller_tweets/.

THIRTEEN

1. Mac Miller, interview by *Fuse*, "Mac Miller Moves Out of His Mom's House," *Fuse*, May 18, 2012, YouTube video, www.youtube.com/watch?v=wCT86Qk3akk&ab _channel=Fuse.
2. Dan Hyman, "21-Year-Old Rapper Mac Miller Isn't Ashamed of Working with Justin Bieber," *ELLE*, October 7, 2013, www.elle.com/culture/music/ news/a18742/mac-miller-lil-wayne-interview/.
3. Erika Ramirez, "Mac Miller Talks Frank Ocean & Pharrell-Assisted 'Pink Slime' Album," *Billboard*, September 7, 2012, www.billboard.com/articles/ columns/the-juice/475224/mac-miller-talks-frank-ocean-pharrell-assisted -pink-slime-album.
4. Rob Markman, "'Pharrell Has 'Two Really Good Records' with Mac Miller," MTV, February 14, 2012, www.mtv.com/news/1679261/pharrell-mac-miller -collaboration/.
5. Mikey Fresh, "Exclusive: Pharrell Says He Recorded 10 Songs with Mac Miller #PinkSlime," *MissInfo*, June 8, 2012, www.missinfo.tv/index.php/ exclusive-pharrell-says-he-recorded-10-songs-with-mac-miller-pinkslime/.
6. Dan Hyman, "Mac Miller's 'Pink Slime' Oozes Again," *Rolling Stone*, December 10, 2013, www.rollingstone.com/music/music-news/mac-millers-pink -slime-ep-oozes-again-236057/.
7. "Reefer Madness Pleases Young Crowd," *Philadelphia Inquirer*, Monday, August 6, 2012: C04.
8. Insanul Ahmed, "Mac Miller: King of the Hill," *Complex*, January 28, 2013, www.complex.com/music/2013/01/mac-miller-2013-online-cover-story.
9. Mac Miller, interview by Naomi Zeichner, *Fader*, June 5, 2013, www.thefader .com/2013/06/05/interview-mac-miller.
10. Nadeska Alexis, "Mac Miller Was 'Skeptical' About Doing 'Most Dope' TV Show," MTV, February 25, 2013, www.mtv.com/news/1702606/mac-miller -most-dope-family-tv-show-mtv2/.
11. Miller, interview by Zeichner.
12. Darin Byrne, interview by author, July 17, 2020.
13. Insanul Ahmed, interview by author, May 1, 2019.
14. Mac Miller, interview by Larry King, "Mac Miller on New Album 'GO:OD A.M.,' Battling Depression & Donald Trump," Ora.tv, September 9, 2015, www.ora.tv/larrykingnow/2015/9/9/mac-miller-on-new-album-good-am -battling-depression-donald-trump-0_1hro71x0l77p.
15. Brenton Blanchet, "Mac Miller's Victory Lap: Collaborators, Friends Remember 'Best Day Ever' 10 Years Later," Grammy.com, March 31, 2021, www .grammy.com/grammys/news/mac-millers-victory-lap-producer-rapper -friends-remember-best-day-ever-10-years-later-anniversary.

16. Lauren Nostro, "Donald Trump Threatens Mac Miller with Lawsuit, Calls Him an 'Ungrateful Dog,'" January 31, 2013, www.complex.com/music/2013/01/donald-trump-threatens-to-sue-mac-miller.

17. Ibid.

18. Miller, interview by King.

19. Alexis, "Mac Miller Was 'Skeptical.'"

20. Hyman, "21-Year-Old Rapper."

FOURTEEN

1. Eileen Reslen, "'Most Dope' Rough Cuts: Mac Miller Explains Why He Moved to Los Angeles [Video]," MTV, August 13, 2013, www.mtv.com/news/2385704/most-dope-rough-cuts-mac-miller-los-angeles-move-video/.

2. The Internet, interview by *Complex*, "The Internet Talks About Touring with Mac Miller, Chance the Rapper & 'Live from Space,'" *Complex*, December 20, 2013, www.complex.com/music/2013/12/the-internet-live-from-space-mac-miller-interview.

3. Josh Glicksman, "Five Years Later, 'Faces' Is the Heart of Mac Miller's Career," *Billboard*, May 10, 2019, www.billboard.com/articles/columns/hip-hop/8510929/mac-miller-faces-anniversary.

4. Mikey Fresh, "Mac Miller Talks Former Lean Addiction in VIBE Interview Before Death," *Vibe*, September 7, 2018, www.vibe.com/music/music-news/mac-miller-former-lean-addiction-in-vibe-interview-before-death-605085/.

5. Dan Rys, "Mac Miller Talks Sea Turtles, His New Album and Rapping About Movies," *XXL*, n.d., www.xxlmag.com/mac-miller-talks-sea-turtles-his-new-album-and-rapping-about-movies/.

6. Mac Miller, interview by Mikey Fresh, "Mac Miller on His New Album 'Watching Movies': 'I Just Did What I Wanted,'" June 17, 2013, *Vibe*, www.vibe.com/news/entertainment/vibe-interview-mac-miller-his-new-album-watching-movies-i-just-did-what-i-wanted-162530/.

7. DJ Semtex, "Mac Miller Interview 2013," Vimeo video, vimeo.com/412382907.

8. Daniel Isenberg, "Mac Miller Speaks on Settling Lord Finesse's $10 Million Lawsuit," *Complex*, January 15, 2013, www.complex.com/music/2013/01/mac-miller-speaks-on-settling-lord-finesses-10-million-lawsuit.

9. Ahmed, "King of the Hill."

10. Mac Miller, interview by Will Lavin, "Mac Miller Talks 'Watching Movies with the Sound Off,' Big L vs. Jay Z, and Making the Forbes List," November 1, 2013, www.complex.com/music/2013/11/mac-miller-interview-watch-movies-with-the-sound-off.

11. Mac Miller, interview by Naomi Zeichner, *Fader*, June 5, 2013, www.thefader.com/2013/06/05/interview-mac-miller.

12. Kelefa Sanneh, "Where's Earl?" *New Yorker*, May 16, 2011, www.newyorker.com/magazine/2011/05/23/wheres-earl.

13. Earl Sweatshirt, interview posted by nc, "Earl Sweatshirt on RZA Day, His Purpose and Paul McCartney (Interview 2013)," YouTube video, www.youtube.com/watch?v=z_2rYy53JvY&.

14. Naomi Zeichner, "Stream: Earl Sweatshirt f. Mac Miller, 'Guild,'" *Fader*, May 23, 2013, www.thefader.com/2013/05/23/stream-earl-sweatshirt-f -mac-miller-guild.

15. Sweatshirt, interview posted by nc.

16. Delia Cai, "17 Reasons Why Ariana Grande and Mac Miller Are Exquisitely Perfect Together," BuzzFeed, November 5, 2017, www.buzzfeed.com/deliacai/ mac-n-ari-4-ever?utm_source=dynamic&utm_campaign=bfsharecopy&sub =0_118838281#118838281.

17. Ibid.

18. Ibid.

19. Ibid,

20. Ibid.

21. Ibid.

22. Ariana Grande, interview by HOT 97, "Ariana Grande: Sings, curses and talks kissing Mac Miller!," HOT 97, September 4, 2013, YouTube video, www .youtube.com/watch?v=PySx6TrEKJc&ab_channel=HOT97.

23. Ibid.

24. Ariana Grande, interview by Power 106 Los Angeles, "Ariana Grande Rates Mac Miller as a Kisser w/ J Cruz," Power 106 Los Angeles, July 19, 2013, YouTube video, www.youtube.com/watch?v=lB-GRKdwGAs&ab_channel =Power106LosAngeles.

25. Jocelyn Vena, "Mac Miller + Ariana Grande Forever? Nope, She's Just A 'Homey,'" MTV, April 30, 2013, www.mtv.com/news/1706581/mac-miller -ariana-grande-relationship-rumors/.

26. Grande, interview by HOT 97.

27. Ibid.

28. Mac Miller, interview by HardKnockTV, "Mac Miller talks Album, Ariana Grande, Celebrity Culture. Says he thought he was on way out," Hard KnockTV, August 9, 2013, YouTube video, www.youtube.com/watch?v =9M4toIUR6Ho&ab_channel=hardknocktv.

29. Glicksman, "Five Years Later."

30. The Internet, interview by *Complex*.

31. Miller, interview by Zeichner.

32. Jimmy Iovine, commencement address, May 17, 2013, news.usc.edu/51153/ commencement-address-by-jimmy-iovine/.

33. Justin Sayles, "A Deal with the Devil: The Triumph and Tragedy of 'All Eyez on Me,'" Ringer, February 12, 2021, www.theringer.com/music/ 2021/2/12/22279018/tupac-shakur-2pac-all-eyez-on-me-history-death -row. 2021).

34. Tony Gervino, "JAY-Z's 'Blueprint' for a City's Rebirth," Tidal, September 11, 2019, tidal.com/magazine/article/jay-zs-blueprint-18/1–56334.

35. Mikey Fresh, "Mac Miller Talks Former Lean Addiction in VIBE Interview Before Death," *Vibe*, September 7, 2018, www.vibe.com/music/ music-news/mac-miller-former-lean-addiction-in-vibe-interview-before -death-605085/.

36. DJ Semtex, "Mac Miller Interview."

37. Dan Hyman, "Mac Miller's Last Days and Life After Death," *Rolling Stone*, November 15, 2018, www.rollingstone.com/music/music-features/mac-miller-legacy-loss-756802/.

38. Insanul Ahmed, interview by author, May 1, 2019.

39. Donna Claire-Chesman, "Rostrum's Benjy Grinberg Remembers Mac Miller," DJBooth, December 5, 2018, djbooth.net/features/2018–12–05-benjy-grinberg-remembers-mac-miller.

40. Chris Thomas, "Machin Gun Kelly ft. Diddy—'Champions' [Video]," Hip HopWired, February 18, 2013, hiphopwired.com/217405/machine-gun-kelly-ft-diddy-champions-video/.

41. Andrew Noz, "Mac Miller: Find Yourself," *Fader*, August 14, 2013, www.thefader.com/2013/08/14/mac-miller-find-yourself.

42. Jordan Sargent, interview by author, March 5, 2020.

43. Ibid.

44. Jordan Sargent, "Mac Miller Is Cool Now," *Spin*, July 18, 2013, www.spin.com/2013/07/mac-miller-watching-movies-tour-interview/.

45. Craig Jenkins, review of *Watching Movies with the Sound Off*, by Mac Miller, Pitchfork, June 24, 3013, pitchfork.com/reviews/albums/18202-mac-miller-watching-movies-with-the-sound-off/.

46. Review of *Watching Movies with the Sound Off*, by Mac Miller, *XXL*, June 18, 2013, www.xxlmag.com/mac-miller-watching-movies-with-the-sound-off-album-review/?utm_source smclip&utm_medium=referral.

47. Drew Millard, "Mac Miller Opens Up," *Vice*, May 2, 2013, www.vice.com/en/article/rk3pzr/mac-miller-opens-up.

48. Mac Miller, interview by *Billboard*, "'Watching Movies with the Sound Off' Track-By-Track Video Interview," June 25, 2013, www.billboard.com/video/mac-miller-watching-movies-with-the-sound-off-track-by-track-video-interview-1567374.

49. Ibid.

50. Mac Miller, "S.D.S.," Genius, April 23, 2013, genius.com/1702176.

51. Semtex, "Mac Miller Interview 2013."

52. Scott Mervis, "Mac Miller puts the party on pause in mature second album," *Pittsburgh Post-Gazette*, July 11, 2013, www.post-gazette.com/ae/music/2013/07/11/Mac-Miller-puts-the-party-on-pause-in-mature-second-album/stories/201307110267.

FIFTEEN

1. "Mac Miller: My Plan for 2014 Is D.A.D.D—Do As Drake Does," VladTV, January 14, 2014, YouTube video, www.youtube.com/watch?v=D4kMSUwPtOs&ab_channel=djvlad.

2. A.D. Amorosi, "Pot smoking gets rap endorsement at show," *Philadelphia Inquirer*, August 6, 2012, www.inquirer.com/philly/entertainment/20120806_Pot_smoking_gets_rap_endorsement_at_show.html.

3. Brendan Smith, "Rapper Mac Miller shows versatility in Pageant performance," *St. Louis Post-Dispatch*, July 29, 2013, www.stltoday.com/entertainment/music/reviews/rapper-mac-miller-shows-versatility-in-pageant-performance/article_768e92b8-f551-52b6-a2f1-965192d97c5c.html.

4. Jenevieve Ting, "Mac Miller and Friends Pack L.A.'s Palladium for Space Migration Tour," *Hollywood Reporter*, August 9, 2013, www.hollywoodreporter.com/news/music-news/mac-miller-friends-pack-palladium-603546/.

5. Mac Miller, interview by Naomi Zeichner, *Fader*, June 5, 2013, www.thefader.com/2013/06/05/interview-mac-miller.

6. Nomi Leasure, "Why Do I Keep Writing About My Ex?" *Peek* (blog), October 11, 2020, peek-mag.com/why-do-i-keep-writing-about-my-ex/.

7. ——, *Peek* (blog), March 19, 2012, peek-mag.tumblr.com/post/19562365653/my-life-is-fascinating-and-no-not-just-because.

8. ——, *Peek* (blog), November 10, 2011, peek-mag.tumblr.com/post/12592113434/its-so-hard-to-see-everyone-else-love-you-i.

9. Ibid.

10. ——, *Peek* (blog), December 1, 2011, peek-mag.tumblr.com/post/13579418756/x.

11. ——, *Peek* (blog), October 10, 2012, peek-mag.tumblr.com/post/33285421569/okay-a-million-and-ten-questions-about-my.

12. ——, *Peek* (blog), May 26, 2013. peek-mag.tumblr.com/post/51367250472/im-currently-cali-livin-my-commute-cuts-through.

13. ——, *Peek* (blog), June 11, 2013, peek-mag.tumblr.com/post/52692557907/six-things-ive-learned-since-being-in-la.

14. Madeline Boardman, "Mac Miller's Tour Kicks Off as He Talks 'Watching Movies with the Sound Off,' Molly, and His Unexpected Success," Huffington Post, July 19, 2013, www.huffpost.com/entry/mac-miller-tour-watching-movies-with-the-sound-off_n_3618059.

15. Miller, interview by Zeichner.

16. "Cash Kings 2013: The World's 20 Highest-Paid Hip-Hop Artists," *Forbes*, September 14, 2013, www.forbes.com/pictures/eeel45efgik/8-wiz-khalifa-14-million/?sh=7971871471e7.

17. Donna Claire-Chesman, "Rostrum's Benjy Grinberg Remembers Mac Miller," DJBooth, December 5, 2018, djbooth.net/features/2018-12-05-benjy-grinberg-remembers-mac-miller.

18. Ibid.

19. Vince Staples, interview by Sway's Universe, "2014 #SwaySXSW- Vince Staples Shares Advice Given to Him by Mac Miller and Freestyles 2014," Sway's Universe, March 17, 2014, YouTube video, ww.youtube.com/watch?v=KXwkMWReXPE&ab_channel=SWAY%27SUNIVERSE.

20. Vince Staples (@vincestaples), "There is no Vince Staples music without Mac Miller, with that being said we about to smash on the gas.," Twitter, September 13, 2018, 4:29 P.M., twitter.com/vincestaples/status/1040336698226356224.

21. Charles Holmes, "Vince Staples Talks Mac Miller: 'The Good Ones Always Die,'" *Rolling Stone*, November 8, 2018, www.rollingstone.com/music/music -news/vince-staples-met-mac-miller-good-ones-always-die-753457/.

22. Keith Nelson Jr., "Studio Sessions | MixedByAli talks shaping TDE's sound this past decade, Mac Miller and Nipsey Hussle memories, and more," Revolt .TV, December 26, 2019, www.revolt.tv/2019/12/26/21037658/kendrick -lamar-tde-engineer-mixedbyali-interview. 2019.

23. "Double Groovy News with Schoolboy Q & Snoop Dogg | GGN," Snoop-DoggTV, March 10, 2020, YouTube video, www.youtube.com/watch?v =YmkAADtUeTs&ab_channel=SnoopDoggTV.

24. Drew Millard, "The Voices in Mac Miller's Head," *Vice*, November 7, 2013, www.vice.com/en/article/rkpme6/mac-miller-interview-delusional-thomas.

25. Mitch Findlay, "Mac Miller's 'Delusional Thomas' Brought Earl and 'Bill' to the Killing Fields," HNHH, November 1, 2018, www.hotnewhiphop.com/ mac-millers-delusional-thomas-brought-earl-and-bill-to-the-killing-fields -new-song.1980891.html.

26. Mac Miller, interview by Music Feeds, "Big Day Out 2014 Interviews: Mac Miller," Music Feeds, January 28, 2014, YouTube video, www.youtube.com/ watch?v=BBNZwRxI-J0&ab_channel.

27. Millard, "Voices in Mac Miller's Head."

28. Mac Miller, interview by Larry King, "Mac Miller on New Album 'GO:OD A.M.,' Battling Depression & Donald Trump," Ora.tv, September 9, 2015, www.ora.tv/larrykingnow/2015/9/9/mac-miller-on-new-album-good-am -battling-depression-donald-trump-0_1hro71x0l77p.

29. Millard, "Voices in Mac Miller's Head."

30. Craig Jenkins, "Fell Asleep and Forgot to Die: Mac Miller's Good Morning," *Vice*, September 25, 2015, www.vice.com/en/article/rmjpv8/mac-miller-go -od-am-2015-profile.

31. Chris Heath, "Prince's Closest Friends Share Their Best Prince Stories," *GQ*, December 8, 2016, www.gq.com/story/prince-stories.

32. "Who Stole Mac Miller's Dog? Mac Miller & Ralphie," iDudeMan, July 22, 2014, YouTube video, www.youtube.com/watch?v=Z1LMruTcGQo&ab_channel =iDudeMan.

33. "Mac Miller Finally Comes Outside, Launches New Material & Reminds Us He's Funny as F*@k!," *Ebro in the Morning*, HOT 97, August 7, 2015, YouTube video, www.youtube.com/watch?v=fxNvmVDiwD8&ab_channel =HOT97.

34. Adam Fleischer, "Mac Miller's New Video Is Dedicated to His Dog," MTV, September 5, 2014, www.mtv.com/news/1922201/mac-miller-diablo-video/.

35. DJ Semtex, "Mac Miller Interview 2013," Vimeo video, vimeo.com/412382907.

36. "These four chords are at the heart of every pop song," Classic FM, Febru-ary 28, 2019, www.classicfm.com/discover-music/music-theory/four-chords -every-pop-song/.

37. "Behind the Track with Mac Miller on 'Grand Finale,'" Highsnobeity, Sep-tember 25, 2014, YouTube video, www.youtube.com/watch?v=p4ufTwERhcs &ab_channel=Highsnobiety.

38. Alex Gale, "Mac Miller on Sobering Up, His Nemesis Donald Trump and the Drake-Meek Mill Beef," *Billboard*, August 12, 2015, www.billboard.com/articles/columns/the-juice/6663072/mac-miller-interview-donald-trump-drugs-drake-meek-mill-good-am-album.
39. "Behind the Track with Mac Miller," Highsnobiety.

SIXTEEN

1. Jimmy Murton, "Always Going Somewhere," Kickstarter, n.d., www.kickstarter.com/projects/1441551046/always-going-somewhere.
2. Paul Cantor, "I Interviewed Kendrick Lamar Before He Blew Up. This Is What He Said.," *Paul Cantor* (blog), October 13, 2020, paulcantor.medium.com/i-interviewed-kendrick-lamar-ten-years-ago-this-is-what-he-said-242f428e9ab9.
3. Melissa Locker, "Grammys 2014: Macklemore Says Kendrick Lamar 'Was Robbed' on Best Rap Album," *Time*, January 27, 2014, time.com/2103/grammys-2014-macklemore-says-kendrick-lamar-was-robbed-on-best-rap-album/.
4. Andres Tardio, "Scarface Says 'Hip Hop Is White Now,' Blames Record Executives," HipHopDX, April 25, 2013, hiphopdx.com/news/id.23704/title.scarface-says-hip-hop-is-white-now-blames-record-executives#.
5. J. Cole, interview by Angie Martinez, "J. Cole on 'Be Free' Performance: I Watched Eric Garner Video Before to Get in the Mindframe," The Angie Martinez Show, January 4, 2017, YouTube video, www.youtube.com/watch?v=50aH0Tu-xfM&ab_channel heAngieMartinezShow.
6. Adam Fleischer, "Childish Gambino Writes Poem About Being Black in America, and Refuses to Apologize for It," MTV, August 24, 2014, www.mtv.com/news/1899822/childish-gambino-poem-black-america/.
7. "The Nightly Show—Mac Miller Unloads on Donald Trump," Comedy Central, March 10, 2016, www.youtube.com/watch?v=Zm8ISls_TBA&ab_channel=ComedyCentral.
8. Soren Baker, "Mac Miller Questions White Rap Listeners Regarding #BlackLivesMatter," HipHopDX, December 18, 2015, hiphopdx.com/news/id.36700/title.mac-miller-questions-white-rap-listeners-regarding-blacklivesmatter#.
9. Craig Jenkins, "Fell Asleep and Forgot to Die: Mac Miller's Good Morning," *Vice*, September 25, 2015, www.vice.com/en/article/rmjpv8/mac-miller-go-od-am-2015-profile.
10. Zach Frydenlund, "Mac Miller Was Going to Put Out a Christmas Album with Cam'ron," *Complex*, September 8, 2015, www.complex.com/music/2015/09/mac-miller-a-waste-of-time-podcast-with-its-the-real.
11. Logic, interview by author, September 9, 2020.
12. Caitlin Kelley, "Cam'ron Recalls What Mac Miller Told Him About Staying Independent," Genius, December 19, 2019, genius.com/a/cam-ron-recalls-what-mac-miller-told-him-about-staying-independent.

13. Mac Miller, interview by Larry King, "Mac Miller on New Album 'GO:OD A.M.,' Battling Depression & Donald Trump," Ora.tv, September 9, 2015, www.ora.tv/larrykingnow/2015/9/9/mac-miller-on-new-album-good-am -battling-depression-donald-trump-0_1hro71x0l77p.
14. Rory D. Webb, "Mac Miller's New REMember Music Label Highlights Pittsburgh Acts," *Pittsburgh Post-Gazette*, March 20, 2013, www.pghcity paper.com/pittsburgh/mac-millers-new-remember-music-label-highlights -pittsburgh-acts/Content?oid=1630192.
15. *Shangri-La* (documentary miniseries), directed by Morgan Neville and Jeff Malmberg, aired July 12–August 2, 2019, on Showtime.
16. Ibid.
17. Miranda Johnson, "My Way," *XXL*, September 29, 2015, www.xxlmag.com/ mac-miller-good-am-xxl-interview/.
18. Ibid.
19. Sha Money XL, interview by author, July 18, 2019.
20. Kevin Lincoln, "The Couple Behind Odd Future's Unlikely Empire," Buzz-Feed, July 19, 2013, www.buzzfeed.com/kevinlincoln/christian-and-kelly -clancys-unlikely-empire.
21. Ibid.
22. "Rap Radar: Christian Clancy," Tidal, July 15, 2019, YouTube video, www .youtube.com/watch?v=HEjFsXQuhTo&.
23. Ibid.
24. Ibid.
25. Alex Gale, "Mac Miller on Sobering Up, His Nemesis Donald Trump and the Drake-Meek Mill Beef," *Billboard*, August 12, 2015, www.billboard.com/ articles/columns/the-juice/6663072/mac-miller-interview-donald-trump -drugs-drake-meek-mill-good-am-album.
26. Gale, "Mac Miller on Sobering Up."
27 *Mac Miller—Stopped Making Excuses* (documentary), directed by Rob Semmer, for *Fader*, 2016, YouTube video, www.youtube.com/watch?v =UQ3w99trVUk&t=27s.
28. Ibid.
29. Montana's addiction struggles would land him in the ICU come 2019.
30. "Famous 'Sizzurp' Cough Syrup Yanked from Market," TMZ, February 14, 2014, www.tmz.com/2014/04/23/sizzurp-cough-syrup-off-market-justin -bieber-lean-codeine-actavis/.
31. Tayler Montague, review of *GO:OD AM*, by Mac Miller, Pitchfork, October 8, 2015, pitchfork.com/reviews/albums/21038-mac-miller-good-am/.
32. Brian F. Johnson, "Mac Miller Awakens with His Major Label Debut 'GO:OD AM' and Prepares to Headline Red Rocks Amphitheatre's First-Ever Halloween Concert," *Marquee*, October 1, 2015, marqueemag.com/ 2015/10/mac-miller-awakens-with-his-major-label-debut-good-am-and -prepares-to-headline-red-rocks-amphitheatres-first-ever-halloween -concert/.

SEVENTEEN

1. Nomi Leasure, "Nomi Leasure on . . . Dating Someone with Depression," *Taylor Magazine*, March 21, 2018, www.taylormagazine.com/nomi-leasure -on-dating-someone-with-depression/.

2. "Shane Says Goodbye to Mac Miller," The Shane Show, September 10, 2018, SoundCloud, soundcloud.com/shaneshow/091018-shane-says-goodbye-to -mac-miller.

3. Patricia Garcia, "Mac Miller on Love, Ariana Grande, and the Last Thing That Made Him Cry," *Vogue*, September 27, 2016, www.vogue.com/article/ mac-miller-the-divine-feminine-album.

4. Madeline Roth, "Ariana Grande 'Loved' Mac Miller Before They Even Started Dating," MTV, March 1, 2017, www.mtv.com/news/2988883/ariana-grande -loved-mac-miller-cosmopolitan/.

5. Dee Lockett, "Watch Ariana Grande Curl Up in a Ball of Embarrassment When Ellen Asks About Her Boyfriend, Mac Miller," Vulture, September 14, 2016, www.vulture.com/2016/09/ellen-embarrasses-ariana-grande-about -mac-miller.html.

6. Mac Miller, interview by Dan Pardalis, "Mac Miller Talks About His Rap Bucket List, Shelved Projects and Wrestling Finishers," *Complex Australia*, December 10, 2015, www.complex.com/music/2015/12/ interview-mac-miller-talks-about-rap-bucket-list-shelved-projects-wresting -finishers/03.

7. Mac Miller, interview by the Breakfast Club, Breakfast Club Power 105.1 FM, September 22, 2016, YouTube video, www.youtube.com/watch?v=omTQNW Pghhc&ab_channel=BreakfastClubPower105.1FM. 2016.

8. Brian Hiatt, "Mac Miller: The 2016 Rolling Stone Interview," *Rolling Stone*, September 7, 2018, www.rollingstone.com/music/music-news/mac-miller -2016-interview-ariana-grande-kendrick-lamar-720847/.

9. MusicmanTy, interview by author, November 4, 2020.

10. Raha Lewis, "Mac Miller on How His Friendship with Ariana Grande Evolved into More: 'Everything Just Happened Organically,'" *People*, September 13, 2016, people.com/celebrity/mac-miller-on-how-his-friendship-with-ariana -grande-evolved-into-more/.

11. Miller, interview by the Breakfast Club.

12. Cee-Lo, interview by author, July 23, 2020.

13. Garcia, "Mac Miller on Love."

14. Mac Miller, interview by Sway's Universe, "Mac Miller Speaks on Addic- tions + Talks Love & Working with Kendrick & Anderson .Paak," Sway's Universe, September 21, 2016, YouTube video, www.youtube.com/watch?v =gs9E6lFzSE4&ab_channel=SWAY%27SUNIVERSE.

15. Garcia, "Mac Miller on Love."

16. Natalie Finn, "The Truth About Ariana Grande's Complicated Relation- ship with Mac Miller," E! News, October 23, 2018, www.eonline.com/

news/979732/the-truth-about-ariana-grande-s-complicated-relationship
-with-mac-miller.

17. Robert Glasper, interview by author, February 27, 2020.

18. "Robert Glasper—Studio Stories with Mac Miller, Erykah Badu, & D'Angelo
2016," *Fader*, September 14, 2016, YouTube video, www.youtube.com/watch?v
9BHsmstTiM&ab_channel heFADER.

19. Miller, interview with the Breakfast Club.

20. Ibid.

21. Mac Miller, interview by Zane Lowe, "The Late MC Opens Up," July 2018.

22. Big Jerm, interview by author, October 4, 2019.

23. Camraface, and Jennifer Rovera, as told to Mike Pearl, "I Photographed a
Former 'Survivor' Contestant at the Lowest Point in His Life," *Vice*, May 28,
2014, www.vice.com/en/article/gq8je7/i-photographed-a-former-survivor
-contestant-at-the-lowest-point-in-his-life.

24. Craig Jenkins, "Mac Miller Visits Our Office to Discuss The Divine Feminine
and What He Learned from Pharrell," Vulture, September 27, 2016, www
.vulture.com/2016/09/mac-miller-on-the-divine-feminine.html.

25. Jay-Z (@sc), "Too many . . Fab , black people really magic . Mac Miller nice too
though .," Twitter, June 15, 2017, twitter.com/sc/status/875532022847909889.

26. House listing, Zillow, www.zillow.com/homedetails/11659-Valleycrest-Rd
-Studio-City-CA-91604/20031848_zpid/?.

27. Ryma Chikhoune, "Mac Miller on Coachella, Girlfriend Ariana Grande, and
Settling into His Happy Place," *W*, April 24, 2017, www.wmagazine.com/
story/mac-miller-coachella-2017-interview.

28. "Ariana Grande speaks out on Manchester concert attack," ABC News,
August 22, 2018, YouTube video, www.youtube.com/watch?v=oo43I4n4
RKQ&ab_channel=ABCNews.

EIGHTEEN

1. Nerisha Penrose, "Mac Miller's Blood Alcohol Level Was Twice the Legal
Limit in DUI Crash: Report," *Billboard*, May 22, 2018, www.billboard.com/
articles/columns/hip-hop/8457357/mac-miller-blood-alcohol-level-dui-car
-crash.

2. "Mac Miller Arrested for DUI, Hit and Run," TMZ, May 17, 2018, www.tmz
.com/2018/05/17/mac-miller-arrested-dui-hit-and-run-crash/.

3. Sarah Hearon, "Ariana Grande Opens Up About Mac Miller Split: 'Unconditional Love Is Not Selfish,'" *Us Weekly*, May 10, 2018, www.usmagazine
.com/celebrity-news/news/ariana-grande-opens-up-about-mac-miller-split/.

4. Karla Rodriguez, "Ariana Grande and Saturday Night Live's Pete Davidson Are 'Casually' Dating," *Us Weekly*, May 21, 2018, www.usmagazine.
com/celebrity-news/news/ariana-grande-snls-pete-davidson-are-casually
-dating/.

5. Rob Haskell, "Ariana Grande on Grief and Growing Up," *Vogue*, July 9, 2019,
www.vogue.com/article/ariana-grande-cover-august-2019.

6. @FlintElijah, "Mac Miller totalling his G wagon and getting a DUI after Ariana Grande dumped him for another dude after he poured his heart out on a ten song album to her called the divine feminine is just the most heartbreaking thing happening in Hollywood," Twitter, May 21, 2018, 7:56 P.M., twitter.com/FlintElijah/status/998714302080040961.

7. "Shane Says Goodbye to Mac Miller," The Shane Show, September 10, 2018, SoundCloud, soundcloud.com/shaneshow/091018-shane-says-goodbye-to -mac-miller.

8. Ryma Chikhoune, "Mac Miller on Coachella, Girlfriend Ariana Grande, and Settling into His Happy Place," W, April 24, 2017, www.wmagazine.com/ story/mac-miller-coachella-2017-interview.

9. "Shane Says Goodbye," The Shane Show.

10. Miller, interview by Lowe.

11. Ibid.

12. DJ Clockwork, interview by author, August 1, 2019.

13. Allison P. Davis, "You Know He Got That Big Dick Energy," Cut, June 26, 2018, www.thecut.com/2018/06/pete-davidson-ariana-grande-big-dick -energy.html.

14. Craig Jenkins, "Producer Jon Brion on the Gutting Task of Completing Mac Miller's Final Album After His Sudden Death," Vulture, January 21, 2020, www.vulture.com/2020/01/mac-miller-circles-jon-brion-interview.html.

15. Reggie Ugwu, "Mac Miller and Jon Brion Had a Vision. It Almost Came True.," New York Times, January 20, 2020, www.nytimes.com/2020/01/20/ arts/music/mac-miller-jon-brion-circles.html.

16. Chikhoune, "Mac Miller on Coachella."

17. David Sexton (@d_sexton20), "Just shook @MacMiller's hand before his Tiny Desk, nbd," Twitter, August 1, 2018, 11:23 A.M., twitter.com/d_sexton20/ status/1024677104573730816.

18. Thundercat, interview by Michel Martin, "Thundercat on 'It Is What it Is,' Losing Mac Miller and Learning to Do Nothing," All Things Considered, April 4, 2020, www.npr.org/2020/04/04/826900093/thundercat-on-it -is-what-it-is-losing-mac-miller-and-learning-to-do-nothing.

19. Miller, interview by Lowe.

20. Andrew Barber, interview by author, January 8, 2020.

21. Post Malone, interview by Zane Lowe, "Post Malone: 'Hollywood's Bleeding' Interview," Apple Music, September 6, 2019, YouTube video, www.youtube .com/watch?v=XMJsJMv_-q4&ab_channel=AppleMusic.

22. Miller, interview by Lowe.

23. Gia Hughes, interview by author, August 14, 2020.

24. Nomi Leasure, Peek (blog), August 28, 2018, peek-mag.tumblr.com/ post/177469146465/the-art-of-healing-part-v-return

25. "Mac Miller Hotel Cafe Footage (Behind the Scenes)—Part 1," JVO Productions, May 15, 202, YouTube video, www.youtube.com/watch?v=ucl IKMlzf7o&ab_channel=JVOProductions.

26. Palermo Stone, interview by author, July 11 and 22, 2019.

27. Dan Hyman, "Mac Miller Wants You to Know He's OK," *Rolling Stone*, August 3, 2018, www.rollingstone.com/music/music-features/mac-miller -swimming-interview-profile-706164/.

28. United States v. Cameron James Pettit, www.justice.gov/usao-cdca/press -release/file/1199456/download.

29. Mac Miller, interview by HardKnockTV, "Mac Miller talks Album, Ariana Grande, Celebrity Culture. Says he thought he was on way out," August 9, 2013, YouTube video, www.youtube.com/watch?v=9M4toIUR6Ho.

30. Haskell, "Ariana Grande on Grief."

31. Miller, interview by HardKnock TV, "Album, Ariana Grande."

32. Miller, interview by Lowe.

EPILOGUE

1. Mac Miller, interview by KarmaloopTV, "Boston Police & Blue Slide Park," August 16, 2011, YouTube video, ww.youtube.com/watch?v=pwi1dPYw6h4&ab _channel=KarmaloopTV.

2. "Report: Comedian Mitch Hedberg Died of Accidental Drug Overdose," Associated Press, January 13, 2005, www.foxnews.com/story/report-comedian -mitch-hedberg-died-of-accidental-drug-overdose.

3. Mac Miller, interview by Daniel Isenberg, "In the Lab with Mac Miller," *NahRight*, 2013.

4. Tee-WaTT (@TeeWatt), "He sent me this earlier today and today's news made me feel so empty. It hurts but let's pray for his family, his team, and Ariana. We lost a great guy and we need to remember depression is something serious and we need to spread love not hate.," Twitter, September 7, 2018, 10:40 P.M., twitter.com/TeeWaTT/status/1038255639569551360/photo/1.